SACRED RITUAL, PROFANE SPACE

STUDIES IN CHRISTIANITY AND JUDAISM
Series editor: Terence L. Donaldson

The Studies in Christianity and Judaism series publishes volumes dealing with Christianity and Judaism in their formative periods, with special interest in studies of the relationships between them and of the cultural and social contexts within which they developed.

The series is sponsored by the Canadian Corporation for Studies in Religion whose constituent societies include the Canadian Society of Biblical Studies, Canadian Society for the Study of Religion, Canadian Society of Patristic Studies, Canadian Theological Society, Société canadienne de théologie, and Société québécoise pour l'étude de la religion.

1 SACRED RITUAL, PROFANE SPACE
The Roman House as Early Christian Meeting Place
Jenn Cianca

SACRED RITUAL, PROFANE SPACE

The Roman House as Early Christian Meeting Place

JENN CIANCA

MCGILL-QUEEN'S UNIVERSITY PRESS
MONTREAL & KINGSTON · LONDON · CHICAGO

ISBN 978-0-7735-5332-3 (cloth)
ISBN 978-0-7735-5333-0 (paper)
ISBN 978-0-7735-5424-5 (ePDF)
ISBN 978-0-7735-5425-2 (ePUB)

Legal deposit second quarter 2018
Bibliothèque nationale du Québec

Printed in Canada on acid-free paper that is 100% ancient forest free (100% post-consumer recycled), processed chlorine free

This book has been published with the help of a grant from the Canadian Federation for the Humanities and Social Sciences, through the Awards to Scholarly Publications Program, using funds provided by the Social Sciences and Humanities Research Council of Canada. Funding has also been received from Bishop's University.

Funded by the Government of Canada | Financé par le gouvernement du Canada | Canada | Canada Council for the Arts | Conseil des arts du Canada

We acknowledge the support of the Canada Council for the Arts, which last year invested $153 million to bring the arts to Canadians throughout the country. Nous remercions le Conseil des arts du Canada de son soutien. L'an dernier, le Conseil a investi 153 millions de dollars pour mettre de l'art dans la vie des Canadiennes et des Canadiens de tout le pays.

LIBRARY AND ARCHIVES CANADA CATALOGUING IN PUBLICATION

Cianca, Jenn, 1978–, author
Sacred ritual, profane space : the Roman house as early Christian meeting place / Jenn Cianca.

(Studies in Christianity and Judaism series ; 1)
Includes bibliographical references and index.
Issued in print and electronic formats.
ISBN 978-0-7735-5332-3 (cloth). – ISBN 978-0-7735-5333-0 (paper). – ISBN 978-0-7735-5424-5 (ePDF). – ISBN 978-0-7735-5425-2 (ePUB)

1. House churches – Rome. 2. Sacred space – Rome. 3. Domestic space – Rome. 4. Christianity – Rome. 5. Rites and ceremonies – Rome. 6. Rome – Religion. I. Title. II. Series: Studies in Christianity and Judaism series ; 1

BV601.85.C53 2018 250.937 C2018-900075-9
C2018-900076-7

This book was typeset by Sandra Friesen in 10.5/13 Minion.

For Mark, after all

Contents

Figures

Acknowledgments

This book began at the Department for the Study of Religion at the University of Toronto and is the product of collaboration with many wonderful scholars encountered there. To John Kloppenborg, I am deeply grateful for generosity, advice, and good humour. John Marshall provided helpful and constructive critique throughout the process. Jennifer A. Harris offered mentorship, insightful theoretical framing, and friendship.

Terry Donaldson read a version of this work early on and then read it again (and again) as editor for this series at McGill-Queen's University Press. He offered many thoughtful recommendations which improved the quality of the manuscript considerably. I am grateful also to Kyla Madden and the whole team at MQUP, for careful reading, editing, and shepherding during the process of putting this work together for publication. The two anonymous reviewers of the manuscript offered streamlining and clarifying suggestions for which I am thankful. The Senate Research Committee of Bishop's University generously supported the publication of this book.

Innumerable thanks are also due to my graduate school colleagues at the University of Toronto. Nicole Libin was first comrade and continues to inspire and motivate. The members of the Mullins Seminar read rough drafts of these ideas over many pints and always with a spirit of friendship. To Christina Reimer, beloved and trusted friend, I owe more than I can say.

Much of this work was written in a space I consider sacred: Divinity House at Bishop's University. Its sanctity is in no small part due to the people who have occupied it. Jamie Crooks has been a dear and constant friend for almost twenty years, and nearly no thought has passed through my head that has not been generously received by his ears, usually without desert. Michele Murray and Daniel Miller made seamless the transition from teacher to friend over the course of the years. Other important folk sanctifying this space include Bruce Gilbert, Kerry Hull, Jordan Tronsgard, Harvey White, and honorary Divinity denizen Dale Stout.

Lastly, I am grateful to my parents, for raising me to challenge everything, if perhaps unintentionally. Thank you especially to my father for those early conversations about origins and destinations, and for giving me the permission I didn't know I needed in order to pursue questions of religion.

SACRED RITUAL, PROFANE SPACE

Introduction

The first three centuries CE,[1] the earliest years of Christianity, are increasingly seen in modern scholarship as sites of complexity. Rather than a homogenous community of believers, forging a single new identity in Christ, early Christian groups were grappling with often opposing beliefs, doctrines, and styles of leadership. This variety was perhaps nowhere more striking than in the house-church communities. Before the days of purpose-built architecture, adherents to the Jesus movement met in private spaces, adapting their domestic practices to accommodate their worship practices.[2] This negotiation of daily life with ritual life was already part of the domestic sphere, at least in living spaces occupied by traditional polytheists. These inhabited spaces were rich sites, replete with daily practices that complicated the practice of ritual. The emergent Christian rituals and beliefs were, by their nature, at odds with the polytheistic practices of the Roman Empire, in both private and public contexts. Christian rituals were still developing in the first three centuries, before there was an established system of liturgical and ritual practice. Further, there were no materially articulated places set apart for these rituals in the house churches, which created an atmosphere for the practice of ritual that was quite different from the places of worship in and after the fourth century. Given this lack of permanent, dedicated ritual space, the task of understanding sacred space in the house church is a difficult one.

Perhaps due to this absence of material articulation, notions of early Christian attitudes towards space, when the subject is addressed at all, tend to focus on the rejection of space, especially of sacred space. Among the more common characterizations of early Christian space (and its accompanying ideology) is the idea that these earliest believers were not very concerned with the world around them. According to this view, because the earliest believers considered themselves to be awaiting an imminent eschaton, there was no need for the permanent articulation of sacred space. Sacred loci for the practice of ritual were unnecessary, since the collective body of believers was the primary (and in some interpretations, only) mode of spatiality.[3] Indeed, this view is consistent with much of what is written in the letters of Paul. While the idea of sanctity residing only in bodies, individually or collectively, is an attractive way to resolve the problem of Christian rituals coexisting with daily life or polytheistic practices, it does not acknowledge the places where Christians met in their own right. This view assumes that the domestic spaces in which house-church Christians gathered were neutral or empty of other signification. To assume that domestic spaces in the Roman world were neutral, however, is to negate the structures, both material and ideological, that formed the basis of daily life. This assumption also too heavily prioritizes the literature of early Christianity, in which the ideal, rather than the real, situation is presented as normative.

For this reason, it is essential that material evidence for the earliest Christian meeting places be engaged in the reconstruction of these communities, especially with regard to their use and conception of space. It is clear that communities of believers met in domestic spaces in this early period, until they began to construct buildings of their own for worship. These unrenovated, inhabited spaces hold the key to understanding many of the seemingly irresoluble conflicts experienced by the house-church Christians. Exploring the spaces in which Christians met is integral to understanding ritual practice, the identity and formation of community, and the development of a Christian notion of sacred space.

Discussions of house-church Christianity have rarely explored notions of sacred space in these communities. This lack of attention to sacred space may be predicated on the aforementioned assumption that the body of believers was sufficiently sacred space for the practice of rituals. It may also be based on an understanding or definition of sacred space that is linked only to purpose-built environments. If sacred space is understood as being bound up with environments of that sort, it stands to reason that, until a specifically Christian place of worship was constructed (namely, the building of the Lateran by Constantine ca. 313), sacred space in Christianity would not have been identifiable or perhaps even possible. Further, the conception of sacred space is sometimes understood as having overtones of purity or, at the very least, separateness; that is, in order to have Christian sacred space, that space could not be polluted by or contain elements or practices that are in opposition to it, including domestic life and Roman domestic cult worship. According to this conception of space, the domestic spaces in which the earliest Christians met would have been doubly unsuitable to the construction of sacred space, given that they were neither purpose-built nor pure.[4] While seemingly logical, these assumptions about sacred space in general, and sacred space in relation to house-church Christians, serve to negate the space in which these earliest groups congregated. It is clear that a more broadly conceived definition of sacred space is needed in order to understand ritual gatherings taking place outside of purpose-built structures.

In recent studies, a good deal of attention has been placed on the development of early Christian architecture away from domestic space and toward purpose-built spaces. Rather than focusing on the house church in its own right, these studies emphasize the development of sacred space, often in conjunction with the development of formalized ritual and liturgical practice. While valuable in terms of architectural development, such studies offer little in the way of negotiating the question of the shared or coexistent space of the house church.[5]

The current study, then, focuses specifically on the early Christian house church in its dual function, as inhabited space and ritual space, both Roman and Christian. The purpose of the study is twofold. Its first goal is to understand the types of spaces in which the Christians met, including their layout, population, practice, and function. These spaces will be presented always with a view to understanding them primarily as domestic spaces, and only secondarily as places of worship. The study's second goal is to attempt to understand the ways in which house-church Christians may have constructed sacred space in these places, despite the necessary negotiations demanded by this mixed environment. Here, it will be understood that any conception of sacred space as constructed by the house-church groups must also have allowed for the continuation of domestic life in all its forms.

Throughout this work, I will argue that, despite a lack of materially articulated or physically separate space, the house-church Christians were indeed meeting in sacred space. How that space was constructed would have been predicated on the unique demands made by a new community, meeting in a place not specifically appointed for their needs. It will also be shown that among the practices normative to these domestic spaces were practices problematic to house church meetings, including not only practices of the body (such as sex, defecation, and death), but also practices of the domestic cult. Despite the fact that the domestic cult operated in a polytheistic context, I maintain that its practices did not necessarily cease in those places used for worship by the Christians. In addition, I argue that continued domestic cult practice did not preclude the house-church Christians from understanding themselves to be meeting in sacred space and performing sacred rituals. In other words, the conception of sacred space in house-church Christianity did not demand the negation or rejection of traditional domestic cult practice. Thus, I will argue that the house-church Christians employed ritual in their construction of sacred space, but that this sacred space was itself temporary, existing only during ritual practice. This temporary sanctity, then, would have found its place inside the context of Roman domestic life, which included the domestic cult.

My research centres on the house church as meeting place for many of the earliest Christians. It is necessary to explain what I mean by the term "house church." The term is used here to indicate any unrenovated, inhabited living space used by the Christians for worship, including not only houses, but apartments, workshops, shared tenement blocks, and rural or farm estates. Any place in which Romans lived, regardless of whether it was a true *domus*, is understood here to be a domestic space potentially available to early Christians for meeting. In these spaces, there would not have been any movement as yet toward an articulation of Christian ritual space. Indeed, they were spaces shared by both a household and a religious community. Generally, house churches flourished in the first three centuries. Later stages of Christian worship space, such as the one reflected by the Christian building at Dura Europos, involve renovation and therefore fall outside of what I term "house church"; Dura is better termed a *domus ecclesiae*.[6]

The major roadblock to reconstructing house-church practice is the paucity of material evidence for house churches in general. It is true that very little evidence remains that can be claimed unequivocally as a house church in this early period. Indeed, an unrenovated, unmodified space is by its very definition dispossessed of those markers which could identify it as Christian. It is for this reason that literary data is often relied upon over against material data in this period. This reliance, however, is problematic. Literary data is not always indicative of practical, lived experience, reflecting as it frequently does the attitudes and concerns of the educated elite. Architectural data from the first three centuries, then, ought to be engaged in the study of these early communities. Despite the fact that this architectural data is not identifiably Christian, it is certainly consistent with the types of spaces that the house-church communities would have been using. Indeed, the lack of identifiably Christian markers in the archaeological record from this period is testament to the level of adaptation and coexistence embraced by the house-church Christians in the time leading up to renovated and purpose-built architecture.

Making connections between what is known from literary data and what is known from material data leads to a more nuanced picture of earliest Christianity. It is exactly this exchange between literary and archaeological sources that I propose. In my discussion of house-church Christians, the connection between literary and archaeological sources will be achieved by (a) isolating and interpreting texts that deal with house church worship; (b) isolating and interpreting examples of domestic spaces that correspond with the social and geographical locations of early Christian communities; (c) superimposing the claims and ideas expressed in Christian texts onto these architectural models, in order to see whether the image presented in texts corresponds to the practice reflected by the interpretation of material data; and (d) using modern theoretical studies of sanctity, space, and ritual in order to understand any conflicting data that may arise. The literary and material data are not always consistent, and this inconsistency raises questions concerning the activity of the house church, its interaction with preexisting religious traditions and its material presence in domestic spaces, the hierarchical structure of both church and household, and most importantly, the house church's sanctity.

The data for these house churches will be taken from the domestic spaces of the ancient Mediterranean, with a special focus on Italy. The accident of preservation means that the majority of evidence for domestic architecture in the Roman Empire comes from the Italic peninsula, especially Campania. Wherever possible, however, examples from outside Campania (including Rome and Ostia) and from the provinces will be used to demonstrate the wide variety of housing options available to the Romans and, of course, to converts to the Christian movement. It should be noted that the focus of this monograph is on *Roman* domestic space; that is, rather than an exhaustive exploration of what might be termed Graeco-Roman (or ancient Mediterranean) spaces, including domestic spaces inhabited by Jewish Christ-confessors, the focus here will be on spaces used by communities who self-identify as Roman. The model presented in this work is used to explore sacred space in conjunction with markers of Roman identity, especially via the Roman domestic cult, but it can and ought to be applied to different types of spaces as well.[7]

From time to time, models of later Christian architecture (from the mid-third to the fourth centuries) will be engaged in conjunction with general models of earlier domestic architecture. The renovated space of

Dura Europos, for example, provides a valuable point of comparison in terms of sacred space, worship practices, and ritual enactment. In discussing later or renovated spaces, however, it will always be made clear that these spaces are not identical to house churches, and that their spatial organization is different from inhabited spaces.

While there is inevitably a desire to create a complete or definitive picture of house-church space, it must be admitted that such an enterprise is impossible. The material and textual evidence of house-church space is simply too limited to be conclusive. By the same token, the models of domestic architecture in the Empire are too varied to be typologized. In the same way that the social makeup of early Christian groups ought not to be perceived as monolithic, but instead, as representing a broad demographic of the ancient Mediterranean population, so too ought the spaces of these communities be understood as diverse. Thus, there is no need to establish a typology of space and place which could then be applied to early Christian groups of all kinds. Rather, a framework of sacred space, constructed via ritual and superimposed on multiple models of domestic space, can be employed in creative imaginings of house-church sacred space.

In the current project, then, there will be no claim to understanding how all house churches functioned and were organized. The approach taken here will focus instead on a series of options to be explored. Looking at the material in this way also allows difference to be highlighted, rather than rejected, in the reconstruction of early Christian practice. Differences can be used in order to understand the myriad ways in which the house churches and their Christians would have functioned. The ultimate goal is not to paint commonalities between these spaces. Rather, it is to flesh out, as completely as possible, an image of how different communities may have strived for ritual sanctity in their own ways.

In order to deepen the investigation of this ritual sanctity, a number of theoretical approaches to space will be engaged. An investigation of space and place, as well as the relationship between the body and its environment, will help to animate the archaeological data. Theoretical conversations about sacred space, also, will problematize long-held assumptions about early Christian space, and offer some new avenues for exploration. Overall, the image of house-church sacred space will be fed by literary evidence, archaeological evidence, and theoretical explorations of space, place, and the human experience.

While chapter 6 is dedicated to establishing a definition of sacred space, it would be beneficial to state from the outset that traditional modes of assigning sanctity to space, especially those modes pertaining to purpose-built structures, fall short when applied to the house church. Thus, I provide here a brief working definition of what I mean when I say "sacred space," with the caveat that this definition will be examined and problematized in detail later in the volume. Any definition of sacred space must recognize the inextricable relationship between rituals, the bodies that perform them, and the spaces in which they are practised. Sacred space must be dynamic. Thus, the model of sacred space I use here is one that is composed of the following elements: space that is set apart from "ordinary" space; space that is constructed as sacred by the practitioners and inhabitants who occupy it; space that is bounded either through material articulation or through performance; and space that is used for ritual. Each of these elements will be discussed in detail in chapter 6, especially in relation to the house church.

An approach such as this one is needed for many different types of early Christians. In the current study, however, the focus will be on a specific group: Christ-followers and converts to the Christ movement who worshipped in Roman domestic space, and whose cultural or ritual background was polytheistic in nature. The term "Christian" is arguably problematic in this early period; the terms "Christ-confessor" or "Christ-follower" are perhaps more accurate, reflecting the complexities of conversion in the first three centuries. I suggest that the term "house-church Christians" be used wherever possible in this discussion, in order to focus on the specific group of people who met in domestic spaces, as members of a community, in order to worship Christ. Sometimes the term "Christian" will be used on its own for the sake of clarity, or to indicate a broader group (especially when discussing third- and fourth-century spaces, as in chapter 4); sometimes the term "Christ-confessor" will be used (especially when discussing textual data that does not necessarily pertain to members of a house-church community). Jewish Christians or Christ-confessing Jews will not be discussed at length, although future work ought to apply this approach to those groups as well. The focus here will be an exploration of Roman culture and society, as represented by and enacted in the Roman house, and the ways in which this materially present cultural and social matrix interacted with the ritual practice of Roman house-church Christians.[8]

Chapter 1 provides background and context for the exploration of house-church space. The timeline and chronology of house-church Christianity is provided first. Next, I present the social structure and demographics of house-church Christianity, indicating a mixed character.

The size of the groups and their ritual practices are also investigated. An overview of literary references, inscriptions, and papyrological data then indicates the widespread nature of the use of domestic space as worship space. What little material data is available in terms of specifically Christian use of domestic space will also be presented and discussed. Overall, this chapter demonstrates: first, the fact that many Christians indeed used domestic space as worship space; second, that the social status of these Christians was varied; and third, that the housing models to be used in the reconstruction of house-church Christianity ought also to be varied.

Chapter 2 will examine the many different types of housing available to inhabitants of the ancient Mediterranean in the first three centuries. As mentioned above, the focus will be on "Roman" houses; this distinction does not limit the spaces to houses in Rome, or even in the Italic peninsula, but rather refers to the spaces of inhabitants who self-identify as Roman. Types of spaces to be investigated will include elite Roman *domus* and villas, country estates, apartments, shops used both for commercial and residential use, and smaller apartments (perhaps best termed as "tenements"). This chapter also turns to life in these spaces – the quotidian experience of Romans in their homes. I will discuss the Roman family, including the population of the household, leadership in the household, and the roles and expectations of members in the household. The debates over public and private axes, activity areas in the houses, and the use of space will be marshalled here with a view to establishing models of lived experience in the Roman house. Finally, this chapter discusses self-representation and the relationship between identity (especially *Romanitas*) and architecture in the domestic spaces of the Roman Empire, emphasizing the inextricable link between them.

Chapter 3 examines the cultic and ritual practices in these Roman domestic spaces. The chronology of Roman domestic cult practice, as well as the key deities celebrated and the central rituals of the cult, are presented here through both literary and material evidence. The material evidence of household shrines, in all their incarnations, is given pride of place. In addition to elite Roman houses, I examine apartments, shops, and other non-elite dwellings for evidence of the Roman domestic cult. Again, the connection between Roman identity and material expression is emphasized, demonstrating that the domestic cult was not one that could be easily cast aside, but rather was a fundamental part of what it meant to be a Roman. The material evidence for traditional polytheistic attitudes and practices demonstrates that cessation of the cult would have been unlikely.

Chapter 4, following on the material and literary data for the practice of Roman domestic cult, establishes the argument that many Christian households, including those who were responsible for hosting the meetings of the earliest Christians, would have continued to practise elements of the Roman domestic cult. In order to do so, this chapter first outlines the common attitudes expressed toward Roman domestic cult by Christian writers, demonstrating that the relationship between Christian belief and domestic practice was complex and varied. Next, two case studies of known Christian meeting space are explored in detail: the villa at Lullingstone and the so-called Christian building at Dura Europos. These case studies examine the presence of material data in support of continued adherence to, or tolerance of, polytheistic cult. The villa at Lullingstone contains elements of decoration and, possibly, of practice associated with polytheistic cult; the building at Dura Europos contains vestiges of the practice of the ancestor cult. While both of these sites are examples of renovated spaces, rather than house churches proper, the existence of both polytheistic and Christian practices in these spaces reveals the likelihood of this coexistence in house churches as well. Indeed, the juxtaposition of these practices, remaining even after time and money was invested to renovate these spaces, emphasizes how much more likely a juxtaposition would have been in places that had not been adapted for Christian use. Further, both of these sites are usually defined as sacred space, or as containing sacred space (in some of their worship-dedicated rooms), thereby indicating that the coexistence of supposedly incompatible practices does not negate the sanctity of the worship space.

Chapter 5 will move from Roman domestic ritual to specifically Christian ritual. The chapter sketches the rituals of the house churches as they are known, and focuses especially on the rites of the *agape*, the eucharist, and baptism. A brief discussion of the ritual of gathering is also noted here. The emphasis on these rituals offers a glimpse into the prioritization, in early Christian writings, of practice over place. Specific placement of the rituals is rarely discussed in these writings, but the attitudes of early Christians towards sacred or ritual space are varied. The variety of attitudes and conceptions of sacred space in early Christianity does not preclude the construction of house-church sacred space, however, and so these attitudes are explored as well. Ranging from outright rejection of space to a recognition of special or sacred space, these attitudes reveal the nature of sacred space in some of the earliest communities.

Chapter 6 outlines theoretical approaches to sacred space, ranging from the sacred/profane dichotomy of Durkheim and Eliade to the social constructivist views of later theorists. This section provides a working definition of sacred space, including a discussion of boundaries, both material and temporal. Embodiment is a key element in the construction of sacred space, as is emplacement; this chapter emphasizes both elements in the construction of space. An examination of theories of sacred space reveals the tendency to prioritize the built, rather than the adaptive, environment, demanding that other approaches to the construction of sacred space be found. Finally, ritual practice, especially through the lens of performance and practice theories, provides insight into the formation of temporally constructed sacred space – a space that is impermanent, and which allows for the continuation of Roman domestic life in its normative context.

The study that follows will challenge, reexamine, and introduce key issues pertinent to the earliest Christian communities. I will challenge the idea that the early church and its space was conceived only via the "body of believers," a group of disembodied, displaced worshippers whose eschatological hope erased the fundamental human need to be emplaced. I will also argue that these house-church Christians were not necessarily interested in the "purification" of their space, through the removal of conflicting religious practices from their earliest worship spaces (the house churches). Despite a lack of materially articulated worship space, the earliest Christians necessarily formulated their own ideas about sanctity in their house churches, ideas borne out by the eventual establishment of sacred space in the Christian spaces of the Late Empire and after.

The engagement of space and place is essential to the understanding of the earliest Christians. Without this engagement, it is all too tempting to imagine the ideal experience of conversion, which involves a rejection of all that came before. Lived experience is rarely so accommodating. Finally, I will not present a theory of early Christian sacred space that claims to be universally applicable in every house church in every outpost of the Empire. At the same time, it is worth considering the power of place in the reconstruction of any community, as well as its impact on identity, both individual and communal. My working theory is that the sacred spaces of the house churches were likely multivalent spaces, accommodating Roman domestic cult practice, daily life and practices of the body, and of course, the ritual practice of the earliest Christians. This rich sense of place likely also contributed to multiple affiliations or identities, incongruous to the modern eye, but exceedingly liveable in the contemporary world of the house-church Christians.

Chapter One

The Context of House-Church Christianity

PLACING THE HOUSE-CHURCH MEETINGS

The last fifty to sixty years of early Christian sociological scholarship has moved towards situating the earliest Christians in their space. Many of these studies focus on the development of early Christian architecture, asking the all-important question of how the community that began as an unorganized group of Jesus followers, content to meet in the houses of their leaders, became an organized episcopate with the architecture to match.[1] Rather than focusing on this development, however, this work focuses on the house church in its own right. It is necessary, therefore, to provide context and parameters for the investigation of house-church Christianity.

This chapter will present first a timeline of house-church Christianity. Because house-church Christians met only in those places that were made available to them, and not in purpose-built structures, socio-economic factors obviously dictated the types of space that one can imagine for a given group. The social status, economic standing, and general demographics of house-church groups will also be investigated. Next, this chapter will present the literary evidence for domestic space as worship space, including the writings of authors from the first to the third centuries. Finally, available material evidence for domestic space as worship space will be presented, including a discussion of the *tituli* and later renovated spaces. What will become apparent from the discussion is the importance of imagining a number of different contexts and experiences, both architectural and social, for a wide variety of house-church groups.

TIMELINE OF HOUSE-CHURCH CHRISTIANITY

The period of the house church extended far beyond the first century and the loosely connected Pauline communities reflected in the earliest Christian writings. The Christians continued to meet in domestic spaces, without purpose-built structures of their own, until the peace of Constantine and the massive building programmes that followed. There is no evidence to the contrary. There is evidence indicating that some of these private spaces were modified for worship in the third and fourth centuries, and in one case – that of Dura Europos – that these modifications included the termination of domestic life altogether. The case of Dura should not be taken as evidence for Empire-wide practice, however; too often this single example is taken as the model for all third-century Christian space, rather than a model of Christian space in a particular outpost of the Empire at a particular time.[2] Therefore, one should not set Dura as a *terminus post quem* for the use of unmodified houses as early Christian meeting places. Until the building programmes of the Christian Empire reached every corner of the provinces, the house-church model, in some form or other, should be seen as dominant. In fact, it has been argued that Roman Britain, and other western provinces, were slow to see the changes that began in Rome and the East.[3] Indeed, one might expect to see a good deal of overlap between the use of house churches and the use of monumental, purpose-built structures, at least in terms of time, if not place.[4] Thus, the chronological framework for house-church Christianity should extend from the mid-first century to the early fourth century, an end point that is quite conservative.[5] Any discussion of the social makeup of the house-church Christians, then, should not be limited to the Pauline communities, but include also those second and third century communities leading up to and overlapping with the Constantinian peace.

SOCIAL STRUCTURE OF HOUSE-CHURCH CHRISTIANITY

The types of meeting space available to house-church Christians would have been predicated, of course, on the socio-economic status of the group. Because of both chronological and regional variants, however, it should be immediately apparent that there is no way to truly typify house-church Christians. Thus, there will be no attempt here to elide the differences between the community of, for example, first-century Corinth as presented in the Pauline correspondence, and the community of the late first- or early second-century Roman church as represented by the letters of Clement or the *Shepherd of Hermas*. While texts can provide valuable clues as to the nature of early Christianity in specific locations, these clues cannot be applied wholesale to all of the communities in Rome and her provinces. Rather, a series of potential or likely situations should be investigated.

Knowledge of first-century Jesus movement groups is, of course, largely connected to the letters of Paul. The regional centres known to have been visited by Paul, or communities with which he corresponded, have long enjoyed pride of place in the understanding of Christian origins in the empire. Rome and Corinth, for example, are centres of the debate over the social structure of these earliest Christians. The demographics of the house-church Christians are important in the understanding of their space, as meeting places would have been wholly dependent upon those willing to host or play patron to the church.

The discussion of the early Jesus movement has ranged from consensus to new consensus and back again; here the briefest of surveys of first-century Christian social demographics will suffice. The debate over urban groups, especially those in Rome, has long raged over whether communities were composed almost entirely of working poor and slaves or freedpersons, or whether members of the group also came from the upper strata of elite society. Abraham Malherbe reported in his 1977 work on the social structure of early Christianity that a "new consensus" had been reached. This new consensus hinged on a key factor: namely, that early Christians were not composed entirely of the lowest strata of the population, but that there were also members who were wealthy and, perhaps, members of the elite.[6] That is, early Christian groups drew from most levels of society.

Some criticisms were levelled against Malherbe's supposed consensus, especially in relation to claims that the earliest Christian communities would have had any elites among its members. Perhaps the strongest voice of dissent came from J.J. Meggitt.[7] Included in the consensus with which Meggitt disagreed was the work of other scholars, including Gerd Theissen and Wayne Meeks.[8] Meggitt was virulent in his criticism, claiming that there was no evidence for members of the upper strata of Roman society in Pauline communities, and further, that although different levels of economic means are perhaps apparent in Paul's letter to Corinth, these levels should be interpreted as being within the classes of the working poor and lower.[9] For example, Meggitt argued that no members of the church would have held political office, based on an interpretation of Romans 13:1 ("Let every person be subject to the governing authorities").[10] Meggitt also argued that the "Pauline Christians *en masse* shared fully the bleak material existence which was the lot of 99% of the inhabitants of the Empire."[11] In other words, in Meggitt's view, there were no members of the early communities who held any status above the working poor. He claimed that these members supported each other through "mutualism," a term that indicates collective responsibility and action within the community designed to aid the less fortunate.[12] This claim, however, feels hollow in the face of his assertion that members of the community had no money at all. Meggitt also does not contend with the question of where these working poor might have been able to meet, if all of them were operating at subsistence level.[13]

While the "new consensus" as purportedly offered by Meeks, Malherbe, and Theissen is not without its flaws, Meggitt's portrait of Pauline communities seems to swing wildly in the opposite direction.[14] Meggitt's claim that poverty was endemic to the Roman Empire is correct, but what is lacking is the recognition that some Christians would have had access to the same system of patronage available to other citizens of the empire. Meggitt's notion of "mutualism" is theoretical only, with little evidence to support it, and it does little to counter the longstanding system of patronage that Meggitt rejects for the Christians.

Other scholars have posited social demographics similar to Meggitt's, but with a more reasoned approach. James Jeffers, for example, also sees the vast majority of early Roman Christianity as having been composed of "poorer and less respected foreigners."[15] Overall, Jeffers sees Rome's earliest converts as poor slaves or former slaves from the East, who spoke Greek and were, if not Jewish in origin, perhaps initially converted through Judaism.[16] Wayne Meeks concludes that the majority of the urban Christian population in the first century was neither slave nor aristocrat, and drawn mainly from the class of "free artisan or … small trader."[17] A more recent study, including the work of Steven J. Friesen and Walter Scheidel, has indicated the presence of a "middling group" or groups in the economic structure of the Roman Empire at large.[18] While not negating the fact that the majority of the Empire's inhabitants did in fact dwell at the subsistence level or below, this study proposes that the bulk of the Empire's wealth resided not only with the elites, but also in the hands of middling groups.[19] Friesen and Scheidel do not argue for a middle "class," but rather, seek to explore options for a more diversified distribution of wealth in the Empire.[20]

Returning to the so-called "new consensus," Malherbe's claims do not necessarily indicate a preponderance of upper-strata members; they simply allow for their existence in the community.[21] Gerd Theissen's work has suggested a similar approach, acknowledging the possibility of higher-status members.[22] Certainly, the acknowledgment of some wealthy members, in the Corinthian community at least, corresponds with the debate over the Lord's Supper in 1 Cor 11. It seems clear that here, there are problems arising between members of differing social status levels.[23] Other scholars, including David Balch and Carolyn Osiek, have suggested that the majority of Jesus followers would have come from the middle levels of Roman society, noting that there is no evidence in the first century for Christians of the senatorial class.[24] They too note the seeming evidence for stratification and socio-economic difference in 1 Cor 11, though they posit that the "extreme top" and the "extreme bottom" were absent from this scenario.[25] Peter Lampe notes that it is not until the 90s that wealthy members are mentioned (*plousioi*); after this point, Lampe sees the Christian community as acquiring more members of the wealthier classes.[26] The textual evidence available for Pauline Christianity strongly indicates at least some members of means, since shared meals are the central act of meeting (Acts 20; 1 Cor 11), and, of course, because Paul names hosts himself.[27]

By the second century, and perhaps even the late first century, it is clear that wealthier members of society had begun to patronize the church. While it remains unclear whether these wealthier members were in fact of the aristocratic or senatorial class, or of the imperial household, certainly by this time there were members of the community who had access to funds, and could therefore act as hosts or patrons of the church. In this period, the success of the church was predicated upon financial growth and the conversion of moneyed members to the faith.[28] Balch and Osiek, who posit a first-century Christian community whose members came from the middle levels of society, recognize the development of patronage and the conversion of upper-class members by the third century and after.[29] The texts of *1 Clement* and the *Shepherd of Hermas* also indicate the presence of wealthier members or patrons, which at times led to conflict in their communities.

It is generally agreed upon that, by the second century, there was a growing hierarchy in church leadership, including the development of an episcopate. In the literature of the late first and second centuries, it appears that a conflict in leadership was arising, based on the difference between host and bishop or leader. In the *Shepherd of Hermas*, there is seemingly a disagreement arising between members of the community of Hermas, who have divided over the issue of leadership. It seems as though some wealthier members of the community were using their financial contributions as leverage to lead the group, bringing them into conflict with the bishops, who claimed apostolic authority or charismatic gifts.[30] The issue of authority was at this point becoming a growing concern, given the many interpretations of the faith that had by now emerged, including heresies and other dangerous subgroups. By the second century, the church was concerned with creating and preserving an orthodoxy, with right texts, right interpretation, and right leadership. If wealth were an allowable indicator of leadership, the church would run the risk of being led by members of the community who had their own private interests at heart. That these groups were still meeting in houses is also apparent from the fact that would-be leaders used their own domestic spaces to woo members to their side in schismatic arguments.[31]

Wealthier members within the Christian community are also indicated in the text of the *Shepherd* by criticism of their actions. Hermas calls to the readers' attention the fact that some Christians in the community are focusing more on their external affairs than the affairs of the church (*Sim.* 9). What seems to be occurring is that wealthier Christians, who would obviously need the support of the broader, polytheistic community in order to succeed financially, were prioritizing their businesses over the integrity of the Christian faith.[32] Ironically, this financial success among Roman polytheists would have been essential to the upkeep of the Christian community!

1 Clement also reflects a growing concern with hierarchy in the church. The institutionalization of leadership seems to be the primary concern here, partly due to ideological differences which arose as the community grew away from its origins in apostolic authority (*1 Clement* 40–4). For Clement, institutionalization is explicitly connected to the desire for unity and the prevention of further schisms (ibid., 94–7).[33] Both Clement and Hermas reflect the need to marshal the growing sectarianism of the post-apostolic age. It is important to note, however, that this institutionalization or centralization of leadership is still occurring within the confines of the household, and involves concerns over leadership and purity only insofar as beliefs and doctrine in these communities are concerned.

Overall, then, it is safe to say that the house-church Christians were a diverse group, representative of a broad range of status types. Certainly, beginning in the second century and continuing throughout the third and fourth centuries, there were more members of economic means, and perhaps members of the aristocratic elite. In any case, there was a greater number of wealthier members in the community as it grew and developed. With more economically stable members available, it is possible that more house churches were supported by patrons, in larger spaces than those of the earliest communities. House-church Christians, then, were drawn from every economic group in the Empire, especially in the second century and after.

HOUSING TYPES AVAILABLE TO THE HOUSE-CHURCH CHRISTIAN MOVEMENT

Even those who disagree on the socio-economic status of the earliest Christians agree that Pauline Christianity was predominantly an urban movement.[34] It makes sense, then, to visualize the earliest Christian domestic spaces in their urban contexts, which were, in most cities of the Empire, apartment blocks or *insulae*.[35] Apartments or insulae do not demand that a community have members of the senatorial class or other persons of aristocratic lineage. Many successful tradespersons, for example, could have lived, either as tenants or as owners, in medium-sized apartments, which would have afforded the space for meeting.

Places inhabited by the impoverished have also been suggested as potential meeting places for house-church congregations. Robert Jewett, for example, has posited a kind of "tenement church" in the early days at Rome, creating a model for understanding early groups who perhaps did not have a benefactor in their ranks.[36] It is difficult to see how some of the rituals known to have been practised by house-church Christians could have been performed in these small spaces (baptism, for example), although it must be acknowledged that, for some groups, these types of spaces may have been the only ones available. At the same time, the evidence of the Pauline correspondence certainly suggests that hosts and patrons were part of the communities with which he was acquainted, and so the tenement church should perhaps not be taken as the norm. A sort of compromise between the wealthy villa host and the tenement church dweller has also been posited. Jeffers, for example, who sees the smallest apartments as insufficient for house-church meetings, suggests that "Christian house congregations which met in the homes of believers probably met in the first-floor 'deluxe' apartments."[37]

By the second and third centuries, the growth of wealthy members (and the spread of Christianity into rural and provincial areas) likely meant that larger houses, such as *domus* or villa estates, were also common places of worship. Therefore, given the broad range of socio-economic types in house-church Christianity, there should also be an accompanying range of housing types. Those rituals that we know from textual evidence to have been performed in house churches must be accommodated in every space, from a villa to a tenement.

SIZE OF THE HOUSE CHURCHES

Understanding the placement of rituals, as well as the understanding of house-church communities altogether, is predicated on the size of the communities that met in houses. The number of house churches in a given city or region, especially in the first century, is unknown. Hypotheses concerning the overall numbers of converts to this new religious movement vary widely, depending on the proposed social makeup of the group at a given time and in a given region.[38] The churches and their hosts mentioned in the Pauline correspondence (and the pseudo-Pauline correspondence) give clues to the size of the communities, but these clues are by no means easily interpreted.

The Letter to the Romans, for example, is the centre of a longstanding debate about numbers of churches, because of the specific naming of persons in Romans 16. There are a number of reasons why Paul might have named specific people separately in his letter. They might have represented hosts of specific church communities; that is, each of these people might have had the members of their communities meeting in their houses, apartments, or workshops as a self-contained group. These persons might also have represented rotating hosts of a single church; that is, the burden of hosting and patronage might have been shared between a few wealthier or fairly stable community members. It is also possible that Paul is simply mentioning people of whom he has particularly heard in relation to the Roman church community.[39]

Each of these situations could be true, and each raises different issues. In the first case, if there were small, only loosely related cells of Christianity within a given city (in this case, Rome), it is not clear how or whether they might have communicated with each other. If these groups were separate from each other, or at least met separately, is it responsible then to speak of a "Roman church" as though it were a single group with shared ideologies and practices? In the second case, a single church is suggested, with a series of meeting places, each hosted by a generous member of the community. This case raises questions about accommodation. How many Christians is too many, when the meetings are occurring in a single domestic space? The same question holds true also for a single church that always meets in the same space. That is, if the people named were not all patrons, but rather members of a single church which met all together, the same issue of numbers and accommodation would apply.

It is most likely that a community in a given city (and certainly in Rome) was split into a series of smaller groups, meeting in a number of domestic spaces. Wayne Meeks has argued that the first-century Roman church was composed of a series of small house-church cells, spread throughout the city.[40] Osiek and Balch have also pointed out that a house church, once it grew too large, would likely have been capped, and another church would be founded, keeping the cells small.[41] If this were the case, the letters sent from Paul may well have been read in each of these house churches, which were separate from one another due to practical, rather than ideological, concerns.[42] Looking at other regions gives a similar, if muddied, picture. In Colossians 4:15, for example, two separate groups are named. First, "the brothers [and sisters] in Laodicea" are mentioned; second, "Nympha and the church in her house" is named. It seems clear that these are two separate groups, and that Nympha's church was mentioned by name not because it was the only church, but because it was the only one hosted by a person known to the author.[43] Below, in the discussion of early Christian ritual, I will return to size of the groups in conjunction with the celebration of the *agape* and the eucharist. An average number of members is difficult to propose, given the broad range of spaces available to the groups, but any estimate should always bear in mind the limitations of the domestic sphere.[44]

EARLY CHRISTIAN LITURGY AND RITUAL PRACTICE

Before attempting to understand how worship might have taken place in house churches, it is necessary to outline the elements that constituted this worship.[45] Again, since the chronological or temporal range of the house churches spans three centuries or so, one can expect the modes of worship to change over time, especially in terms of organization and formalization. The earliest period exhibited no signs of formal liturgy, but specific rituals and shared events are evident in the earliest texts associated with the Jesus movement, including Paul's letters. By the time Constantine's measures were put into place, the new official cult of the Empire was already a flourishing movement, with hierarchical leadership structures, formalized liturgy (including creeds, accepted readings, hymns, and a festal calendar), and a fledgling canon. While some spaces would have been adapted in order to facilitate this growing formalization, the sheer paucity of material evidence for this adaptation should indicate that some communities did not have the resources to renovate and adapt their spaces. The domestic spaces of the earliest Christians, which served well in a period of eschatological imminency, needed to serve also the needs of a developed community with formalized ritual. Unadapted domestic spaces, then, needed to accommodate all manner of ritual proceedings. Indeed, domestic spaces are recorded as the locus for early Christian activities of all kinds from the first to the third centuries.

TEXTUAL EVIDENCE FOR THE USE OF DOMESTIC SPACES BY THE EARLY CHRISTIANS

Although the archaeological record is sparse in terms of specific material evidence for house churches, there is textual evidence that suggests that Christians used various kinds of domestic spaces to gather and to worship. Textual evidence for the use of space in the earliest days of the nascent Christian community can be found in the Pauline corpus, Luke-Acts, and apocryphal and non-canonical writings. There are, of course, interpretive issues with some of these sources. The Pauline corpus is the most straightforward, as it describes and reveals contemporary practice. So too do the writings of Clement and Justin, who describe their own period. Using narrative descriptions in later works, however, including the Gospels and the apocryphal acts, can sometimes be problematic, reflecting as such works do a later conception of earlier days. Data from these works, therefore, should be compared wherever possible against sources contemporary to the period being described.

Recent scholarship has attended to the question of meeting space for the early Christians, especially of the Pauline communities.[46] Concerning the accounts in Luke-Acts, a number of fine analyses are available of the types of space said to have been used by Jesus and his disciples during their missions.[47] There were likely no permanent meeting places in this period, although certainly, groups of believers – predominantly from Jesus's and his disciples' own Jewish communities – were beginning to gather.[48]

In the Pauline corpus, textual references to domestic space as the gathering place of the Christians abound. Because Paul writes to many communities, dispersed across the Mediterranean basin, it is probable that this use of domestic space was the standard for the new movement regardless of geographical location. By the time of Paul's writings, patrons of the community had already emerged, indicating people (and their places) who played host to the church on an ongoing, and perhaps even semi-permanent, basis. In Paul's Letter to the Romans 16, he names Prisca and Aquila and "the church in their house" (Rom 16:5), and Gaius, who hosts both Paul himself and "the whole church" (Rom 16:23). Both of these references make clear that places have been set up in the homes of these patrons in order to provide Paul and other leaders the service of ongoing hospitality, giving them places to stay.[49] It is clear also that these people are named for their acts of hospitality and patronage toward the church, and not necessarily for spiritual leadership. 1 Cor 16:19 names Prisca and Aquila once again.[50] The letter to Philemon 1–2 thanks both Philemon and his "sister in Christ," Apphia, who were also hosts to the church. Paul's naming of specific persons here indicates that there are particular, specific places that are known to insiders as worship space, thanks to the hospitality of a few key members.[51]

As is apparent from the references to domestic gathering in Luke-Acts, the movement in the time of Jesus was understood by the second-century author to depend heavily on the hospitality of members of the movement or people sympathetic to those members, who allowed Jesus and his disciples to speak in their homes. While the writer of Luke-Acts gives a characterization of these meeting places in the time of Jesus and his first followers, the image presented of places of meeting is perhaps more consistent with the author's own time. As described in Acts 12:12–19, for example, the meeting places are described as the homes of immediate followers, as in the case of the mother of the disciple John Mark, where Peter goes when released from prison. The gospel writer also places the teaching of Jesus in the home of Simon the Pharisee, where Jesus reclines and shares a meal with his host before sharing his teachings with the so-called sinful woman as well as the invited guests (Luke 7:36–50).

Another example of a meeting of Christians by the same author is found in Acts 20:7–12. In this passage, a young boy named Eutychus dozes off while Paul is teaching to the gathered community of believers. The meeting is taking place in an upper room, and the boy falls to his death "three floors below" (Acts 20:9). In this passage, there are a number of points of interest. First, this community at Troas is described as meeting on a particular day of the week: "On the first day of the week, when we met to break bread" (Acts 20:7). Second, it is possible that the place where they met is understood to have been a place where this community was accustomed to meeting, as there is no mention of needing to find a special place to hear Paul's teaching. In other words, the author of Luke-Acts understands these Christians to have their own places of meeting. Third, the place described is in an upper storey of a building. If this were a domestic space (and it seems to have been, especially with reference to the breaking of bread as a central occasion of the meeting), it would have been one of a relatively humble nature, such as a small apartment or tenement. Generally, due to the dangers of fire, the more luxurious apartments, owned by or rented by persons of some means, would be located on the lowest storeys of large apartment blocks or *insulae*.[52] Since this apartment is located on an upper storey – specifically, three storeys above the ground – it was likely not an especially large or well-appointed apartment.[53] In general, these descriptions in Luke-Acts reveal much more about the second-century perception of first-century meeting places than they do about the meeting places in Jesus' own time. The depiction of meeting places as domestic – including both houses and upper storeys or apartment blocks – is consistent with other second-century data for meeting places of early Christians.

In non-canonical and apocryphal texts from the second century, more data emerges that indicates domestic space as worship space. While not numerous, these references are key pieces of information about the early church and the growing importance of patronage. In the Acts of Justin the Martyr, Justin (d. 164) is said to have declared that, when he is in Rome, he lives in an apartment above the baths of Myrtinus, where the Christians congregate. He says also that he "knows of no other place besides this one" (*Acta Just.* 3.3).[54] This passage bears further reflection. First of all, it is an apartment that is specifically mentioned here, not a house; second, Justin claims to know of no other place besides this apartment. Presumably at this point the community in Rome would have been too large to have been accommodated by a single apartment, no matter how spacious.[55] On the one hand, it seems that Justin is simply noting the place where he knows that Christians meet. At the same time, he may be attempting to conceal other meeting places from the inquiring prefect, Junius Rusticus. Regardless of whether or not Justin's claim that the meeting place above the baths was the only one available to the Roman Christian community, that it was domestic space is clear, especially given that he claims to have stayed there.[56] Unlike the evidence of the canonical Gospels and the apocryphal acts, however, the data from Justin's last days indicate contemporary practice, and thus it can be assumed that, in Rome at least, domestic space as worship space was still the order of the day in the mid-second century.

The *Acts of Paul and Thecla*, written in the late second century, likely in Asia Minor, refer back to the time of Paul's teaching, and name the house as the space where Paul taught. The "church which was in the house of Onesiphorus" (*Acts of Paul and Thecla* 2.1) is the place where Thecla hears and grows enamoured of Paul's message.[57] From the *Acts of Peter*, also composed in the late second century in Asia Minor, there is much to be gleaned about house-church communities, patronage, heresy, and sacred space.[58] Throughout the Acts, the house is the base for much of the teaching and assembly in the community that eventually welcomes Peter (near Puteoli). The house of "Narcissus the presbyter" is mentioned as a key meeting place here (*Acts Pet.* 6–7). The house is also the locus for the heretical teaching of Simon Magus, who has wooed a wealthy patron (and senator), Marcellus, to be host not only to him, but to those who would hear his teachings (*Acts Pet.* 8–9). This betrayal is considered a blow to the community, since Marcellus was once a great patron of the church in this area, which included supporting the widows and orphans (*Acts Pet.* 8). Thus, Peter refuses to speak in his home.[59] The homeowner, wishing to host him anyway, "purifies" his home through sweeping and by sprinkling holy water (*Acts Pet.* 19), and he sends a slave to fetch Peter back to his house, asking him to use the space to teach, as indicated in the following quotation:

> After these sayings of Peter were completed Marcellus arrived unexpectedly and said, 'Peter, for you I have completely cleansed my entire house of the vestiges of Simon and thoroughly swept it of his dust … And now, most blessed one, I have directed the widows and the aged to meet in common with you in (my) house, in order that they may pray with us.' (ibid.)[60]

The data from the apocryphal acts, like that of the Gospels and Acts, may reflect a retrojection of later tradition onto earlier activity, and thus cannot be taken as hard evidence for specific meeting places, but what is clear is that the house is understood to be the default location for the meetings of first-century Christians.

That Christians met in private spaces seems to have been understood by people outside the community as well. An example of this knowledge can be found in the *Octavius* of Minucius Felix, an apologetic document which includes, among other things, a discussion of the strange practices of the Christians. Caecilius, an opponent of Christianity, asks,

> Why have they no altars, no temples, no acknowledged images? Why do they never speak openly, never congregate freely, unless for the reason that what they adore and conceal is either worthy of punishment, or something to be ashamed of? (*Octavius* 10.2)

Implicit in the accusation of Caecilius is that Christians do not build temples not because they are unable, but because they are unwilling. For Caecilius, this is tantamount to an admission of shame, for in his opinion, they are guilty of horrific acts which demand secrecy.[61] In the reply given by Octavius, it is said that the Christians do not refrain from building temples out of shame, but because there is no temple which can contain God.[62] Octavius asks, "What temple shall I build to him, when this whole world fashioned by his work cannot receive him" (*Octavius* 32.1–2). While this explanation has the clear purpose of acknowledging that God is uncontainable, it is also important to note that Octavius does not dispute the fact that the Christians do not have temples or altars built to God. His response is not a corrective, but an attempt to explain the ideology that drives the decision to meet in houses rather than temples.[63] Octavius tells us that, although they could very well build their own places in which to meet (indicating a thriving community with money and resources), they insist upon "hiding away" and meeting in private. He also mentions that he arrives at the "house" where the Christians gathered to worship. It would seem that the Christians, though obviously well known to those outside their group by this period, are perceived still as people who meet in private spaces.

In the Pseudo-Clementine literature, a large number of people are converted to belief in Jesus Christ through the charismatic preaching of Peter. A great man of Antioch, Theophilus, "dedicated the great basilica of his house in the name of a church" (*Recognitions of Clement* 10.71) as a result.[64] A number of interesting points arise from this brief mention of worship, including the naming of Theophilus as patron, and the recognition that he was "more exalted than all the men of power in that city" (ibid.). That his house is described as a "basilica" perhaps mitigates the unlikelihood of "the whole multitude assembling daily" to hear the further teachings of Peter (ibid.).[65] The texts pertaining to apostolic preaching, both canonical and non-canonical, must be treated in a different way than inscriptions, or references contemporary to the post-apostolic age. For one thing, the gathering of the people to hear the special preaching of a visiting evangelist, and one who was associated directly with Jesus, should not be seen as typical of worship practice. For example, the *Recognitions* note that the multitude of believers gathered every day to hear Peter's preaching, as opposed to the weekly worship more consistent with second and third century Christianity.

The early third-century Gnostic text, the *Acts of Thomas*, also refers to domestic space as meeting space for the apostolic community. This text, originally composed in Syriac, outlines the travelling missionary work of the apostle Thomas as he travels to spread the word of Christ to India. Of interest here is the invitation extended to Thomas by Siphor (an important person of the king's court) to teach in his house. He offers to prepare his *triclinium* (dining room) for the purpose of meeting and teaching (*Acts of Thomas* 131).[66]

Inscriptional and papyrological evidence also points to the use of houses or other domestic spaces by early Christians. Many of these have been catalogued and translated by White, and so only a brief example will be offered here.[67] *P.Gen.*Inv.108, from Egypt, is a third- or fourth-century papyrus listing the buildings in a particular city (Panoplis). Included among the many buildings of different types are a number of houses; among these, there is made mention a "house which is also the ... of the church."[68] Frustratingly, the lacuna in the text is at a crucial point; it is clear, however, that there is a connection being made here between a church community and an *oikos*.[69] Many references include valuable information about the nature of the assembly and so will be discussed in conjunction with the formation of Christian space.[70]

MATERIAL EVIDENCE FOR THE USE OF DOMESTIC SPACE BY THE EARLY CHRISTIANS

Having discussed briefly some of the literary evidence for domestic space as worship and meeting space for the earliest Christians, it is necessary to look at the material evidence for the same. It is true, as discussed above, that the earliest period of house-church Christianity leaves much to be desired in the way of material evidence. There are simply no extant examples of the houses used by the Christians, mentioned above in both canonical and non-canonical texts. Given that the literary evidence quite clearly indicates the use of domestic space as worship space in these early days, however, one can feel confident that domestic spaces were in fact used. Later meeting spaces can be of some aid in the discussion, also, and while it would be irresponsible to retroject evidence from later meeting spaces onto the earlier period, later examples of worship space can help to contextualize the state of the question concerning the earlier spaces. Thus, a few examples of this later Christian space will be included here.

There are, essentially, three different types of material evidence that should be engaged in the discussion of house churches: first, later places that have a historical or legendary association with the earliest days of Christianity (including the *tituli* of Rome); second, later renovated domestic spaces which were certainly used by Christians at some stage; and third, Roman houses in general, which do not have specific associations with Christian meeting places, but which provide an important context for the discussion. Each of these types of material evidence has its own contributions to make, as well as its own issues and problems. The bulk of the following section will be concerned with the third category, but the first two categories will be discussed briefly as well.

The first category of spaces is perhaps the most problematic, although its candidates also held a special place in the Christian imagination. This category is typified by those sites that have later, frequently monumental structures built upon earlier foundations of domestic space. In most cases, the sites of these later churches were purposefully chosen in order to continue the tradition of early Christian activity on that spot. Often, earlier foundations do exist, and generally, these foundations are consistent with domestic space. The problem is that, while earlier foundations do indicate domestic space, these earlier sites are not demonstrably Christian. There is rarely any evidence to indicate that Christians used these specific spaces before renovation, construction, or adaptation occurred.[71] In the case of the *tituli* at Rome, extensive hagiographies and liturgical calendars have been based on the assumption that basilicas were built on preexisting Christian worship spaces, and it is therefore difficult to negotiate the boundaries between legend and fact. Rather than listing the catalogue of these types of spaces, which has been done elsewhere, a few examples will be discussed here, which will make clear the concerns and issues associated with these spaces.

The so-called *tituli* have been used as evidence of early Christian house-church worship in Rome. The *tituli* have also been used to attempt to place Christianity in specific regions of Rome, making them important resources for the social makeup of Christianity.[72] In the work of Krautheimer especially, but also Petersen and White, the discussion of the *tituli* is central to the understanding of the Roman Christian community.[73] A number of fourth-century basilicas were hosts to continuous Christian use from the earliest period of Roman Christianity. Ostensibly, these basilicas have histories that claim shared foundations with houses originally used by the house-church Christians. The locations of these new, permanent basilicas were chosen in order to monumentalize and memorialize this legendary past. These places were also associated with a prominent figure in the early church, either a leader or a patron. The use of the word *titulus* does seem to indicate ownership, rather than leadership, though most of the *tituli* were eventually named for and likely dedicated to saints and martyrs.[74] According to tradition, the *tituli* were hosted by these important figures in the church, and grew along with the Christian population in Rome, following the same patterns of expansion as the community itself, until eventually, after the peace of Constantine, basilicas were constructed on their foundations.[75] At the same time, although legends date these basilicas to the earliest days of the Christian movement in Rome, the associated material evidence cannot be positively connected to the practice of Christianity until later, when renovation and new construction on their foundations began.

Generally, the *tituli* of Rome are located in the following regions of the ancient city: on either side of the Via Appia, on the Esquiline Hill, in the Campus Martius, and in modern-day Trastevere.[76] The so-called *titulus Byzantis* (or Vizantis), the house under the Basilica of Saints Giovanni e Paolo in modern-day Rome, is a good example of the way in which the *tituli* can function in the broader conception of worship space. The Basilica of SS Giovanni e Paolo is located in the Clivus Scauri, on the Caelian hill. Beneath this basilica is a maze of buildings, including houses (dated to the second century CE), commercial spaces, and unidentified spaces.[77] While the earliest houses here date to the early second century, Christian worship cannot be absolutely placed there before the second half of the third century.[78] During this period, a number of the buildings in this area were converted into use by a Christian community; renovations included the amalgamation of a number of buildings as well as the removal of walls in an upper room, in order to create a larger room for assembly. Paintings, still extant, demonstrate the presence of Christianity, including subjects such as the so-called *confessio*, the central figure of which is a martyr in an *orans* pose.[79] Therefore, it is clear that the space was used by Christians at least by the third century. Both Krautheimer and Petersen see the continuity of space for Christian worship (that is, the continuation from this renovation of an insula to the construction of a basilica in the fourth century) as an indication that the Christians most likely used the space for worship before the third century as well.

The same argument has been used for Dura Europos. That the Titulus Byzantis was used for Christian worship prior to the third century is a distinct possibility, but White discourages the idea, given the fact that the material evidence simply does not prove it.[80] Thus, there is little more that can be said with certainty than this: the space was used by Christians to meet and worship at least by the second half of the third century, and possibly earlier. The same holds true for other *tituli*.[81]

Early scholarship on the house-church communities took it as fact that these *tituli* represented actual houses and places where the Christians met, but it must be acknowledged that there is no proof that these spaces were used by the earliest Christians. The earliest references to known *tituli* date to the late fourth or fifth century, and despite the claims of these sources for first or second century use, there is no hard evidence to prove it. Peter Lampe has noted the problems inherent in seeing fifth- and sixth-century literary sources (he calls them, rightly, "legends") as evidence for first- or even second-century use of the *tituli*.[82] He argues, however, that when the legends place Christian worship in *tituli*, they tend to place this worship in particular areas of the city. Lampe notes that it is "interesting that late antiquity's legend-tellers prefer certain quarters of the city when they fabricate Tituli [*sic*] stories about the first and second centuries."[83] Lampe's work focuses on building a topography of Roman Christianity, but implicit in this work is the notion that Christians were meeting in houses in Rome, and in particular areas of Rome at that. It is plausible, then, that while specific places known from the fifth century and after as *tituli* may not have been the exact sites used in the first and second centuries, it is clear, at least, that the original spaces used by Christians were houses. The transformation of these houses into basilicas (whether on sites actually used by first-century Christians or not) denotes a desire for continuity in meeting places. If the fifth-century Christians were not able to locate the *actual* house of Clement, any house in a region known to have been populated by Christians would do. While there is still a lingering lack of material evidence for specific *tituli*, this late antique tradition of titular basilica-building supports the argument that domestic space of a "typical" variety in these neighbourhoods is a good place to start when discussing early Christian meeting space.

Similar to the problem of the *tituli* are a number of sites in the Roman East. Of special interest, perhaps, is the so-called House of Peter at Capernaum, since it is widely considered to be among the earliest places for Christian meeting. The fourth- or fifth-century church excavated on the site does have the foundations of a first-century domestic complex beneath it, and legend does associate the place with Peter.[84] If this place were the "House of Peter," then this would date the community's use of this space to the earliest days of the Jesus followers.[85] The archaeological record, however, provides no certain use of any structures on this site by Christian communities before the early fourth century.[86] A similar situation exists at Umm al-Jimal, in the so-called church of Julianos (or Julianos's church), built in the fourth century, as well as at Khirbet Qana.[87] These places, once the plots of first- or second-century houses, are understood to have been used by Christians prior to any church construction, but there is nothing that indicates unequivocal use by Christian communities prior to the fourth or fifth centuries.[88]

Early material examples that give proof positive of domestic space converted to early Christian worship space, then, are few and far between. In fact, there are really only two examples that can truly fit into this category, and these two come from the furthest points of the Empire. The earlier and most well-known example of domestic space adapted for worship by early Christians is of course Dura Europos, in Syria. The other is the post-Constantinian chapel complex at Lullingstone, in Roman Britain.[89]

At Dura Europos, the structure, which most call a *domus ecclesiae*, or "house of the church," was adapted from a preexisting house, built in the early third century.[90] The foundations of an earlier, first-century house were found under the third-century house, but as White has pointed out, there is no way of knowing for sure whether this house was also used by Christians. In fact, there is no concrete evidence demonstrating Christian use of the third-century house prior to its renovation.[91] The signs of adaptation for a Christian house-church community began in the mid-third century, and extended only until 256, the year that Dura itself was razed to the ground by invaders.[92] The adaptation was relatively extensive, including the creation of a large assembly room, formed by knocking down the wall between what had once been a dining room and a smaller room next to it. The walls in this room were whitewashed, and a raised dais was placed at one end, from which preaching and teaching were likely performed. Perhaps more famously, there was also a small baptistery constructed in a room in the opposite corner of the house, complete with baptismal font and paintings of an unmistakably Christian character.[93]

Being a renovated *domus ecclesiae*, Dura is different from the spaces used by the earliest house-church communities. At the same time, it does reveal a few important details about early Christian worship, namely: that domestic space was the type of space the Durene community members had available to them; that renovations transformed the house from inhabited space into exclusively worship space; and that an adapted domestic structure, rather than a purpose-built structure, was used (at least by this community) until the mid-third century.[94] It is not possible to create a typology of third-century Christian space based on the example of Dura Europos, and it is certainly illogical to make too facile a comparison between spaces in the east (Syria) and places in the west (Rome). It is possible, however, to note that domestic space (in this case, renovated) is the locus for Christian worship in Dura Europos, which can then be compared with examples elsewhere in the Empire.

Interestingly, the only other example that can be said with certainty to have been an inhabited domestic structure adapted for Christian use is on the westernmost reaches of the empire.[95] At Lullingstone (Kent) in Roman

Britain, a villa underwent a number of structural changes throughout its period of occupation, which ranged from the first to the late fourth or early fifth centuries.[96] At some point in the mid-fourth century, a central room in the villa was adapted to become a chapel for Christian worship. It is clear from archaeological evidence (including evidence of a lengthy vacancy, major structural changes, and so forth) that it was not one family who continuously inhabited this villa throughout its history. It is also clear that the evidence for Christian worship cannot be guaranteed before the mid-fourth century, when the first pieces of material evidence emerge. Unlike at Dura Europos, however, it is possible to find at Lullingstone that supports the concurrent use of this villa as both living space and worship space.[97] At Dura, there is no proof that the house was lived in and used by Christians before it was adapted, rather than purchased in order to adapt it. The same is not true at Lullingstone. There, the construction of the chapel is clearly dated to a period during which the villa was inhabited.[98] The example of Lullingstone, as well as Dura Europos, will be discussed in much further detail below. In terms of early Christian space, however, the examples above are among the earliest on offer.[99]

CONCLUSIONS FROM AND LIMITATIONS OF THE AVAILABLE EVIDENCE

What is clear from the discussion of the literary and material evidence for early Christian worship is that, across the Empire, domestic spaces were used for the congregation of the early church. This brief review simply demonstrates the validity of the term "house-church Christians." Further, the brief examination of the social and economic makeup of house-church Christianity indicates that a wide variety of domestic spaces ought to be employed in the imagining of house-church worship space.

Because the archaeological record lacks material evidence for specific spaces used, it is not possible to construct a typology for early Christian worship space. That is, one cannot extrapolate from the available evidence that Roman Christians met in houses of a specific size, with baptisteries and assembly halls, since there are not enough examples of this style of meeting place. Attempts to find architectural continuity between meeting places can only be effective when applied to the third century and after, and even then, the hapax of Dura is hardly enough to formulate a large enough set of data. While the temptation to draw parallels between later spaces and their adaptations may be fruitful for the later period (for example, in the late third century or after the Constantinian peace), it is simply impossible, and in fact, irresponsible to retroject these models of worship space onto the first two and a half centuries of Christian worship. What, then, is to be gained from yet another discussion of early Christian worship space?

In short, rather than placing Christians and their rituals in specific places, with specific architectural features, the approach here will be to creatively, but responsibly, present a series of options for worship space. Each of these options would have presented unique challenges, ranging from simple problems of reasonable accommodation for its membership to more complex issues of shared ritual space and concerns over sanctity or purity. House-church Christians may have found themselves worshipping in a *domus*, the dwelling of an elite Roman.[100] They may also have assembled with their peers in smaller spaces, above shops, in upper rooms of apartment buildings, or in spacious apartments above baths or other commercial spaces.[101] The evidence does not prioritize one of these options over another. Thus, an examination of a number of different types of domestic space available to house-church Christians in the first three centuries will set the stage for the discussion of how they might have grappled with the issues of identity, sanctity, and ritual practice in these inhabited spaces.

CHAPTER TWO

Roman Domestic Space

The earliest Christians did not have built spaces of their own in which to meet. Instead, they used the domestic spaces offered to them by members or friends of their communities. These domestic spaces, of varying sizes and types, would likely not have been modified for the church's use. The dominant function of these spaces was still as *home*, or dwelling place. The house-church Christians, then, did not necessarily find themselves meeting in a place amenable to the demands placed on them by their new religion and its new rituals. Financial and ideological factors meant that the Christians did not build worship spaces of their own until after the Constantinian peace.

The discussion of early Christian worship and meeting space is not a straightforward one. On the one hand, textual evidence indicates that the earliest Christians met in domestic spaces; on the other hand, there is very little material evidence that positively identifies a particular space as a house church. There are a number of explanations, however, for this relative lack of material evidence, not the least of which is the nature of the house church itself. Indeed, the very nature of the unrenovated house church demands its invisibility in the archaeological record. This lack of conclusive material evidence has been argued as further proof that the spaces used by these house-church Christians were unrenovated, domestic spaces.[1] It is for this reason that it is important to investigate Roman domestic space in its own right, rather than analyzing only those spaces which reveal a Christian presence in the material record.

As discussed in the introduction, a house church should be characterized as a place inhabited by a family group that was used by members of the nascent Christian community to gather and offer worship to their new deity. Because these spaces were still inhabited spaces, unlike the churches and Christian buildings of the third century and after, they were naturally devoid of the markers of this new religious practice. Once the Christians started adapting, renovating, decorating, and modifying their worship spaces, they moved out of the house-church phase and into the later phase, which has been identified as the phase of the *domus ecclesiae*, perhaps best represented by the Christian building at Dura Europos. These spaces, though probably adapted from domestic structures, were no longer inhabited by the families who once lived in them, and can therefore not be classified as house churches. As discussed above, a house church is defined by its dual function as a place inhabited by a family group *and* a place used by the new religious community of the Christians.

In this chapter, I will introduce and explain the types of Roman domestic space most commonly understood as candidates for the house church. The inhabitants of these spaces will also be discussed. It is not the house-church Christians who will be in the foreground here, but rather those "typically" polytheistic Romans who would have inhabited these spaces before they became meeting places for Christians. These inhabitants, the Roman *familia* in all its incarnations, will be "placed" in their homes. A discussion of the roles in the *familia,* and the spaces in the house where these roles were performed, is essential to fleshing out the portrait of Roman domestic space. Finally, I will explore the relationship between social status and the desire for self-representation through domestic architecture. By "populating" the Roman house, it should become clear that the Christians were not meeting in empty, neutral spaces, but rather in real homes, where all of the activities of daily life flourished.

ROMAN DOMESTIC SPACE: SOME BACKGROUND ISSUES

In the section that follows, the discussion will focus on the domestic spaces of typical Romans, in preparation for a discussion of sacred space in the early church. There are, of course, a number of terms that must be unpacked from the outset. In the context of this work, the term "typical Roman" is taken to mean any person (citizen or otherwise) living in the Roman Empire who adheres to the values as set out, espoused, and practised by those who live in the Italic peninsula, and especially its capital, Rome. This definition allows for some provincial citizens to be called Romans, whether they are Rome-born or not, including, for example, magistrates living and working for Rome in distant provinces. It also allows for freedmen and those of the merchant class who either adhere or aspire to the cultural mores of Imperial Rome, whether or not they are citizens and whether or not they live in Rome proper. Therefore, a "typical Roman" here is a member of the Empire's population whose civic and private practice reflects the values of Rome. Those described as "polytheists" or "cult practitioners" are here meant to be members of the populace who perform the cultic rites and duties, in both a civic and a domestic context, expected of any pious Roman. These cultic rites and duties will be discussed in further detail in chapter 3; at this point, it will suffice to note that acts of sacrifice to the emperor (public/civic), and sacrifice to the domestic deities (private/domestic), are the baseline for involvement in Roman rites and rituals.

Since this work focuses on converts to Christianity out of Roman polytheism, and the interaction between these groups, the cultural and religious mores of the Jewish communities that also made up large numbers of the early Christian population (including in the city of Rome) will not be discussed here. Because of the nature of the space of the Jewish communities in the same period (the first three centuries CE) – which included the Jerusalem Temple before 70 CE (in other words, a centralized sacred space), and the mourning of its loss after 70 – the notion of sacred space to a convert to the Jesus movement from Judaism was naturally different from that of a convert who saw herself as coming out of a Roman polytheistic tradition.[2]

As the focus of this work is on the kinds of Christians who came from polytheistic Roman backgrounds, so too will the focus of the architectural survey be on those types of domestic spaces used by "typical" Romans. It is naturally very difficult to define a typical Roman, especially if many different social strata are engaged. It is important, therefore, to engage many different types of domestic space, since the demographics of the house-church Christians indicate a broad range of social strata. In order to reflect this broad range, the following section will present an overview of the types of housing available to Romans (and therefore, to Christians) throughout the Empire. Because of the accident of preservation, the majority of the evidence for housing comes from the Italic peninsula, at least until the fourth century and after. Wherever possible, examples from outside Italy will be engaged in the course of this work.[3] Thus, the examples will include: *domus*, which are atrium or atrium-peristyle houses of the wealthy elite; large apartments in *insulae*, occupied by those of fair economic status but perhaps not of aristocratic status; smaller apartments or tenements located on upper storeys of *insulae* in the city; and shops and one-room living spaces.

The most commonly invoked model of domestic space in the conversation about house churches is the *domus*, or atrium house. The reasons for this invocation are vast, and centre on the attempt to create a forerunner to the basilical model which overtook Christian architecture after Constantine.[4] Despite the fact that the notion of the atrium house as "source pattern" for basilical architecture has been largely disproven, a lingering attachment to the atrium house as locus for the Christian meetings has continued.[5] Still, the atrium house is one of the options for early Christian meeting space, and when recognized as a part, rather than the whole, of the answer, insights gleaned from its investigation can be helpful in the discussion of sacred space. It bears repeating, however, that the atrium house should not be viewed as a model for the later basilica.

The atrium house is the place where it is possible to superimpose the mores of Roman aristocratic life onto its accompanying architecture. It is necessary, then, to discuss the function of the rooms of the atrium house in relation to their inhabitants and their social status. Comparing these models to other types of housing and their inhabitants will reveal how much of the atrium house model applies or does not apply to housing of different types. Thus, the discussion will begin with an architectural analysis of a "typical" Roman atrium house, followed by a discussion of its inhabitants and their place in the house, and then a discussion of the function of each of the rooms as laid out in the architectural analysis. Next, other types of housing will be considered, along with whatever similarities or differences of function from the atrium house that might emerge, in order to round out the picture.

THE ROMAN HOUSE OR *DOMUS*: WEALTHY ROMANS AND THEIR LIVING SPACES

Based mainly on Pompeiian evidence, the plan of an atrium house consists of various rooms situated around a central courtyard, or atrium.[6] The atrium house is the type of house considered ideal for the aristocratic elite, according to Vitruvius (*On Architecture* 6.3), and its layout is conducive to the domestic rituals of a *pater familias* of elite social standing.[7] In the late Republican period and the early Imperial period, the atrium house developed into the atrium-peristyle house, which incorporated the colonnaded garden of the Greeks with the already common atrium layout. Generally, these houses had atria and peristyles on a single, continuous vertical axis, though of course, as houses were expanded and developed, this vertical axis was sometimes compromised.

While on the one hand, the atrium houses of Pompeii and Herculaneum can be said to have extremely similar characteristics, it is, on the other hand, nearly impossible to provide a floor plan that accounts for all of the exceptions, inconsistencies, and differences in atrium house architecture. There are, however, a number of rooms that were nearly always found in an atrium house, many of which are described by Vitruvius.[8] The first is the *fauces*, or the "jaws" of the house, through which all people wishing to enter or exit the house had to pass. In wealthy homes, this narrow passage would often be guarded by a slave, whose duty it was to ensure that no one prohibited from entering could do so.[9] There would have been a steady flow of people through the *fauces*, especially those who came during the morning ritual of *salutatio*, which took place in the rooms discussed next: the atrium and the *tablinum*.

The house of a wealthy Roman was centred on the atrium, a courtyard that served as the main congregating area of the house. Entering from the *fauces*, visitors would find themselves immediately in the wide open space of the atrium, a space filled with light and, often, elaborate decoration. The atrium would nearly always house an *impluvium*, a depression in the centre of the room in which rain water would be collected, having come through the *compluvium* above. The *compluvium*, a large rectangular hole in the roof of the house, would also serve as a major light source for this part of the house, making the atrium often the brightest part of the house. As will be discussed below, this space lent itself to a wide array of household activities, depending on the time of day and the season. It was here in the atrium, depending on the wealth and status of the house's owner, that the most expensive and elaborate furnishings could be found. In Pompeii, many examples are available that indicate the importance of this room for presenting the image of the *pater familias*, whose status would be underscored by his selection of rich colours in wall painting, marble revetments or columns supporting the atrium's roof, and elaborate *lararia*, or domestic shrines, set up to venerate the household gods or the ancestors.[10] In general, the areas of the house most frequently travelled by guests would also be the most elaborately decorated. Since the atrium was the gathering place for all guests, whether they proceeded further into the house or not, it stands to reason that its decoration was the most important, and the material evidence from Campania bears out this assumption.

Directly adjoining the atrium was the *tablinum*, which served as the focal point of the entire courtyard area. The *tablinum* was the room in which the *pater* received his clients, guests, slaves, business relations, and any other visitors, during the *salutatio*. This morning ritual was a key moment in any elite *pater*'s day, during which he would have face time with those people who helped him keep his business running smoothly.

The *tablinum* was often fronted with a large table, behind which the *pater familias* would sit.[11] Directly behind him, in an atrium-peristyle house, would be a large window, doorway, or opening, behind which the outside space would gleam in the bright sun. One can imagine the impact such a scene would make on a slave or client, come to beg favours of a wealthy *pater familias*. Indeed, the ideal construction of an atrium house was meant to create an impact; this vertical axis, running from the *fauces* to the peristyle, impressed upon the morning visitors the power and wealth of the house's owner.[12] Domination was expressed not only through the actions of the *pater*, but through his surroundings as well.

Surrounding the atrium were smaller rooms, often windowless, which received what little illumination they could from the light streaming from the adjacent atrium or peristyle. These *cubicula*, often now referred to as bedrooms, were rooms to which visitors did not have free access. One would normally have to be invited into a *cubiculum* to gain entry, most often by the head of the household. *Cubicula* did serve as bedrooms and, in some cases, bedroom furniture and arrangements are extant. However, these rooms also served as workrooms and meeting rooms for the inhabitants of the household, depending on the time of day. In very wealthy households, these rooms could be decorated with elaborate wall paintings. In fact, it is surprising how elaborate the decoration is in many *cubicula*, indicating that these rooms were perhaps not as private as one might expect.[13] In many houses, however, the *cubicula* were often decorated quite simply or monochromatically. Rooms labelled *cubicula* could also have been storerooms or workrooms. The function of these rooms is not always clear, especially where there is not clear artifactual evidence, or where "household assemblages" are not taken into account.[14]

Another key element of the atrium house was, of course, the dining room, or *triclinium*. So called because of the tripartite couch arrangement common in both Greek and Roman dining traditions, the *triclinium* was the site of many important social and business transactions. In some larger houses, there were multiple *triclinia*, and these *triclinia* were sometimes used according to the season; an outdoor *triclinium* to be enjoyed in the summer would be miserable in the rainy winter. Like the atrium, these formal dining rooms were often elaborately decorated with wall paintings and mosaic floor decoration, the latter of which usually indicated the layout of the three dining couches. One would not enter a *triclinium* of a wealthy Roman without invitation, and as dinner parties were the primary loci of both entertainment and networking, these invitations were coveted indeed.[15]

Other spaces varied widely, depending on location, wealth, status, and personal taste. These spaces could include: a *cucina*, or a kitchen, which was the location of the domestic hearth and the place where slaves would prepare meals for the banquets; the aforementioned peristyle, whose colonnaded garden and peaceful atmosphere would serve as an escape from the noise of the city outside; storerooms and exedrae, multi-purpose and seasonal rooms; rarely, sacellae or rooms set aside for the practice of the domestic cult; and a kitchen garden, where vegetables and herbs would be grown for the family's consumption. All of these variations are present to some degree in the material evidence, and discussed by Vitruvius (6.3). In terms of the "bare bones" of the *domus*, however, the *fauces*, atrium, *tablinum*, *cubicula*, *triclinia*, and frequently, the peristyle, were the spaces that made an atrium house what it was: not just a home, but a physical declaration of wealth, status, and import among the Roman aristocratic elite.

The population of the *domus* is key to understanding the function of its rooms and of the house as a whole. The Roman *familia* was composed not only of the *pater familias*, the *mater familias*, and their children, but a retinue of other connected persons who could live in the house with them. As Andrew Wallace-Hadrill has said, one might better refer to these households as "housefuls"; extended family members, slaves, and a steady flow of visitors meant that houses of wealthy Romans were bustling centres of activity.[16]

In the section that follows, the population of the house and its use of the available space will be sketched. This discussion is by no means a new or a simple one; issues of public or private access, as well as temporal versus architectural distinctions in the use of the space, have dominated the scholarship of the Roman house and of the Roman family in recent years. The complex relationships between members of an elite *familia*, as well as their slaves and extended networks of freedpersons, should be placed in the house in order to better understand social interactions.

The actions of the *pater* have already been discussed somewhat in the section above. The ritual of *salutatio*, during which an elite *pater familias* greeted his clients, business associates, and freedmen, took place in the atrium and the *tablinum*, and was the earliest activity of the day. This ritual, of course, was especially prevalent in the Republican period, but continued into the early Principate, at least until the end of the first century. After this morning ritual was completed, most Roman men would take themselves out of the house and into the public sphere, where the remainder of the day would be spent. In Rome, as well as in provincial cities built on a Roman model (including Pompeii), activities between men took place in the forum, at the baths, and in the juridical and political centres of the basilica and the house of the senate or magistrate. These "public" activities of the *pater familias* are the key to understanding the ways in which the rest of the house's occupants used its space. The question of whether a particular part of the house is private or public cannot be answered without a clear understanding of the movements of the *pater*.[17]

Frequently, the division between public and private in the Roman house is thought to have taken place along vertical and horizontal axes. That is, the visitors of the *pater* entered through the *fauces*, waited in the atrium, and were then met by the *pater* in the *tablinum*. If further conversation was needed (away from the prying eyes of others waiting, as well as slaves and other members of the *familia*), the rooms used were those on the horizontal axis: that is, the *cubicula*. Other key events in the *pater*'s social matrix, such as dinner parties, were held in the *triclinia*, also located on the horizontal axis. The axis of *fauces*-atrium-*tablinum*-peristyle was open to nearly everyone, while the horizontal axis, including *cubicula* and *triclinia*, was open only to those who received invitations from the *pater familias* or another member of the *familia*.

This notion of axes, wherein particular rooms were either private or public, has been problematized by a number of Romanists, but especially Andrew Wallace-Hadrill, who argues that these axes oversimplify the function of the rooms of a Roman house.[18] Wallace-Hadrill argues that axes of public and private access only applied at certain times of day. The gate to the *fauces*, for example, was not *always* unlocked; it was only unlocked for those hours during which external business took place in the home. At night, of course, the gates to the house would be locked and guarded by a slave. As Michele George has pointed out, the use of a particular space within a house would change throughout the day, creating "diurnal distinctions in spatial use," as opposed to concrete ones.[19] What was in the morning "public" space – for example, the atrium – became, if not private space, household-specific space in the afternoon. Once the morning business was finished, the atrium was used for weaving, cooking, sewing, and all manner of other activities, performed by slaves for the upkeep of the *familia*.[20]

The much-discussed debate over the best model for public and private access in the elite Roman house is not the focal point of this discussion, however.[21] The question here is how and whether the access and traffic into and out of the elite Roman *domus* would or could have affected a Christian community that met there. It would seem that the influence is twofold: first, traffic of outsiders into the house would have meant an awareness of what was happening within; and second, the owners of a *domus* would have been cognizant of this traffic, and would have been aware of the importance of appropriate self-representation to these outsiders. The first point is less important, mainly because consensus has long acknowledged the unlikelihood of "secret" meetings in the earliest Christian communities. The second point, however, is one of some significance in the broader context of early Christian meeting space, a point to which I will return in later chapters.[22] At this point, it will suffice to note that the issues of access, activity, and population in the *domus* are essential to laying the groundwork for early Christian sacred space. It will therefore be necessary to sketch, however briefly, the basic outlines of these issues.

For the women of the household, daily activity could be quite different from that of the men of the house. On occasion, in the absence of a husband acting as *pater familias*, or in the case where a Roman matron was *sui iuris* (that is, free from the *potestas* of both father and husband), a woman could and did act as mistress of the house and of her affairs.[23] In this situation, the woman would essentially be a *mater familias*.[24] While many women did not have a great deal of public power, they did move freely throughout the house, especially the *matrona*, who had specific duties she was greatly appreciated for if she executed them well.[25] These duties included the responsibilities of slave management, the discipline of children, supervision of her children's education, and acting as hostess at banquets in her home.[26] Unlike an Athenian mother and wife, a Roman matron would not be restricted from any specific areas in the home. While it is true that a Roman woman may well have avoided the areas of atrium and *tablinum* during her husband's or father's morning business, there is no indication that these areas were ever explicitly forbidden for her to enter.[27] Further, there are no specific quarters set aside for women; indeed, the activities of weaving and so forth, touted by Livy as women's work, would have taken place in the atrium, which doubled as the central welcoming area for outsiders. In general, it is clear that a Roman *domus* would normally have been free from a gendered articulation of space.[28]

The same argument can be made for slaves, although this case is slightly more complicated. There have been many debates over the existence of "slave quarters," usually placed in "secondary" parts of the house and left undecorated or unfinished, as would befit a slave population.[29] Perhaps more convincing, however, are those scholars who argue for the invisibility of slaves in the archaeological record.[30] That is, just as a slave would not be considered fully human in Roman terms, so too would a slave not have special space set aside for his or her own use. A slave needed to be where his or her master or mistress was, or where they were sent. Large houses whose spaces were left less elaborately decorated than others are not necessarily suggestive of separate spaces for lower status household members. While the presence of multiple shrines, especially in areas such as the kitchen or storerooms, has sometimes been used to indicate separation between slave and free areas of the household, the fundamental point is that there was nowhere in the house where the *pater* could not go, and nowhere in the house a slave could not be sent.[31]

In sum, this very brief overview of the members of the Roman *familia* has served to introduce some of the issues that might have arisen in the shared space of the Roman household. The function of rooms and the potential outcome of this shared space will be discussed further in later chapters.

APARTMENTS, SHOPS, AND OTHER DWELLINGS OF NON-ELITES

It has long been recognized that a discussion of early Christianity and house churches that focuses only on the *domus*, or the elite Roman house, is not sufficient. As discussed above, Christians came from every stratum of society. Exactly how many of the Christians met in large, elite houses and how many would have met in more cramped quarters is impossible to say; but it is likely that dwellings of both the wealthy and the poor would have been used.[32]

Apartment living was the most common type of habitation for urban-dwelling Romans.[33] The evidence for this type of architecture comes predominantly from the material evidence available at Ostia, and to a lesser extent, Rome.[34] It is frequently thought that large apartment complexes housed only the very poor. At Ostia, however, it is clear that a number of different styles and sizes of apartments existed within these larger complexes. The available evidence from Ostia is invaluable for providing insight into urban life, especially when compared with Pompeii and Herculaneum, both country towns with reputations for hosting the country homes of the urban wealthy. Ostia was the port city of Rome, a hotbed of trade and merchant activity. Slaves and labourers were numerous, but so too were members of a kind of merchant group, whether they were freedpersons or originally of Roman stock. Ostia is sometimes thought to provide evidence of a kind of Roman middle class, which is perhaps anachronistic, but which indicates nonetheless the economic position of these hard-working urban dwellers. Many of Ostia's buildings are preserved, at least their first floors; and, of the preserved domestic buildings, a huge proportion of them are apartment blocks of some kind.[35]

There are a few different types of apartments, or *cenacula*. The discovery and subsequent excavation of Ostia's apartment complexes provided the first glimpse into life in a *cenaculum*. While the largest examples could have been as spacious as a small *domus*, the average size of *cenacula* at Ostia was approximately two hundred square meters.[36] One could expect someone of reasonable means to inhabit this type of domestic space. More often than not, these *cenacula* were rented, rather than owned; the construction of multiple apartments in similar (if not identical) style frequently indicates a single owner with numerous properties.[37] That a large number of owners rented their buildings to tenants is also clear from many ancient sources.[38] These apartments often had communal aspects, such as a central courtyard which provided outside space, a latrine, or a niche honouring particular gods, accessible to all of the apartment dwellers.

As is evident from such structures as the Case a Giardino (Regio III, Insula IX) or the Caseggiato di Diana (I, III, 3–4), some apartments were far from tenements for the poor; in fact, some apartments were quite luxurious. On the first floor of the Caseggiato di Diana, for example, wall paintings, along with mosaic flooring and decorative stone work in cross vaults, indicates some solvency in the finances of the inhabitants. While courtyard spaces were communal in both of these examples, the courts were quite sumptuous, with multiple fountains, shrines, and gardens.[39]

There seems also to have been an effort, at least in the larger apartments, to appropriate some of the room functions from the *domus*. Therefore, one sometimes sees *triclinia*, *exedrae*, and *cubicula* in apartment buildings, although the layout is somewhat different.[40] While the use of *domus* terminology for the rooms in a *cenaculum* or a *medianum* apartment may be misleading, one should expect tenants of large apartments like these to have engaged in some of the same activities as a Roman living in a *domus*: entertaining, greeting business associates, and so forth.[41] Further, there is some evidence to suggest that freedpersons adopted the visual language of citizenship, especially in funerary monuments. This emulation of the freeborn would likely also have carried over into their domestic quarters.[42]

Other types of housing were less sumptuous. In many apartment buildings, while lower floors would be composed of large *cenacula*, upper floor apartments could be very small, perhaps even a single room.[43] In these smaller layouts, the central space, or *medianum*, would often have been used as a shared area with *cubicula* all around.[44] Here, rather than a single tenant family occupying all of the *cubicula*, poorer tenants would have only a single cubiculum and the shared central space at their disposal. Upper storeys were, of course, more dangerous, since there was a constant threat of fire – despite the measures taken by Nero after the fire of 64 (Tacitus, *Annals* XV, 39) – and inhabitants of the upper levels would have found escape difficult. Smoke from cooking would also cloud these upper storeys, making living conditions less than desirable. Most inhabitants of small apartments would have cooked their food on portable braziers, and cramped quarters meant very little circulation; smoke from lower storeys would also drift up to the upper levels. In general, then, it was the lower level that usually housed large apartments, with decreasing size and liveability as one moved up the building.

Shops also provided living quarters for many urban dwellers in Rome and the cities of her provinces. Generally, shops were rented out by tradespeople; they were often attached to a large townhouse or *domus*, or located on the ground floor of apartment complexes. These shops served a variety of functions. The most common were *tabernae* and *macella*, but cobblers, leatherworkers, and other tradespeople also set up shop in these spaces. Shops functioned as places of work during the day, but at night, they were the dwelling places of the people who worked in them, and sometimes their entire families. Shop dwellings were not always cramped and squalid; there is some evidence at Ostia that the upper levels of some shops could be used for domestic life, creating a separate space for the family.[45] Less fortunate shopworkers, however, might have had to squat in the shop itself after working hours ended. More often than not, no material evidence of domestic life in these shops can be found. In a few cases, however, there were recesses in the wall (possibly for beds), stairs to a toilet or latrine, or pits, possibly for kitchen use.[46] Other shops had no articulation between work and living space, meaning that the one-room shop had to double as a workspace and as a one-room house. Still, even these spaces, cramped as they were, represented a relatively fortunate segment of the population, since they could afford the rent, and afford to have a place of their own. Less fortunate inhabitants of the Roman Empire included multiple family units in a small shared space (such as a one-room apartment or shop), while others still were homeless.

In general, the aforementioned spaces conform predominantly to the urban environment, rather than the rural one. Rural dwellings were different, and reflective of the pace of farm rather than city life. Of the sprawling Roman villas, little will be said, since they conform in basic type to the largest of the *domus* or townhouses described above. Where they varied was generally in scale; rural real estate allowed for bigger, better houses, with multiple dining areas, multiple courtyards, and extensive gardens.[47] Climate was obviously a factor in rural villa design as well; whether a home were located by the sea, in the mountains, or on farmland would dictate the design of the most important rooms. Generally, the villas of rural estates, including those in the provinces, reflected the same style and preoccupations of Roman life.[48]

Farm estates represented a vast network of housing, all serving, of course, the main house and its occupants. Again, these main houses usually look like *domus* or villa types (e.g., Lullingstone, in Roman Britain), and continue the modes of representation discussed above. Farms, however, also incorporated housing for the workers, whether they were slaves or freedpersons. Thus, farms often consisted of a large central villa, augmented with outbuildings, barns, and places of residence for workers.[49]

ARCHITECTURE, IDENTITY, AND SELF-REPRESENTATION IN THE ROMAN HOUSE

The discussion of aristocratic housing is generally dominated by the atrium house. It must be acknowledged that, with the exception of some of the northwestern provinces (Roman Britain, especially), the atrium house proper was a product of the Republican period, peaking in the late Republic and initially reflecting Republican values. In the High Empire, however, these Republican values shifted as the role of the aristocratic elite also shifted. The relationship of patron and client was important in a tangible way in the Republic, with freed slaves and clients being a key body of citizens from whom one could expect support, by way of votes in the Senate. In the High Empire, the position of senator was of course greatly diminished, and even those senators who did enjoy some prestige were appointed, rather than voted into their positions. In addition, the body of the Senate as a whole naturally had a greatly decreased impact on lawmaking and other political affairs, given the absolute power of the emperor. At the same time, however, the Senate (along with the Praetorian Guard and high-ranking officials in the military) was still a place where influence could be wielded, and these positions continued to be coveted. In addition, upwardly mobile members of the citizenry (including freedpersons, second-generation citizens, and provincial nobility) continued trying to climb into these positions. They would not have been able to acquire for themselves the history possessed by those of the aristocratic classes, but they would have been able, through appointment to coveted positions, to create a new family narrative for their descendants. Entertainment, too, was as essential a part of belonging in the Empire as it ever was in the Republic, and some of the most sumptuous material evidence for domestic entertainment comes from the Late Antique period. The formula of representation and entertainment described by Vitruvius and espoused by late Republicans of the noble classes was perhaps no longer motivated by Republican ideals, but was still a key part of what it meant to be a Roman in the High Empire. Entertainment, especially through the banqueting tradition, became even more prevalent in the Imperial period and may have peaked in the fourth century CE, both in Italy and the provinces.[50] Indeed, along with the tyrannical power of the emperor came the opportunity for the lower classes to ascend the ranks (along with high-ranking members of provincial families), meaning that emulation of Republican values and mores would have continued.[51]

The physical space of the home reflected this need for self-representation and advertisement in the Roman world. What a Roman represented in his or her house was not necessarily a reflection of individual choice, however. To truly belong to Rome, to have *Romanitas*, demanded a certain effacement of one's individual character, especially if that character reflected an ethnicity, a religious practice, or a family history at odds with prevailing modes of belonging in the Empire at the time. Mark Grahame asserts that status (achieved through behaviour appropriate to a Roman) trumped ethnicity and individuality.[52] It is clear that elite members of society, and those who wished to imitate them, needed to demonstrate loyalty and belonging to their peers in order to be successful. This demonstration of Roman identity was effected through architectural design, decoration, and proper behaviour, including invitations to one's home. These three elements, while not exhaustive, are examples of how domestic space played into the construction of Roman identity, while providing a canvas for the self-representation of the owner.

The debate over what constitutes a typical Roman house is far from settled, as the examples above should indicate. Despite attempts to standardize layouts, even a cross-section of a single town (for example, Pompeii) shows extensive difference.[53] At the same time, there are specific rooms that tend to dominate the houses of the elite (and by extension, their imitators). The most common of these are the atrium, the *tablinum*, and the peristyle. Andrew Wallace-Hadrill notes that "Roman domestic architecture is obsessively concerned with distinctions of social rank, and the distinctions involved are … within the social space of the house."[54] Wallace-Hadrill here points to the Vitruvian description of the ideal construction of domestic space, including the reflection of status, occupation, and responsibility in the architecture of the house; here, there is expressed not only the *right* of the elite Roman to have a particular type of space, but the *responsibility* (Vitruvius 6.5). Later, when wealthy non-elites built houses of their own, they imitated this architecture in imitation of elite status. Mark Grahame indicates that the *fauces*-atrium combination reflects the most important architectural measure of status, as these rooms determine both access and control in the house. This combination was also the architectural form most commonly appropriated by non-elites in the domestic sphere, since it carried with it the visual reminder of a person of status, a person whose responsibilities included the elite ritual of *salutatio*.[55]

In a general sense, wealth and status were communicated through rich materials in decoration and construction. Those rooms which experienced the highest outsider traffic (the atrium and tablinum, especially) were usually decorated in a more ostentatious manner than rooms that likely received less traffic. During the *salutatio*, it was important to demonstrate power through architecture and decoration. *Triclinia*, too, were often decorated and furnished with costly items, since dining was the fundamental element of entertaining. In the Late Empire, reception rooms and apsidal dining halls supplanted these as the central rooms for entertainment, while fulfilling the same function.[56]

Domestic art was also a key expression of Roman identity. Peter Stewart notes that "suitable artistic ornaments do not only *reflect* the cultivation and sophistication of their owner; they also *make* the man."[57] For example, images that reflected knowledge of Greek art or mythological subjects would indicate that the owner of the house was skilled in *paideia* (i.e., Greek education), which was much admired in Rome, and in which the young boys and girls of Rome received training.[58] Stewart goes on to note that "domestic art emphasizes the messages that the architecture is *meant* to communicate about the proprietor's role in society, and it effectively demarcates the different spheres of activity in the house, reflecting the Roman social hierarchy as it does so."[59] Sarah Scott discusses a number of Romano-British villas, including the mosaics at the Piazza Armerina. The so-called Great Hunt mosaic depicts animals "being lured into captivity."[60] This mosaic is not just for decoration, but also for demonstrating the ties that this owner would have had with the amphitheatre. As Scott notes, "It is an overt demonstration of the owner's power and his links with the amphitheatre … The pavement also contains detailed references to the festivals of Rome, again requiring a specialized level of knowledge."[61] The position of owners in society at large, then, was communicated not only through their social interactions, but even (and perhaps especially) through the decoration of their domestic space. In general, the areas that received the highest level of traffic from outsiders, especially important outsiders, would have been decorated with the most care, in order to maximize the opportunity for self-representation.

It was not only the content of the decoration that indicated patterns of activity, function, and of course, the status of the owner. The wealth and luxury inherent in extensive decoration also communicated the status of the owner to guests. As Wallace-Hadrill argues, "The function of decoration is to discriminate and to render the house fit for the pattern of social activity within it."[62] Because certain areas of the home were set apart for public or civic duties, it was necessary that they be decorated in a manner fit for receiving guests, both inferior and superior in status to the owner. Social mobility in the Empire demanded wealth, and that wealth was expressed in domestic space by as luxurious a decorative model as possible. The austere Republican ideal was long gone by the High Empire, and instead, the aristocracy embraced these expressions of personal wealth and status. Further, as Wallace-Hadrill states, the aristocracy set the trend of luxury as an expression of elite status, and it was this luxury that became symbolic of *Romanitas*.[63] This symbolism of luxury was then appropriated by freedpersons, as well as provincial nobility who wished always to emulate the identity of the centre, Rome.[64]

Especially after the shift from Republic to Empire, the trappings of wealth became important for the expression of status. As Simon Ellis argues, while the mores of *Romanitas* were changing in the High and Late Empire, concentrations of wealth and the demands of patronage meant that the home not only continued to represent the owner, but in fact, the owner now took more control over that self-representation. He points out that "the late Roman aristocrat carefully defined the architectural context in which his public encounters took place. He separated public and private and used the architecture to manipulate social encounters in a way that had never been done in earlier periods."[65] As Grahame has argued, the key element of Roman aristocracy in the High and Late Empire was status, wealth, and luxury.[66] Piety, however, was also an ongoing concern, and it is for this reason that more attention will be paid to the domestic cult and its contribution to the formation of Roman identity in the next chapter. Overall, however, the dominant understanding of *Romanitas*, however it may have shifted and changed from the Republic to the High Empire to the Late Empire, was reflected materially in the domestic sphere of the elites, as well as those who attempted to appropriate their status for themselves.

It is clear, then, that it was important for a Roman homeowner to demonstrate that he or she possessed the qualities most valuable to a Roman. Essentially, the house was a canvas on which could be painted the "Romanness" or *Romanitas* of the owner. Among the most important expressions of Roman cultural identity was the practice of the domestic cult, including sacrifices to both the *Lares* and the ancestors. It was common for Romans of some status to display this personal piety, by placing ancestor busts in the atrium where they could easily be seen, and by incorporating shrines to the domestic gods in key places of the household. Personal piety was not only reflective of a Roman's commitment to the household; it was also a reflection of belonging and loyalty in the Empire at large. While elite Romans were likely to be preoccupied with belonging and identity in the Empire, upwardly mobile Romans also were conscious of this need for visual self-representation. In the provinces, as well, markers of Roman identity can be found in domestic spaces.[67]

ROMAN HOUSING AS A MODEL FOR HOUSE CHURCHES

Roman housing was wide and varied, reflecting both urban and rural necessities, and a broad range of socio-economic types. It has frequently been said that early Christianity was predominantly an urban movement, and a focus on urban dwellings has perhaps been rightly placed. Still, rural estates were part of the Christian movement in the provinces (especially Britannia, Hispania, and Gaul), and so these types will also be engaged in the coming chapters. What should be clear from the foregoing discussion is that there was no one model for domestic space in the Roman Empire; it follows, then, that there can be no one model for a house church. Given that house-church Christians came from mixed social and economic backgrounds (as discussed in the previous chapter), one can expect that the domestic spaces used by these groups for meeting were also of a mixed character. This mixed character also extends to ground plans; the Roman house cannot be typologized or standardized in terms of layout and structure. There is far too much difference among the material evidence available, and far too little material evidence altogether, to delineate anything so specific as a typical plan of a Roman dwelling.[68] Indeed, even if it were true that consistency could be tracked in Pompeii, for example, this consistency would not be representative of every house in the Empire. Rather, it would only indicate a specific place at a specific time. Thus, the discussion of Roman domestic space cannot provide a blueprint for an architecturally consistent house church and superimpose upon it the activities known to house-church communities. At the same time, this broad range of housing should suggest to us a broad range of responses to this coupling of sacred and domestic space. In all of these cases, there was a consciousness – whether articulated materially or not – of what an ideal house was like, and what kinds of attitudes should be reflected in the houses of Romans. The ideal house, then, was less about articulated space or room types than it was about communicating identity and belonging.

This communication of identity and belonging is reflected in certain ideological factors that run throughout Roman domestic spaces, both of the elites and non-elites. The functions of rooms were frequently wed to the duties and ideologies of the owner and his or her family. Further, these duties and ideologies were connected to the owners' desires for self-representation. As discussed above, self-representation and display was paramount in the ideal Roman house. This self-representation should not be seen as an expression of individuality, however; it is rather a representation of a homeowner's participation in the framework that identifies a person as Roman. One should expect, therefore, that the house-church Christians found themselves in a place already in use, both on the most basic level (functionality) and on an ideological level (*Romanitas*).

These ideological manifestations were naturally most prevalent in those houses which were used not only for shelter, but as tools of communication. Tenements and shop dwellings would not have been used consciously as tools for self-representation, at least in most cases. People living in subsistence-level spaces, however, would have been aware of the importance of self-representation in the culture at large, and would likely have witnessed it firsthand in larger dwellings and *domus* (or villa estates) in their neighbourhoods. In other words, while a tenement dweller would likely not aspire to the ideal expression of *Romanitas*, he or she would be aware of that ideal, and expect it in places of the wealthy or upwardly mobile.

In terms of sacred space and the use of these places for early Christianity, each type of housing discussed above brings its own special problems and concerns. In aristocratic houses, the public presentation of the *familia* and the material articulation of *Romanitas* in the home were elements with which a patron of the church would have to grapple. In tenements and smaller dwellings, as well as the large houses of the elite, shared space with neighbours who were not members of the Christian religious community would have to be negotiated.

The chapters that follow will explore the implications of this juxtaposition of multiple identities in one place. The most likely candidate for both the expression of *Romanitas* and potential dissonance in the house-church Christian community, across the broadest range of socio-economic types, is the Roman domestic cult. The next chapter, then, will be devoted to its exploration.

CHAPTER THREE

Roman Domestic Worship

Roman domestic worship was ubiquitous from the earliest days of the Republic to well after the rise of Christianity. As discussed above, the earliest Christians met in domestic spaces. Many of these spaces would have been made available to them by members of the Roman elite. These Roman patrons would almost certainly have been polytheistic in terms of their family and ritual history. Given this history, it is likely that they would have practised the Roman domestic cult and performed its rites in their houses. Romans were not, of course, the only ancients who performed household rituals, nor were they the only group from which Christian house churches drew their converts and patrons.[1] Given, however, the focus on Roman domestic space in the foregoing chapter, the current focus will continue to be placed on the rites and practices of polytheistic Romans.

Of primary interest in the discussion to follow is whether these converts and their patrons would have continued to perform the rites of the domestic cult after having converted to Christianity. If they did, the implications are far-reaching for the characterization of early Christian sacred space. In order to engage this question, it is necessary to outline the Roman domestic cult and its presence and practice in Roman homes. Below, a brief sketch of the beliefs involved, the deities invoked, and the literary and material evidence for domestic cult practice in the early Christian period (the first three to four centuries CE) will set the stage for the examination of these domestic spaces as Christian worship space.

As we have seen, the notion that the elite Roman villa, or *domus*, was the only locus for house-church activity in the earliest days of the Christian movement has been rightly criticized.[2] The early Jesus followers were drawn from a number of different social statuses and locations, and would have inhabited different types of spaces. It stands to reason that their communal meeting places, too, would have reflected a broader range of types than the villa and the *domus*. It is necessary, therefore, to discuss the Roman domestic cult not only in the *domus*, but in other housing types as well.

Certainly the Roman domestic cult is especially and powerfully associated with Rome's aristocratic elite. There are two related issues, however, that demand further consideration. First is the acknowledgment that a successful house church needed a successful (wealthy) patron, and that this patron's contribution would be both financial and material in nature. A patron with a large house would wherever possible be selected as the host for a Christian community. Second, it is not only in elite *domus* that we see data in favour of the practice of Roman domestic cult. In both literary and material sources, there are indications that Romans who were *not* of the aristocratic class also participated in many of the rites associated with the household gods.[3] Thus, this chapter will begin by describing the rites of the Roman domestic cult and its associated deities. Next, the material evidence for the Roman domestic cult will be presented, demonstrating its prevalence in the domestic spaces of the Empire. Finally, its cultural context will be examined, demonstrating the inextricable link between *Romanitas* and the practice of the domestic cult.

CHRONOLOGY OF DOMESTIC WORSHIP

Before moving into a discussion of the material evidence for Roman domestic worship, a brief note on the chronology is necessary. It is often recognized that the time during which the household cult flourished was under the Republic; it is lamented by some Roman writers of the Imperial period that the piety of the Roman people had waned to such a degree that even the household deities were no longer honoured. Most of the evidence for family rituals and household religion comes from the cities destroyed by Vesuvius in 79 CE, which is, of course, very early in terms of the Empire's lifespan. However, as will be made clear in the examination of the later evidence in support of domestic worship, shrines to the household gods continued to be constructed into the late second and early third centuries (for example, at Ostia), and even after.[4] That the domestic gods continue to be mentioned well into the Christian era demonstrates their lasting presence in the houses of Romans, despite the common perception that the High Empire was characterized by a move toward Christianity and other "mystery" religions.[5] The notion of the household cult as "archaic" has also contributed to the misinterpretation of the chronology in modern scholarship, supposedly indicating that the Romans would have moved past the traditions of their forbears. It should be remembered that the Romans were not opposed to so-called archaic traditions, and in fact, were frequently especially amenable to religious practices older than their own.

THE DEITIES OF THE HOUSEHOLD

The Roman domestic cult centred around the worship of a few deities: the *Lares*, the *Penates*, the Genius or Juno, and Vesta. David Orr divides the domestic cult into three main focal points: the hearth, the fields or gardens, and the storerooms and cupboards, respectively represented by Vesta, the *Lares*, and the *dii Penates*.[6] Each of these areas represents a locus of important, life-sustaining activity. The hearth was of course where cooking took place, but it also represented the sacred centre of the family, just as the sacred hearth of Vesta, burning with its eternal flame in the Forum Romanum, represented the sacred centre of Rome herself. On agricultural estates, the fields and gardens were obviously important, while in most houses – both domestic and rural – the storerooms and cupboards demanded special protection from insect and rodent pests, as well as thieves. The locus of the family's sustenance and stores, these rooms also held an importance place as the symbols of the family's success. As will be discussed below, the household gods were celebrated in shrines, often called *lararia*.

The Genius (and the Juno, its less commonly attested female counterpart) played a unique role as the "life-double" of the *pater familias*, responsible for maintaining his success and that of his family.[7] The *pater*'s Genius acted as a kind of liaison between the spirit world and the earthly world, mirroring the relationships and rituals demanded of him.

The *Lares* were the deities of the household and the *familia*; specific to each household, their power would not necessarily transfer from one family group to another. They were usually represented as young men, and kept the family and its household safe. There is some confusion as to whether the *Lares* (or *Lares familiares*) were bound to a family (people) or to a house (geographical location).[8] The same is true of the *Penates*, responsible for the protection of kitchens and storerooms. While the origins of the *Penates* are unclear, many Romans believed them to have come from Troy with the fleeing hero, Aeneas. In Vergil's *Aeneid*, the household and family gods of Aeneas and his father Anchises are identified as the *Penates* (2.44–58), and their transplantation to the Italic peninsula represented the founding of a new and glorious civilization, while maintaining the connections to a glorious past. Thus, both the *Lares* and the *Penates* had familial power and importance in addition to their function as protectors of the house.[9]

FAMILY RITUALS IN THE HOUSEHOLD

The occasions for the cult of the household deities were many and varied. On the one hand, there was not a specific festal calendar for domestic cult practice, as there was for public religious practice in Rome. On the other hand, there were certain events in the lives of family members that seem to have shared an important relationship with the household deities. Specifically, these events include the birthday of the *pater*, the birth and dedication of a new child to the family, rites of passage (especially for male offspring), marriage, and death. On each of these momentous occasions, families would make explicit overtures to their household gods in order to protect themselves from harm.

Shrines were decorated with garlands on the Kalends, Nones, and Ides of every month, as well as the birthday of the *pater familias*.[10] There were accompanying rituals for almost every event in the daily life of a *familia*, big or small; as Harmon states, "It was not only on [feast] days, but on every day that the domestic gods enjoyed the worship of the family."[11] Plautus says as much in his monologue of a *lar*:

> I am the *Lar familiaris* of the house out of which you have just seen me come. I have possessed and watched over this house for many years now, already for the father and the grandfather of the man who lives in it now … He has only one daughter. She sacrifices incense or wine to me every day, or prays in some way to me again and again, decorating me with garlands. (*Aulularia* 1–15)[12]

At mealtimes, the gods were also honoured, either with a libation or an offering of food. The *pater* would often pour out a little wine (either into a special plate or *patella* in the *lararium*, or sometimes directly onto the floor,[13] and offer a small portion of the meal to the *Lares*.[14] Vesta, too, was honoured with food offerings; Ovid indicates that this is an archaic tradition that continued in popularity well into the Imperial period.[15] Material evidence, too, indicates that sacrifices took place on domestic altars. Painted *lararia* frequently depict the act of sacrifice (either in the form of libation or of burnt offerings on altars). In addition, evidence of burnt sacrifices, both of vegetable and animal matter, has been discovered in Pompeian houses.[16]

Protective rituals concerning children also involved the household deities, including rituals at childbirth, the passage into adolescence, and the donning of the *toga virilis*, signifying a boy's arrival at manhood. The nine days following childbirth were considered to be especially dangerous, and these days, called the *dies lustricus*, were home to a number of rituals performed to keep the child safe. On the eighth or ninth day, a male child was given an amulet for protection (the *bulla*), which he wore until he passed into adolescence.[17] A child would also receive his or her name on this day, another apotropaic ritual.[18] The protection of children was, of course, of primary concern in a period when rampant illness and disease could all too easily claim their fragile lives.[19] Much more than mere ceremony, the actions of naming and adorning with a protective amulet were key elements in the safety of children, and by extension, the perpetuation of the family.[20] All of these rites were performed in the presence of the household gods.

The domestic gods were also key players in coming-of-age ceremonies; when a male child was ready to join the world of men, he removed his *bulla* and dedicated it to the household deities, and donned the toga in their presence.[21] Once a boy had attired himself in the *toga virilis*, he passed into manhood. Again, this rite was performed in the presence of the domestic gods who had protected him since the day of his birth. Whether the action took place at the hearth or at another shrine or *lararium* in the house is unclear, but what is obvious is that the domestic deities were called upon for these all-important rites to protect the *familia*.[22]

Marriage also involved the household deities, both in the bride's home of origin and her destination. The bride-to-be was pampered at home, much as modern brides are, but there were ritual aspects to this preparation as well. As Harmon points out, these marriage rites were as close to rites of passage as a female member of the family would receive. While male children had the *bulla* and the *toga virilis* to signify their passage into adulthood, female children had the ritual for marriage as their signification of womanhood. Brides were attired and decorated in specific ways on the days leading up to their marriage, and on the day of the marriage itself. The hair of a young bride would be braided specially, into six braids (*sex crines*).[23] Far from being a randomly selected hairstyle, the *sex crines* was an archaic style symbolizing virginity. The description of the hairstyle (see *Festus* 454L) is usually interpreted as three locks on either side of the head.[24] It is interesting that this hairstyle was meant to emulate the hairstyle of the Vestal Virgins, protectresses of the hearth of Rome, just as the Roman matron presided over the hearth in the home. Braiding the bride's hair in this way indicated her virginity, but also her transition out of virginity and into matronhood.[25] Unsurprisingly, the conservative Republican values of family loyalty and modesty were implicit in the ritual adornment of the bride as chaste protectress of her new home.

Funeral rites also composed an essential part of the rituals performed by a family. Many of these rituals were performed outside the home, and so do not necessarily fall under the auspices of domestic cult practice; however, the lying in state of the body for up to seven days (*collocatio*), the rituals concerning the soul of the departed, and meals and libations celebrating the recently dead all took place in the home.[26] The all-important rite of *conclamatio*, a calling of the deceased by name as the soul passes over – like a reverse culmination of the *dies lustricus* – was among the first preparatory steps. The washing and dressing of the body was performed by the family, or in the case of wealthy Romans, by professional funeral managers.[27] The corpse would be festooned with garlands and surrounded by candles and incense (partly, no doubt, for the practical purpose of minimizing odour), and the laments of mourners (both familial and professional) would fill the home. The body would lie in state on a special couch (the *lectus funebris*) in the atrium of the house, usually with its feet facing the door.[28] Images of the funerary rites are preserved on a number of Roman sarcophagi, and in many instances, the presence of the family at these rites is conspicuous.[29]

The transportation of the body to the tomb, the funeral procession, and the process of burial were all highly ritualized – but, as they occur outside the house, they will not be discussed here. Purification, however, was essential in the household after the body was taken away. Although the body of a Roman remained in the house during the days immediately after death and immediately before burial, a corpse was certainly seen as polluting. Dead bodies in general in the Roman world were pollutants; it is for this reason that the burning and burying of bodies was to take place outside the city.[30] Thus it should not be surprising to note that the house of a recently deceased Roman needed to be purified after the removal of the body.

The *feriae denicales* were days set apart for the family to mourn. During this time, the family was in a liminal state – neither actively engaged with the matters of death (the corpse having been buried), nor able to resume business affairs.[31] This liminal period was also the time during which purification was essential, both of the house and of its inhabitants.[32] Just as the responsibility for the worship of the household gods fell to the head of the household, so too did the purification rites after death. If the *pater familias* were the one being mourned, the responsibility for purification would then fall to his heir (as would the continuation of the domestic rites after the completion of the *feriae denicales*). According to Festus-Paulus, this purification of the home after the removal of the corpse included a "sweeping-out" with a special broom; the one responsible for the purification of the home was called the *eurriator* (from *extra uerrere*, to sweep out).[33] The family was also purified after the funeral, in a ritual cleansing involving water and a laurel branch (called the *suffitio*).[34] The *lectus funebris* was of course removed; it would have been brought out of the house and burnt with the body.[35] The *Lares* were also purified through sacrifice; Cicero tells us that a castrated goat or sheep was offered to appease the household gods.[36] On the ninth day after burial (the *novendialis*), a meal was shared at the place of burial, signifying the end of the mourning period.

The so-called cult of the dead – only a small part of which has been discussed here – was an important part of Roman life, as it ensured the memory of ancestors through frequent commemoration. This commemoration also served as a reminder for those left behind that, if they were faithful in their upkeep of these rituals, they too could expect the same kind of living memory after their death. Many of these rites took place outside the home; as discussed above, the meals for the dead (such as the *cena novendialis*), the pouring of libations, and the lighting of candles usually occurred at the site of burial. However, the starting place for the cult of the dead was in the home, immediately following death and preceding the funeral procession; and, in cases where the site of burial could not be easily accessed, rites would be performed in the home.

ANCESTOR CULT

In addition to the rituals specifically associated with death, burial, and funerary preparation in the cult of the dead were ones dedicated to honouring the family's ancestors. The ancestor cult was at least as important as the cult of the *Lares*, especially in the homes of aristocratic Romans from Republican families. Certainly the ancestor cult had protective functions, just as the *Lares* and *Penates* did; keeping the ancestors satisfied and well-maintained meant that they would protect the home from malicious spirits. Conversely, of course, refusal to maintain the ancestor cult and to offer the appropriate sacrifices could result in consequences for the family, either through harmful actions taken by spurned ancestral spirits, or, perhaps more importantly, through a loss of status.[37]

Continued adherence to the ancestor cult meant an unbroken line of inheritance for a Roman *familia*. It is therefore likely that the ancestors also played a role in many of the family's important events: for example, the birth of a child, rites of passage, and funerary rites.[38] As Flower notes, it is difficult to say whether the ancestors were actually "participants" in the rites accompanying these events, or whether they were simply spectators.[39]

As discussed above, part of the reason for maintaining the domestic cults was to demonstrate to visitors to the *domus* that a Roman was wealthy, pious, and deserving of his or her position in society. The same was true of the maintenance of the ancestor cult. Having (and displaying) aristocratic lineage was especially important in the Republican and early Imperial periods. After the Christian era, however, a desire to substantiate one's place in the status system of the Roman world continued to be strong – even, or especially, for freedmen. Wealth could be accumulated; the acquisition of social status was far more difficult.[40] Part of this social status was inextricably linked with one's position in the genealogical connection to the Republic's founding families. If it were impossible to marry into one of these families, the best one could do as a substitute would be to demonstrate (or feign) belonging in a family of good standing and known history. As Hillner asserts, "membership of a multi-generational family was an important component of Roman aristocratic identity."[41] Citizens who desired upward mobility, then, appropriated the practice of displaying ancestor masks or busts, despite the fact that they did not really have a claim to them.[42] Thus, the continued maintenance of the relationship between the living and the dead was essential for both established and status-seeking Romans.

WORSHIP OF NON-TRADITIONAL DEITIES IN THE HOUSEHOLD

Rituals to the ancestors and to the household gods come most immediately to mind when considering Roman domestic worship. Other deities, however, were also worshipped in houses. Depending on the family, and whether its members had any special religious or cultic affiliations (or affinities), deities other than the *Lares* and *Penates* were both materially represented and celebrated in the house. These deities could be represented as votive statuettes or subjects in painted shrines, or they could be mentioned in votive inscriptions. Many deities enjoyed a place in the household shrines, and there were often regional trends that dictated the popularity of certain deities.

For example, in Pompeii, the most commonly attested gods in household shrines, excepting the household gods, were Hercules, Bacchus, and Venus. To a lesser extent, Mercury, Minerva, Apollo, Priapus, and Silenus were also present. These Roman gods had special functions in the city of Pompeii; Bacchus, for example, had an obvious connection to the Vesuvian region, famous for its grape harvest.[43] Foreign gods were also popular in *lararia*; in Pompeii, Isis was quite prevalent, along with her compatriots Anubis and Harpocrates.[44] According to the *Historia Augusta*, even the emperor Alexander Severus had in one of his *lararia* images of heroes and gods from other cultures, including Abraham, Orpheus, and interestingly, Jesus Christ.[45]

However, the worship of deities other than the traditional household gods – especially those from foreign cultures – could occasionally draw criticism. Writing during a time when Rome's citizens were wracked with illness, Livy laments:

> Not only were the bodies attacked by the plague; varied superstition made its way into human spirits too, mostly from the outside … those afflicted by religious madness, by claiming to be seers and introducing new sacrificial customs into the houses … For they saw in every block of houses and in every little sanctuary alien and unknown expiatory sacrifices intended to beseech the gods to show favour. Therefore the aediles were charged to see that only the Roman gods were worshipped, and this in no way other than that inherited from the fathers. (*History* 4.30.9–11)[46]

There are a few points of interest here: first, that household or private worship is assumed by Livy to have been ubiquitous; second, that "alien" gods (or exotic gods) are to be abhorred, especially in times of crisis;[47] and third, that there is an "appropriate" and accepted way to worship in the home – that is, "in no way other than that inherited from the fathers," which is presumably a reference to the cult of the *Lares* and *Penates*. However, the preponderance of data in Pompeii alone indicates that the "traditional" gods were not the only deities honoured in the household; special relationships between families and other gods – including those with a more public presence, as well as those belonging to the foreign or "exotic" group of deities – could be cultivated in the home alongside the domestic gods.

EVIDENCE OF THE HOUSEHOLD SHRINES IN DOMESTIC WORSHIP

Literary sources confirm the widespread presence of the household shrines. Cicero, in an oration concerning the theft and perceived desecration of his house while in exile, muses on the sanctity of houses:

> What is a 'sanctum' to any higher degree, what more protected by every religious practice, than the house of each one of the citizens? Here we find in one and the same place the altars, here the hearths, here the household gods, here the cults, religious practices, and the ceremonies. This place of refuge is so much a 'sanctum' for everyone that it is not permissible to tear anyone away from his house. (*De Domo Sua* 41.109)[48]

As Klauck claims, Cicero understands the house to be holy not by "consecration of the building, but through the forms of religious praxis that are carried out with pious intention by those who dwell in it."[49] It is clear that Cicero, although speaking rhetorically, imagines the typical Roman dwelling to house the domestic gods and their rites.[50]

The majority of the data for domestic worship in shrines, however, comes from extant shrines themselves. It is difficult to construct a typology for all of the different types of shrines across the Empire, especially given the patchy nature of the material evidence. However, Boyce's *Corpus of the Lararia of Pompeii*, as well as Bakker's *Living and Working with the Gods* and Giacobello's more recent *Larari Pompeiani*, provide an excellent overview of the dominant models of shrines in the Roman world.[51]

In addition to houses or *domus*, shrines or evidence of private worship are found in workshops, baths, depots, shops, bars, markets, hotels, and apartments. Every type of space in which people lived and worked has some evidence of the worship of the domestic gods. But how widespread were these shrines? Boyce has catalogued 550 shrines from Pompeii alone; a large number also survive from Herculaneum. The presence of wooden altars at Herculaneum indicates the likelihood of more portable altars in places that did not have a permanent shrine.[52] Domestic shrines can be found at Ostia, and all over the provinces. While the majority of evidence comes from Pompeii and Herculaneum, both literary and material sources confirm their presence throughout the Empire.

Since worship of the household deities was a daily (or nearly daily) practice, it stands to reason that many extant *lararia* have been found in central locations, including entranceways, atria, and peristyles. Others have been found in or near the kitchen, which has been interpreted as an indication of a slave- or kitchen-oriented cult.[53] Regardless of room choice, it is most often the case that shrines are located in an area large enough for the entire *familia* to meet and participate.[54]

TYPES OF SHRINES TO THE DOMESTIC GODS

Extant shrines exist in a number of different forms, with the most common types being simple niches or the more elaborate *aediculae*. Some shrines were also incorporated into wall paintings, and, in rare cases, entire rooms (*sacella*) were set apart for the domestic cult. In modern scholarship, these shrines are usually called *lararia* (sing. *lararium*), as the *Lares* were the most commonly worshipped gods.[55] However, it should be noted that *lararia* also frequently portrayed the Genius as well as the *Lares*, sometimes the *Penates*, and, as mentioned above, other deities altogether. Despite the fact that most shrines found in houses tend to be called *lararia*, this should not be taken as an indication that only the *Lares* were worshipped there.

Niches

The most common form of household shrine, niches are found in a wide range of private housing, from the humblest one-room workshop to the grandest villa. Niches vary in size from very small (enough to house perhaps a statuette and an offering) to quite large (enough to house a number of statuettes and an offering). The niches themselves are generally the same type of niches used for lamps or other general items in the home; however, the decoration of some niches, and the debris left in and around them, helps to determine which are shrines, and which are simply holes in the wall.

Positively identifying niches as shrines has always been problematic. It is often difficult to be sure whether a niche was used as a shrine to the domestic gods, or whether a niche was simply a niche. When niches have evidence of statuary inside them, or if they have been painted or decorated, it is generally safe to say that they were used as shrines. However, even niches that show traces of burning candles or incense ought not to be interpreted automatically as having been shrines; evidence of burning could simply indicate that a niche was used to hold an oil lamp to light an area of the house.[56]

3.1 *Lararium* niche, Caseggiato del Larario, Ostia

There are cases, however, where it is clear that a niche found in a domestic setting was used as a *lararium*. The niche in the Caseggiato del Larario at Ostia is one such example; due to its prominent placement in the atrium of the communal dwelling complex, as well as the architectural detail and "polychrome" tile of the niche, it is safe to say that it was used for special (which is to say, ritual) purposes.[57] Other niches have been found with traces of painted decoration, indicating that they were used for a purpose other than storage or lamplight. Niches that have been plastered, but not painted, are also likely candidates for *lararia*.[58]

The name of the Domus del Larario reveals its obvious relevance to this discussion. In this building (a typical *domus* with living space and workshops attached), a courtyard houses a niche that has been identified as a *lararium*, constructed during the Antonine period.[59] This particular niche is plastered, and shows traces of paint. Other features that identify it as more than just an ordinary niche include an arch, built into the wall of the courtyard above the shrine, and two marble slabs, above and below the arch. The lower one has depressions that Bakker has identified

3.2 Outdoor aedicular shrine, Herculaneum

as pivot-holes, indicating that the shrine would have had doors, somewhat like a cupboard. Although it is impossible to identify which of the household deities were honoured in the shrine, the cupboard style could indicate an ancestor cult (since, as above, the *imagines* were sensitive to light and often kept behind special wooden doors). Generally, however, the data in support of the household cult in the Domus del Larario indicates a primacy of place as well as decoration, indicating its continued importance into the late second century CE.

Aediculae

Aedicular shrines are freestanding shrines with architectural features (thus "*aedicula*," or "little temple"). These shrines are much more elaborate than niche shrines, sometimes featuring painted decoration as well as relief sculpture. Other *aediculae* were built of brick, which would then have been plastered with stucco and decorated. Because of their more elaborate design, this type of shrine was most frequently located in

3.3 Painted *lararium* from the Caupona of Euxinus, Pompeii. The image of the painted *lararium* is from a thermopolium, rather than a domestic space, but is of a type consistent with other examples found in Campania. (For comparison, consider the extensively painted wall in the House of Sutoria Primigenia, Pompeii, and the painted *lararium* with incorporated altar in the House of the Lararium, Terzigno.)

houses owned by Romans of some stature. The public location of *aediculae* – in the atrium or the peristyle, more often than not – also meant that they sent a message of wealth and piety to those visiting the house of a wealthy Roman. These "public" shrines were often incorporated into the broader decorative scheme of the house, and ought to be considered quite permanent.

Most *aediculae* have a space for statuettes of the *Lares*, of the Genius, or of other gods connected to the family; in the case of the *lararium* from the House of the Tragic Poet, that space is a plastered, painted niche. These niches were generally not set with cabinet doors, but rather left open; this construction suggests a public display of the family gods that corresponds well with the evidence of domestic worship. Statuettes found in houses indicate the type of images that would have been displayed in these *aediculae*, and offerings (incense, flowers, and the like) would also have been placed in the niches of these *aediculae*.

Wall Paintings

Many of the *lararia* from Pompeii and Herculaneum are essentially wall paintings, most commonly found in the more public areas of the home. Some of these paintings have accompanying architectural features, such as pediments, pilasters, or shelves, while others are simply figures painted directly on the wall.[60] These painted *lararia* could be constructed around niches, the decoration of which would be incorporated into the larger scheme of the shrine, or around altars, which project from the wall into the space of the room. In nearly all cases, however, these wall paintings are clearly demarcated from the rest of the wall decoration. That is, even in those examples where there are no architectural features, borders or frames have been painted around the visual representation of the household deities, or the shrine is situated on its own wall or portion of the wall. These painted *lararia* should not be viewed with the same eye as the painted decoration on the rest of the walls of a house; they reflect spaces made separate for domestic worship.

In many cases, the painted shrines have a strong presence in the landscape of the home, taking up anywhere from the upper half of a wall to an entire wall of a room. The subjects of these paintings are most often a pair of *Lares*, flanking the Genius of the *pater familias*, and very often accompanied by large, curling serpents. It is unclear exactly what the serpents, sometimes depicted singly, sometimes in pairs, are meant to represent. They may represent the Genius of the *pater familias*, the *Lares*, the *Penates*, or deceased ancestors.[61] Other gods, too, are occasionally represented in painted *lararia*, including Bacchus, who had a special relationship with the city.

A wide selection of this type of shrine shows these subjects in remarkably similar poses and engaging in the same activities. Because of the similarity of the paintings, these painted *lararia* also serve as valuable data for the ritual practice of the home. The Genius, when present, is usually togate, with the hood drawn over his head in the style of the Pontifex Maximus or any priest engaged in the act of sacrifice, as on the Ara Pacis Augustae, which also shows an aedicular shrine. He often has in his hand a *patera*, out of which he is most likely pouring a libation. Sometimes the Genius stands near an altar, and often, he is flanked by the twin figures of the youthful *Lares*. The *Lares* are frequently carrying

3.4 Aeneas sacrificing, Ara Pacis (detail)

different types of sacrificial implements, and sometimes musical instruments. When a serpent or pair of serpents is present, they are often located below the triad of domestic gods, curling around an altar; these serpents are usually bearded. Occasionally there will be painted upon the altar what seems to be sacrifices or first fruits.[62] These activities, though taking place in the spirit or godly realm, must be quite similar to those ritual actions performed by members of the *familia*. The *pater familias* would be performing in the earthly realm the same type of libation sacrifice that his Genius performs perpetually in the painting. As discussed above, the depictions of certain types of fruit and vegetable offerings on painted altars should be seen as permanent visual representations of the offerings that were placed on the altars in the earthly realm as well – an assumption borne out by the evidence for burnt offerings at Pompeii and Herculaneum.

Sacella

A less common and more elaborate type of worship space for the household gods is the *sacellum*. This type is less a shrine than it is a room; therefore, it would be only the wealthiest (and among those, the most ostentatiously pious) who would have had a *sacellum* in their house. Relatively uncommon in the surviving evidence, *sacella* are rooms set apart as temples in miniature, where the domestic gods – and more often than not, other deities special to the owner of the house –would have been worshipped. *Sacella* can also be characterized as a kind of small chapel. They are often open to the rest of the atrium or other central space, meaning that visitors to the house would be able to see very clearly the cultic affiliation of the household. Heavily and elaborately decorated, a *sacellum* is a good indicator of the wealth of its owner.[63] In general, *sacella* were far less common than more affordable types of domestic shrines, but there are a few instances of them in the Campanian evidence.[64]

Portable Shrines and Altars

In addition to the more permanent shrines discussed above, many portable altars have also been found at Pompeii and Herculaneum. Their sheer numbers indicate the ubiquitous nature of the household cult, a fact supported by the literary evidence. While it is a dubious claim that *all* houses in Roman Italy (and possibly beyond) would have had a shrine to the household gods, it is not unreasonable, based on the evidence of portable altars, to assume that the practice of domestic worship occurred in more than just those houses where permanent altars were found. Portable altars indicate domestic cult presence beyond what can be empirically demonstrated by permanent, material evidence.

Portable altars ranged from a simple tripod design, constructed in wood, to more elaborate cabinets.[65] The latter category raises questions about the actual portability of these so-called portable altars; perhaps "semi-permanent" is a better appellation for these types. One of the finest examples of a semi-permanent altar comes from the aptly named Casa del Sacello di Legno, at Herculaneum. The city of Herculaneum, of course, is famous for its carbonized wood, a product of the eruption of Vesuvius that has provided numerous examples of furnishings, doors, window frames, and other artifacts usually absent from archaeological sites. The aforementioned cabinet was found in the atrium, and had the combined function of cabinet and shrine (*aedicula*).[66] This kind of chest, whether an *armarium* (a place to store valuables), a *lararium*, or simply a strongbox, was also used to house the gods if necessary.[67] The cabinet in the Casa del Sacello di Legno can be categorized as a *lararium* because of two factors: first, statuettes of Hercules and Venus were found inside the upper portion of the cabinet, indicating that this portion of the cabinet

3.5 The so-called Symmachi-Nichomachi Diptych

was used for their veneration; second, delicate columns flank the upper portion of the cabinet, a feature common to household shrines, whether painted, constructed in the round, or carved in relief.[68] Given the nature of the ancestor cult and its accoutrements, it would also make sense that this type of cabinet, complete with folding doors, could have been used to house ancestor masks, especially if they were located in the atrium (the locus, generally, of the ancestor cult).

Other types of altars are known mainly from their representation in painted *lararia* or in other artistic media. Among the finer examples is an ivory diptych, showing a matron, accompanied and assisted by a slave, making an offering of incense on a household altar.[69] There are a number of interesting features that come to light in the examination of this diptych, especially the less-damaged right portion. First, if the dating is accurate, then it is clear that household worship was still being performed in the fourth century CE. Second, the altar is positioned in an outside space; a tree in the background clearly indicates that the offering is being made in either a garden, a peristyle, or on the grounds of a rural estate. That the altar is consecrated to the household cult is not in question, given the presence of serpents encircling the two visible sides of the altar. It is also interesting that a matron is depicted offering the incense; this may be meant to depict the wife of the man who has just successfully won the consulship.

The same kind of altar is pictured numerous times in wall paintings at Pompeii.[70] In some cases, the serpent or serpents are entwined around the altar, while in other instances the serpent is slithering in the space immediately adjacent to the representation of the altar. In terms of placement, many of these altars seem to be in outdoor space, although again, it is unclear whether the altar is in a peristyle, garden, or field. The most commonly occurring altars are round, while others are rectangular, and most of these types seem to be constructed from stone, making them at the very least semi-permanent (rather than portable). Also depicted in wall paintings (frequently in *lararia* themselves) are altars used by the Genius for sacrifices. While the diptych clearly shows a human subject making an offering to the household gods (represented by the serpents on the altar), other representations show the altar residing in the spirit world, where the Genius makes offerings in perpetuity on behalf of the family. Examples of this type are generally rectangular, as opposed to the round altars that frequently accompany the serpents.[71]

IMAGINES OF THE ANCESTORS

Veneration of the ancestors was another facet of the rites of the domestic sphere. There is little evidence to suggest that ancestors of elite families were honoured in the same shrines as those used for the domestic deities. However, images of the ancestors (called *imagines*) were kept in many Roman houses. These *imagines* were usually portrait faces, made of wax or terracotta, although marble or costly metals could be used in families of some wealth (and certainly this was the case in the imperial household).[72] The *imagines* had a primary function in funerary rites (as described above), but they were also kept on display in the atrium of an elite Roman house. Appeasing the ancestors was part of their veneration, but so too was the advertisement of one's family status. Thus, it was important for a Roman family to have their *imagines* in the public eye.

In general, the *imagines* of the ancestors would have been kept in a cupboard specially made for them, which would have displayed the masks to the many clients and guests who visited the atrium on a daily basis. These cupboards would generally have stood open, and on special days, masks would have been decorated and festooned with garlands, just as the *lararia* were.[73]

LOCATION OF SHRINES TO THE DOMESTIC GODS

Where shrines were placed in houses varied. Generalizing about domestic shrines is, as ever, limited somewhat by the fact that the majority of the data comes from the Campanian towns of Pompeii and Herculaneum. It is difficult to determine whether the patterns of activity and location in these southern towns would have been the same as those in Rome, to say nothing of provincial locations. Still, a comparison between Ostia and Pompeii or Herculaneum can provide us with a more complete cross-section. Ostia was, of course, a merchant or "working-class" settlement, whereas Pompeii and Herculaneum were more heavily populated with villas used by wealthy vacationers.

As mentioned above, there have been some attempts to catalogue the location of shrines. Portable shrines, of course, are impossible to place, but permanent and semi-permanent altars can be organized. Much of the impetus to catalogue the locations of shrines seems to come from a desire to pinpoint patterns of activity in the Roman house, especially as they relate to interactions between members of the *familia*. There are several schools of thought on this subject, and it is worth discussing them briefly here. Placement of the shrines to the household gods has some bearing on the interpretation of space that will be employed later; whether the head of the house or the slaves of the house likely used the shrine(s) will be germane to the discussion of shared space.

Shrines can be used to potentially identify areas that would have been frequented by specific members of the family, especially in the Pompeian evidence. For example, the *tablinum* is widely recognized as having been used by the *pater familias* to conduct his morning business. So too can elaborate decoration sometimes indicate the purpose of or access to a particular room. For example, while *cubicula* in many houses are left undecorated, thereby offering no real clues about their inhabitants, some *cubicula* are so heavily adorned that they positively identify their occupant as a person of status.[74] It is doubtful that a room with expensive furnishings or paintings would have been used by a slave or lesser member of the *familia*.

There have been attempts to catalogue shrines according to the status of the worshipper, and the data are often suggestive.[75] If shrines are found more frequently in kitchens, storerooms, and near cisterns, it could indicate that the worshippers who used these shrines were slaves and labourers, since these areas of the house were the focal areas of their responsibilities. However, even if the data were conclusive (which they are not), caution is necessary when interpreting what this actually meant for worshippers in a house. Attempts to show that worship occurring in these more service-oriented quarters of the home was geared specifically toward slaves, or indeed, that slaves had their own shrines, are problematic. Slaves may certainly have borne the responsibility of daily maintenance of these shrines, but there is little to suggest that the *pater familias*'s role as the arbiter of a pious home would have been absent from any place in the house, no matter how humble. Further, while slaves may have been responsible for the majority of the work in the kitchens and storerooms, the safety and maintenance of these rooms and their contents were, in fact, integral to the continued prosperity of the *familia*, and should not be perceived as areas "belonging" to slaves. As discussed above, the entire *familia* would assemble to participate in the rites of the domestic cult on special days, and there is no reason to assume that the kitchens or storerooms would have been viewed as slave-only areas.[76] It must be acknowledged that it is nearly impossible to designate worship areas – and by extension, specific deities or practices – according to status.

In some of the larger villas or *domus*, there are shrines in more than one area of the house. These separate shrines may sometimes represent separate family groups, especially if shrines are located on upper floors which seem to have had separate access, such as an external staircase, or if there were replications of major room types, such as another atrium or *triclinium*. For example, House v.17 in Herculaneum has an upper floor which probably housed a family separate from the one on the first floor; this conjecture is based on the fact that there is a second hearth and a second *lararium* there. As Wallace-Hadrill points out, both the hearth and the *lararium* indicate "separate worship and family unity."[77] Both of the areas have their own shrines. The shrines are thus self-identifying as well as protective, denoting a separate group. On the other hand, we have already seen houses that have more than one shrine to the household gods, and it is not always clear that there would have been more than one family group, especially if there is no clear architectural separation.

Available data also seems to suggest that many shrines were kept in the more public parts of the home: for example, the atrium or courtyard and the peristyle. The houses of the Vettii and of Menander, both from Pompeii, have famous *lararia*, and in both houses, the *lararia* are located in a central courtyard or atrium.[78] These shrines are also quite elaborate, indicating their importance. The well-known *lararium* in the House of the Vettii is classified as a wall-painting type; however, it has accompanying architectural features that indicate its function as being similar to that of a temple (or similar to an *aediculum*).

A temple-style pediment and two flanking columns, along with a base or shelf decorated in relief, project from the wall. Painted onto the wall itself are representations of the deities being worshipped: two *Lares*, represented as dancing, garlanded youths, and the Genius, represented as a togate figure in the act of sacrifice.

There is also literary evidence to suggest that some domestic shrines were outdoors, especially on farms or rural estates. For example, Horace's *Ode* 3.22 notes a dedication of a pine tree to Diana, in her role as mistress of childbirth.[79] The farm's owner commits to offering the goddess a sacrifice each year in a particular place on his property, which he has dedicated to her. Some images of altars, as in the diptych of Quintus Aurelius Symmachus, discussed above, also indicate an outdoor location.

SHRINES IN WORKSHOPS AND COMMUNAL LIVING SPACES

Although the focus of this study is on the shrines in the *domus* of the elite Romans, it is worth noting the presence of the domestic gods in other types of spaces. Some of these spaces are not solely domestic, due to their central function as places of business. At the same time, it is clear that some proprietors of shops would have used their work space as their living space as well, and thus, the space of the shop would then become a domestic space. Other types of spaces include, as discussed earlier, apartment buildings (*insulae*), or at Ostia, communal living quarters (*caseggiati*). These communal living spaces also exhibit signs of private worship, but in a slightly different way. Especially in the *caseggiati*, there are data suggesting that a single shrine or private worship area served the entire community who used the space.

For example, the shrine in the entrance to the Caseggiato del Larario in Ostia (I, IX, 3) indicates the likelihood of a single shrine serving an entire group. The shrine is very large, and centrally located; it is the focal point upon entrance to the courtyard.[80] Surrounding the courtyard are a number of shops, and it has often been described as a kind of shopping or business centre. There is some debate over the use of the shrine, however. Obviously, the naming of the *caseggiato* indicates the excavators' belief that the shrine was used to honour the household gods. Bakker, on the other hand, points out that the shrine's size would accommodate a large single statue – indicating a different deity than the *Lares*. Regardless of the deity or deities worshipped in this niche, there is a definite presence of ritual and religious practice, a connection being made between the owners of the shops and the deities that protect their businesses (and keep the customers coming in). Although the *caseggiato* is not strictly domestic space, the niche does indicate a communal offering on the part of the members of the guild. The upper floors, if they were indeed apartments, most likely had shrines of their own.

CULTURAL CONTEXT OF THE DOMESTIC CULT

Having discussed the nature of the rites and practices associated with the domestic cult, as well as the material record of the types and function of shrines, it is important to situate the domestic cult in the greater cultural consciousness of the Roman Empire. As with the civic cults of Rome, piety and *Romanitas* were reflected in private worship by consistent religious praxis. As is so often stated, the Roman house functioned as a microcosm of the state; domestic rituals were essential to the health and prosperity of the family as well as the Empire as a whole.[81]

As discussed in chapter 2, the homes of the wealthy or the elite were a reflection of their owners' status and associations. Shelley Hales discusses the need for "Romanness to be architecturally expressed in individual domestic units," just as political and religious affiliations were expressed in public, monumental architecture.[82] In the same way that Augustus flooded the Empire with images of his victory in Egypt, the Roman *pater familias* filled his home with markers of his identity. Because Roman houses, especially those of the wealthy, were both private and public, it is important to recognize that a house was not a neutral container; it was purposely filled with imagery which would communicate a particular message. Vitruvius also discussed the obligation of a *pater familias* to have a home that reflected his social status and mores; the house, therefore, was suffused with rhetoric.[83]

This *Romanitas*, reflected in the dwelling places of Romans, would naturally demand the presence of shrines to the household gods. In Petronius's *Satyricon*, an ostentatious aedicular shrine to the *Lares* is prominently displayed, a testament to Trimalchio's desire for a sense of belonging and *Romanitas*.[84] A *pater familias* would have chosen subjects for his shrine that reflected his cultic affiliations; the household shrine was, as Foss called it, "a unique and personalized ritual topography at home."[85]

It must be noted that, *Romanitas* notwithstanding, the rites of the household were sometimes perceived as dangerous to the public good. Private worship could sometimes represent uncontrolled, unmonitored worship. Certainly this would have been the case with regard to the mystery cults as well as to Christianity. It is highly unlikely that domestic rituals were monitored by Roman lawmakers; surely such an undertaking would have been impractical, if not impossible. The relationship, however, between private and public cult could be complex. On the one hand, the domestic cult in its traditional sense – that is, the veneration of the *Lares* and *Penates*, and to some extent, the emperor – both upheld and honoured the civic cult. On the other hand, as Klauck states, "the domestic cult also had an antagonistic effect above all by providing a detour along which foreign cultic forms could become established."[86] Giving Romans free rein to worship whomever and whatever they chose in their homes could be viewed as a dangerous affair, since close monitoring would have been impossible. Indeed, the Christians sometimes bore the brunt of this fear.

PLACE AND RITUAL ACTIVITY IN ROMAN IDENTITY FORMATION

Of special interest in the current conversation is the relationship between the domestic deities and the "place" of the home. Since domestic rites were ubiquitous, it is clear that their accompanying shrines occupied a certain pride of place in the homes of pious Romans. Further, it is important to recognize that household religion demanded a household. That is, a *familia* (defined not only as the "nuclear" family, but including extended family, slaves, clients, and freedpersons) needed a place to congregate in order to perform the rituals that bound the *familia* to each other and to their continued success. Perhaps most obviously manifest in the practice of ancestor worship, there was a definite connection between the *domus* and the *familia*, and that connection was nurtured through the domestic cult. The practice of the household cult was a key factor in the maintenance of the family as a group of human beings, but the house itself – the locus for this practice – was also essential.

There has been, in recent years, a good deal of discussion concerning the formation of identity in the Roman world, as well as the early

Christian world. Literary sources of course confirm the responsibilities of a pious Roman, just as New Testament texts (such as the letters of Paul) contribute to the understanding of the roles and responsibilities of a new Christian. In addition to these literary sources, however, material sources contribute positively to the search for ancient identity construction. These material sources – in this case, the data pertaining specifically to the domestic living space of the Romans and the practices of the domestic cult – indicate *place* as a major factor in identity.[87] In general, the domestic cult is understood to be a part of the overall ritual responsibility of the Romans to their gods, forming a key part of the *pax deorum* and, by extension, their identity as Romans. Shelley Hales argues that the "observation or avoidance of appropriate rituals conveyed assent to or dissent from Roman society," a factor apparent in both the civic and domestic spheres.[88] Should a homeowner refuse to participate in the traditional expression of piety through the domestic cult, it would have been noted as dissent by visitors to the home. Material representation of the domestic cult would have signified to visitors that the inhabitants of the house were behaving in a manner befitting their status.

Identity through piety is especially prevalent in the domestic cult. Bettina Bergman has argued that Roman houses, and specifically the houses of the Roman elite, are geared to prompt memory. This memory is not only individual, but collective; the display of the ancestors in the domestic sphere acts as a repository for the collective understanding of *Romanitas* as a whole.[89] She notes that "a Roman's house was perceived as an extension of self, signaling piety to divine protectors and social and genealogical status to the world outside."[90] While Bergman's exploration of the House of the Tragic Poet underscores that the presence of domestic cult worship is an important mode of expressing *Romanitas*, she also argues that this expression can be mitigated by a combination of family and social factors, including personal choice and piety.[91] John Bodel also recognizes this confluence of both external factors and choice.[92] The expression of domestic piety, then, is somewhere between private piety and institutionalized piety. While on the one hand, the gods chosen for worship in domestic shrines are left up to the owner's discretion, on the other hand, visitors to the house would expect to see particular figures represented, including the *Lares* and the ancestors. Thus, the ritual landscape of the Roman house reflects identity, both collective and individual, but always marshalled through expectation, tradition, and status (actual and aspirational).

To return to Cicero's *De Domo Sua*, the relationship between the place of the home and his identity is clearly demarcated. It is obvious that his return from exile will never be complete until he is reinstated in his house (which was taken over by his sworn enemy, Clodius). He cries:

> If you place me in my house, then I do plainly see and feel that I am restored, which is what all through my cause you have been always labouring to effect by your displays of zeal, by your counsels, and influence, and resolutions; but if my house is not only not restored to me, but is even allowed to continue to furnish my enemy with a memorial of my distress, of his own wicked triumph, of the public calamity, who is there who will consider this a restoration, and not rather an eternal punishment? (37.100)

Cicero goes on to complain about the "tomb" of Clodius that is now present in what was once his home. This violation is not simply one of property, but also of sanctity. The house of a Roman is a place where specific family rituals take place, where the ancestors and the ancestors' gods are therefore accessible. For a Roman, especially a pious one like Cicero, to have someone else take over one's house is the deepest affront. Throughout Cicero's treatise it is clear that the usurping of his space is a religious violation (and indeed, it is important to note that his speech is addressed to the college of priests, rather than the Senate). Clodius's attempt to maintain ownership of the house by claiming that he has "consecrated" it is exactly the issue at hand; Cicero argues that the house has already been "consecrated," through the presence of his own ancestral gods and the habitual practice of their cult.[93]

Recently, Stanley Stowers and John Bodel have discussed the ways in which the religious practices of the household both create and substantiate the importance of a specific place. It can sometimes be argued that the household deities travelled along with the important members of their families; indeed, this seems to have been the case in the story of Aeneas and his flight from Troy.[94] At the same time, however, the family gods were also perceived by the Romans to be representative of a specific place, which in turn indicates ownership of that place by the family who owns the gods. The oft-cited lament of Cicero indicates the intensity of the violation incurred by the removal of his household gods from the place where they ought to reside.[95] Indeed, as Stowers (following J.Z. Smith) has pointed out, "the religion of household and family … is the ultimate religion of place."[96] The reason for this is that domestic space – whether a home, a *domus*, or an apartment block – is itself the ultimate expression of place.[97] If a temple is the place (or home) of the god, then it stands to reason that the place (or shrine) of the god(s) dedicated to the household would be doubly emplaced. It is necessary that they remain with their "people" as well as in their "place." This emplacement ensures that the "place" will continue to belong to the right people – the *familia* that owns and operates the *domus*, and which performs the rites of the household gods. Further, the ongoing ritual activity dedicated to the gods upholds the relationship between them, while also entrenching the place of the home in the practice of domestic piety. There is an inextricable link between the place of a household and the worship of the domestic gods.

It is clear, then, that the sacred rites of household religion in Rome were key to formulations of identity, ownership, and emplacedness. The space of the house, a site of self-representation and *Romanitas*, could therefore create obstacles to the practice of a new ritual group. It will be necessary to discuss both the ritual practices of the Christians and the negotiation of space in order to determine the ways in which this seeming divisiveness could have been overcome.

SOME CONCLUSIONS

In the foregoing chapter, an assemblage of literary and material evidence for household worship has demonstrated the essential connection between the Roman domestic cult and the life of the *familia*. Not only was the Roman domestic cult an expression of piety toward the gods; it was also essential as an expression of *Romanitas*. Furthermore, and perhaps most importantly, the success, safety, and longevity of the family was intimately bound up with its practice. These rites performed by the family bound them to each other, to their places, and to safety. Given this profound connection between the Roman domestic cult and the family, one ought to question whether it would have been possible – let alone probable – for converts to Christianity to have rejected the rites and practices that not only commemorated their existence, but formulated and maintained it.

It is worth asking, then, how domestic cult practice might have continued in the homes of Christians, including those Christians who donated their space to the house-church communities. Further, it is important to understand that this confluence of polytheistic and Christian activity may have resulted in a dual ritual landscape in the domestic houses used by house-church Christians. In other words, both specifically Christian and specifically domestic rituals would need to have been housed in the same space.

CHAPTER FOUR

House-Church Christianity and Roman Domestic Worship

The material and literary data of the Roman domestic cult reveals the latter's integral character in the fabric of Roman daily life and ritual practice. The question remains, however, whether the practices of the Roman domestic cult would have continued in houses that were inhabited by Christians or used by Christians for worship. Some might say that the answer is obvious: Christians would not have tolerated images of and practices pertaining to Roman gods in their houses or house churches. Certainly, the testimonies of some early church fathers suggest that the separation between Roman polytheist and Christ follower extended not only to public cult, but to the domestic cult as well. At the same time, there is a good deal of evidence for the continued use of polytheistic iconography in both Christian funerary art and, more importantly for this discussion, *domus ecclesiae*. In order to determine whether it is likely that members of some Christ-confessing communities may have continued to practise the domestic cult, the spaces used by these communities need to be explored in detail.

In this chapter, I will explore first the literary evidence for Christian attitudes towards the domestic cult, with a view to establishing the orthodox view on domestic cult. While, as one might expect, the majority of relevant writings clearly reject idolatrous practices, attitudes towards the domestic cult in particular are not always obvious or consistent. Next, with a view to materializing this literary perspective, I will present two case studies for mixed iconography – and, in one case, perhaps even mixed ritual practice – in late Roman house churches. The Christian building at Dura Europos and the villa at Lullingstone in Roman Britain reveal a fascinating juxtaposition between Roman polytheistic and Christian iconography, ideology, and practice, suggesting a lived experience of conversion to Christianity that is not consistent with a wholesale rejection of polytheistic elements. In looking at these literary and material data, it ought to become clear that, for some householders at least, accepting Christ did not necessitate rejecting the domestic cult.

CHRISTIAN ATTITUDES TOWARDS ROMAN DOMESTIC CULT

Since the earliest Christians met in domestic spaces, one would expect that they had responses to and notions about these spaces, and to the practices that occurred there. Perhaps surprisingly, there are very few examples in early Christian writing that refer specifically to domestic space, and fewer still relating to the practice of the domestic cult. After the advent of purpose-built architecture for specifically Christian practice, more attention is paid to the use and function of that space, including its potential sanctity, purity, and the violation thereof.[1] In the earliest period, however, this kind of preoccupation with space seems to be absent. As suggested in earlier chapters of this work, conceptions of sacred space are indicative of the later, established church, rather than the house-church movement. In chapters 5 and 6, the concept of sanctity in house churches will be investigated in detail, especially in relation to ritual practice. To facilitate that discussion of sacred space, however, it will first be necessary to investigate what we do know about the attitudes of Christians toward domestic cult and domestic space.

The domestic cult hardly enjoys a prominent place in texts pertaining to Roman religious practice. The data for Roman domestic cult comes predominantly from material, rather than literary, sources. It should hardly be surprising, then, that the early Christians also had little to say concerning the rites of the household. There are no references to the domestic cult in the Pauline corpus or the canonical Gospels, or indeed, anywhere in the New Testament. The discussion of the domestic gods only exists in later writing, beginning with Tertullian in the late second century. Because there is little reference to the domestic cult in early Christian writings, I will also discuss the attitudes of early Christians toward Roman cults in general – and more specifically, the worship of idols. A strong case can be made that the figurines and paintings of the household gods, present in many houses across the Empire, are similar to the idols worshipped in Roman temples. It is also clear that gods other than the typical domestic gods were worshipped in household shrines and represented by figurines; Bacchus, Minerva, Hercules, and other deities were present in many homes via pictorial or sculptural representation.[2] The *Lares* and *Penates*, too, were represented as small-scale figurines and placed in household niches. A large number of niches in homes were there to house just this type of figurine. That some early Christians might have viewed these figurines as idols is very likely.[3]

Paul condemns idol worship in a number of his letters, and the practice of idolatry is discussed as something to be abhorred in many of the canonical books of the New Testament.[4] The most obvious example for house-church communities can be found in 1 Corinthians 8–10. In these chapters, Paul broaches the difficult subject of how an idol is identified, and what difficulties other deities present, given the fact that, for Paul (and those who understand and embrace the concept of monotheism), they do not actually exist. In 1 Cor 8:4–6, Paul states:

> Hence, as to the eating of food offered to idols, we know that 'no idol in the world really exists,' and that 'there is no God but one.' Indeed, even though there may be so-called gods in heaven or on earth – as in fact there are many gods and many lords – yet for us there is one God, the father, from whom are all things and for whom we exist, and one Lord, Jesus Christ, through whom we exist.

The debate here is between the so-called strong and weak members in the Corinthian community.[5] Some members of the community feel free to eat the meat offered to idols, because they understand that idols and other gods are nothing, that they are empty of divinity. Other members of the community, however, are struggling with the fact that such members continue to eat meat offered to idols when they are supposed to be living a life dedicated only to God. For converts to the Jesus movement out of polytheism, eating meat offered to idols would have been explicitly connected to festivals and feast days held in honour of particular deities; to consume that meat would be a reminder of religious rites and practices of the civic cult.[6]

Paul's task here is twofold: first, he confirms the emptiness of the idols, in accordance with the understanding espoused by the strong members of the community; second, he upholds the concerns of the weak members by discouraging the consumption of idol meat on communal, rather than moral or spiritual, grounds. While Paul seems to share the view of the strong, which is that there is no danger in consuming meat offered to idols (1 Cor 10:23–26), he also demands that they recognize their social responsibility to their own community, and, therefore, that they do not fall into the trap of living like their idol-worshipping neighbours.[7] This contradiction is made even more apparent in 1 Cor 10:19–20, where Paul states:

> What do I imply then? That food sacrificed to idols is anything, or that an idol is anything? No, I imply that what pagans sacrifice, they sacrifice to demons and not to God. I do not want you to be partners with demons. You cannot drink the cup of the Lord and the cup of demons.[8]

Thus, the consumption of meat offered to idols is to be avoided, since it is not of God, but of demons. More important than the place of idols or other gods in a cosmological context, however, is the place of the so-called strong and weak members in the Corinthian community, both internally – as people socially obligated to one another in communal love – and externally – as people differentiated from the community at large. While this passage does not specifically mention the domestic cult, it does highlight the difficulties that could arise in a community in the process of negotiating between its new beliefs and its environment. The boundaries between the Christ-confessing group and the broader Corinthian community are blurred, and the level of engagement with idolatrous or polytheistic practices is, for some members, unclear.

Tertullian, too, condemns the worship of idols, and discusses the domestic cult in particular. He specifically mentions the household deities in his *Apologia*, stating:

> As for the household gods, whom you call the Lares, you treat them with a householder's power, pawning them, selling them, or changing them, sometimes making Saturn into a cooking pan or Minerva into a ladle. (*Apol.* 13.4)[9]

Tertullian is expressing his contempt for the seemingly fickle nature of those Romans who worship their domestic deities. Although the domestic gods are supposed to be deities, the humans still exercise power over them. The implication is that these divinities are impotent, a fact that their worshippers prove by their own actions. It is not only the domestic gods who suffer mockery at the hands of their adherents, according to Tertullian (*Apol.* 13.1–9). All of the gods of the Roman pantheon are subject to the same inconsistencies and personal preferences of their worshippers, and these inconsistencies strengthen Tertullian's basic argument that these deities are meaningless.[10]

In his treatise *De Idolatria*, it becomes clear that Tertullian in fact has a twofold position on idols. While the previous example indicates that Tertullian sees idols as meaningless, here the idols represent evil demons, and the worship of idols prohibits the worship of God. He states, for example:

> On this account the zeal of faith will deliver its laments, crying out, 'Does a Christian come from idols into the church, from the workshops of the adversary into the house of God; does he raise to God the Father hands that are the mothers of idols, to worship with those very hands which outside are worshipped in opposition to God; does he lay on the body of the Lord those very hands that confer bodies on demons?' (7.1)[11]

Tertullian's concern seems to be with hypocrisy, but there is also the implicit notion that those who worship idols, or present offerings to them when they are not with the church community, bring into the assembly of Christ a certain degree of pollution. Implicit also in this passage is the notion that there is a "house of God" at all; it seems clear that Tertullian is speaking of a specific place of worship, which is being polluted by hypocrites and believers in false gods. If we see the community of Tertullian as having met in houses, however, then this "house of God" would have been first and foremost a house – or some kind of domestic space. The question, of course, is whether the domestic cult (and its associated paintings and figurines) would be construed as idolatry in the same sense that is meant by Tertullian's understanding of civic cult practice. Based on this passage, it could be assumed that houses used for assembly by the church would have been cleansed from the polluting elements of domestic idolatry. At the same time, there are no specific injunctions demanding the cessation of domestic cult practice in house churches, or indeed in houses at all, before the fifth century.[12]

Another passage to consider from the writings of Tertullian is from his work *De Anima*. Here, he discusses the *superstitio* of the rituals that accompany childbirth, and equates the attendant deities with Satan:

> For to what individual of the human race will not the evil spirit cleave, ready to entrap their souls from the very portal of their birth, at which he is invited to be present in all those superstitious processes which accompany childbearing. (39.1)[13]

As described above, a traditional Roman family would engage in protective rituals upon the birth of a child, including the processes of cleansing and naming the child. Tertullian argues that these rituals, meant to be protective, are in fact commending the spirit of the child into the hands of evil spirits. The assignment of *genii* at the point of naming is another way of welcoming demons into the child (39). He discusses the ubiquitous nature of these childbirth rituals, saying, "does anyone fail to devote to idolatrous service the entire head of his son, or to take out a hair, or to shave off the whole with a razor … on behalf of the clan, of the ancestry, or for public devotion?" (ibid.). He goes on to note: "Hence in no case (I mean of the heathen, of course) is there any nativity which is pure of idolatrous superstition" (ibid.). Tertullian is clearly well versed in the practice of childbirth rituals, and fears their continued practice, as the children themselves are being polluted through these rituals. Unlike the scornful attitude expressed toward the household gods in the previous passage, Tertullian here is alerting parents to the dangers of the continued practice of the domestic cult.

It is also clear that this danger is being expressed to members of his own community, which indicates that there were likely members of this community who were continuing to offer sacrifices and perform the apotropaic rituals associated with childbirth. Tertullian is not telling Christians about rituals that they did not practise; rather, he is attempting to convince them that the rituals that they perhaps see as normative are in fact dangerous. That Tertullian needs to mention it at all is strong evidence that some Christians were still engaging in domestic cult practice. This continued practice is all the more likely when one considers the lack of a Christian substitute. Tertullian attempts to provide a counterbalance for the converts who wonder what to do with their children, saying:

> It was from this circumstance that the apostle said, that when either of the parents was sanctified, the children were holy; and this as much by the prerogative of the (Christian) seed as by the discipline of the institution (by baptism, and Christian education). (39)[14]

Tertullian is perhaps attempting to assuage concerns that Christian parents could have had about the children they might have brought into the world via these archaic customs. At the same time, even his reminder of sanctification through parental conversion does not provide a ritual alternative for parents wishing to protect their newborn children from death, disease, and evil spirits. The idea that sanctification could occur through conversion (and later, through baptism and Christian education) is a different notion altogether, and part of a different system than the one familiar to those who converted out of Roman polytheism.[15]

In addition, it should also be noted that the audience for this writing would not have been the Christian population at large. In the case of Paul, of course, the audience is clear; his letters are composed as specific responses to communities who have asked his advice (in this case, the community at Corinth). For Tertullian's writings, the audience is much less apparent. Certainly, the language and composition of Tertullian's work indicates a highly literate readership, indicating that very few members of his community would themselves have read or heard Tertullian's arguments about idolatry and the domestic cult. At the same time, despite the polemical attitude expressed by Tertullian, especially in *De Anima* and *De Idolatria*, his writings seem to be meant for an insider audience; his efforts here are reminding those inside the Christ-confessing community of appropriate beliefs and practices.[16] Given the nature of these writings, those able to read and to pass on the contents of these works would have been higher-status members – the most likely people to have been patrons and hosts of the church. These higher-status Christians were also more likely to have been implicated in the practice of civic cult, and so too would they likely have continued to espouse domestic cult practice, unless specifically instructed not to do so. As discussed already, self-representation and piety in the home were powerful markers of upper-status Romans. Yet even here, Tertullian implies rather than instructs, leaving the wealthy literate Christians who were his audience without viable ritual alternatives. If this understanding of his audience is coupled with the idea that the domestic cult was perhaps not even recognized by many Christians as problematic, there is a distinct possibility that domestic cult practice may have continued.

Gods of the domestic cult are also mentioned in later writers. Cyprian, for example, makes brief mention of the *Penates* in his treatise, *Quod idola dii non sint* 4. In this work, he names a large number of the Roman gods, ranging from archaic gods (Castor and Pollux, Romulus) to the Capitoline gods (Jupiter, Juno) to the domestic gods (the *Penates*). These gods, according to Cyprian, are all conquered, not only by the coming of Christ, but more importantly, because they were only ever human beings in the first place, elevated to the status of divinity by human choice and action.[17]

Attitudes towards traditional Roman gods remained inconsistent and confusing even after the Christianization of the Empire began after

Constantine. Writers such as Lactantius, Arnobius, and Augustine continued to grapple with the relationship to the gods in the lives of Christians. Lactantius (d. 325), writing after the peace of Constantine, uses many of the same arguments against the domestic cult that earlier writers did, especially the argument that domestic gods are evil spirits:

> They attach themselves, therefore, to individuals, and occupy houses under the name of *Genii* or *Penates*. To these … libations are daily offered as to the *Lares*, to these honour is paid as to the averters of evils. These from the beginning, so that they might turn men away from the knowledge of the true God, introduced new superstitions and worship of gods. (*Epitome* 28)[18]

Lactantius's admonition against the domestic gods is very similar to what Tertullian expressed in *De Anima*. He also describes the daily enactment of ritual in the home, and characterizes the domestic gods as evil spirits. Perhaps more interestingly, it is clear from Lactantius's treatise that domestic cult practices continued into the fourth century.

Arnobius of Sicca (d. 330) also mentions the domestic gods, albeit briefly. In the *Adversus Nationes* he discusses and attempts to understand the pantheon of gods while acknowledging the one true God of Christianity.[19] Arnobius here sees the domestic deities as empty of all divine nature, as he does all anthropomorphic gods of the Romans. Like Tertullian, the evidence he uses to demonstrate the inefficacy of the domestic deities is the lack of knowledge (or confused knowledge) possessed by their worshippers themselves. If the worshippers do not know whom to call upon for a particular ailment or request, how then, asks Arnobius, might anyone expect relief? He states:

> For every one who seeks to obtain an answer from any deity, should of necessity know to whom he makes supplication, on whom he calls, from whom he asks help for the affairs and occasions of human life; especially as you yourselves declare that all the gods do not have all power, and that the wrath and anger of each are appeased by different rites. (*Adv.Nat.* 3.42)[20]

It is clear that first- and second-century attitudes toward the domestic gods were not always consistent. On the one hand, idols and frying pans do not pose a threat to Christianity, but on the other hand, performing rituals to these same deities can sometimes be seen as actively harmful.

This inconsistency, which will be explored further below, indicates a lack of clear, incisive prohibition of the domestic cult within Christian homes and meeting places.

Even later is the testimony of Augustine (d. 430), writing well after the Roman Empire was transformed into a Christian Empire. In this period, Christians were engaging in image-breaking, a kind of vengeful countermand to the years of persecution they suffered through at the hands of the Romans. In an excerpt from Augustine's *Sermones*, he seems to be responding to accusations that Christians are trespassing on their neighbours' property to seek out and destroy their idols. The use of idols here seems to refer to deities worshipped in the private sphere, which would more often than not indicate the presence of domestic cult. Of course, this issue may have pertained also to estate owners on whose property temples or sacred groves were set up; but in general, it is safe to assume that all domestic worship is coming under scrutiny in this sermon. Here, Augustine claims that these accusations are unfounded, and that Christians will only enter someone else's property in order to destroy idols if they are specifically asked. He does note the importance of this idol destruction for converts and believers, saying:

> We are persecutors of idols; we openly profess it. Are we then to be the preservers of them? I do not touch them when I have not the power; I do not touch them when the lord of the property complains of it; but when he wishes it to be done, and gives thanks for it, I should incur guilt if I did it not. (*Sermones* 62.12.18)[21]

Augustine is clear about the fact that domestic idols are at odds with the faith of Christianity. He goes on to speak rather vehemently about people who enter into the house of God without having removed the idols from their property, or worse, having offered to them: he equates it to entering a workshop with muddy hands. He rails against the hypocrites who dare to come into the house of God knowing that they continue to practice idol worship. He then returns to his discussion of the removal of idols on a person's property, citing a specific case where the Christians were asked for aid in the removal of private idols from an estate whose lands were donated to the church (62.12.18).

In this sermon, Augustine is using both the example of this faithful estate owner and the polemic against the hypocrites who continue to practice idol worship to remind his audience of the dangers of continuing to practise polytheistic ritual, even in a private context. Because

Augustine's writing here is meant for insiders, members of the Christian community, it is not meant to educate polytheists about the dangers of domestic worship. Rather, he is speaking here in order to call out those Christians who seem not to have relinquished their attachment to domestic idols, perhaps not realizing that these are idols in the same respect as publicly placed idols. That Augustine needs to remind his congregation that the worship of private gods is idolatrous should indicate that, even in the fifth century, domestic cult worship was still going on within the Christian community. It is also worth noting that this is the first recorded example that amounts to anything like an injunction against the domestic cult; up to this point, the domestic cult has been treated with contempt and fear, but without specific instructions about how a pious Christian ought to proceed.[22]

Thus, it is clear that there were varied and sometimes contradictory responses to the domestic cult within the early Christian community. It is difficult to negotiate the monotheistic message of Christianity with the polytheistic practice of the domestic cult. It seems right to assert that the ritual practice of the domestic cult was viewed as unacceptable by some early Christian writers. Whether deities were seen as empty of divinity (perhaps by Paul, Arnobius, and sometimes Tertullian), or carriers of evil (sometimes by Tertullian, Lactantius, and Augustine), participating in their veneration should have been as clearly unacceptable as participating in the civic cult of the public sphere. The testimonies above, however, offer a few interesting features to consider: first, the practice of the domestic cult continued at least into the fifth century in some regions; second, the argument that domestic gods were evil spirits, made by some authors, suggests that there was some confusion over the characterization of the domestic gods in some Christian communities; and third, the presence of idols in the domestic sphere did not present problems for all believers, given the fact that this practice continued. On the one hand, it is clear that early Christian writers, from Paul to Tertullian to Augustine, saw all Roman cults, including the domestic cult, as outside the realm of Christian practice. On the other hand, it should also be clear that ideal Christian practice, as represented in the texts of these Christian writers, must have been radically different from the lived experience of the house-church Christians. Given these factors, there is a distinct possibility that domestic cult practice continued in the houses of some Christians, and indeed, in some of the houses used by Christians for worship.

While this assertion may seem to be in opposition to a surface reading of the texts, the literary evidence for Christian attitudes towards the domestic cult, in conjunction with the material evidence for the practice of the Roman domestic cult (presented in chapter 3), suggests ubiquitous practice of that cult in a private context, with no Christian alternative or specific injunction against its practice prior to the fifth century. Indeed, the lack of systematized Christian rituals in the domestic context, especially for life-cycle events (commonly associated with fear and danger), should be reason enough for pause. It is difficult to imagine that a group of former polytheists, steeped in the importance of ritual to mark and protect the family during important life events, would cease to be concerned about this commemoration and protection upon conversion. Until such time as Christian rituals provided adequate substitutes, it is much more logical to surmise that converts out of polytheism would simply have continued to practise the family rituals with which they were familiar, and upon which they and their families were dependent.

In order to see this theoretical framework in action, however, it will be necessary to look at examples of known Christian meeting places, and determine whether or not the model of conflicted space and coexistent ideologies can be upheld. As discussed throughout this work, there is a frustrating dearth of material evidence for specifically Christian meeting places in the period before Constantine. At the same time, the investigation of the different types of spaces available to Christians in this period has demonstrated the importance of speaking more specifically about Christian space. Two sites will be discussed below, each representing different points on the spectrum of Christian worship space: the Christian building at Dura Europos and the Roman villa at Lullingstone. The space at Dura Europos was clearly adapted from domestic space in order to provide a place for worship; it was no longer inhabited by a family, and was therefore not a house church proper, but perhaps better defined as a *domus ecclesiae*.[23] The villa at Lullingstone is dated to the post-Constantinian era and also has articulated worship space, bringing it, too, out of the realm of the house church as it has been defined and discussed here. These sites, however, offer points of interest that can be brought to bear on the discussion of earlier spaces, including the coexistence of polytheistic and Christian elements in a post-Constantinian worship space. Both of these spaces provide further challenges to the conception of early Christian sacred space. In each of the models of domestic space presented below, focus will be placed on specific issues that would likely have arisen due to the juxtaposition of a given space and the practice of Christian ritual. After discussing these two later examples, I will examine the application of their points of relevance to the house church.

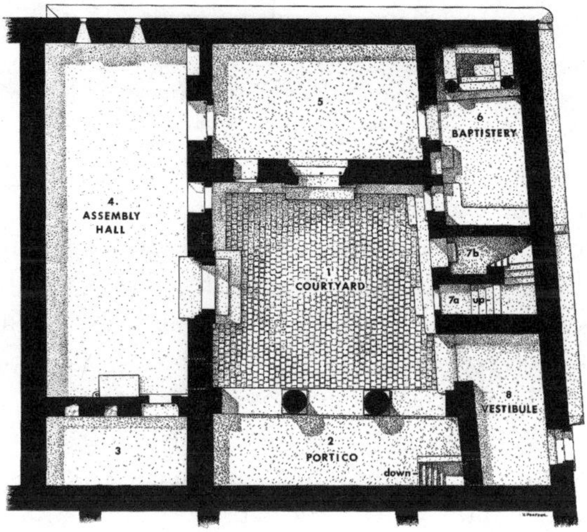

4.1 Floor plan, renovated Christian building at Dura Europos

CASE STUDY ONE: DURA EUROPOS

In the mid-third century, in an outpost in the eastern Empire, a Christian community had enough money, organization, and freedom to create a space in which to hold their meetings. At Dura Europos, the Christians were able to convert a domestic space into a worship space.[24] Unlike the unrenovated house churches, the meeting place at Dura was no longer inhabited by the time it reached its latest stage (d. 256 CE). The final field report on the Christian building indicates that the cesspool associated with the private dwelling was covered over around the mid-third century, indicating the strong possibility that the house was entirely given over to the church and no longer inhabited by a family group.[25] Structural adaptations, which were in some cases extensive, completed the transformation from *domus* to *domus ecclesiae*. Given the lack of inhabitants and the level of renovation of the structure, one might expect to find here, at last, a space in which the Christians could have met, without the problematic elements of domestic life and domestic cult practice.

In order to analyze the space used by the Durene Christian community, it will be necessary to discuss its architectural history. The Christian building at Dura underwent a series of changes in its lifetime. Originally, it was a private dwelling (constructed 232/3). It was later renovated to house the meetings of Christians, but there is no clear indication that the house was used for Christian meetings before its adaptation.[26] The renovations that transformed the dwelling into a permanent meeting place were performed around the year 241 CE, and the building remained in use until its destruction (along with the rest of the city) in 256 CE.[27] The renovations were quite extensive, and included knocking down walls, tiling and paving the courtyard, constructing benches both inside and outside, and plastering the walls. The most important modifications, both structurally and in terms of the creation of worship space, were the expansion of the dining room into a larger assembly hall and the creation of a baptistery in the southwest corner of the house (Room 6). The baptistery marks the earliest material evidence for dedicated baptismal space.

The baptistery at Dura is notable for many reasons, not the least of which is that it houses the earliest non-funerary wall paintings associated with Christianity. On the walls of the baptistery are scenes from both the Hebrew Bible and the New Testament, including Jonah, Adam and Eve, the women visiting the tomb of Jesus, the Samaritan woman at the well, the healing of the paralytic, and the miracle of walking on water. Much has been written about these paintings, from aesthetic analysis to programmatic analysis, and it is not necessary to repeat that work here.[28] The consensus view marks the baptistery as sacred, essential space for the members of the community, with the paintings serving didactic as well as decorative functions.

The baptistery has at its west end a font, which was the locus for the initiation ritual. The font is outfitted with two columns and a curved ceiling, the back of which features a "Good Shepherd" figure, and which is itself decorated with a starry sky.[29] It is generally believed that Room 5, located between 4B and 6, was used as a room for the catechumens, although the designation of this room as such is unclear.[30] Room 5 is ideally located for transitional and overflow space before the initiation ritual; the catechumens could have gathered here before entering, as the baptistery itself is quite small. It certainly seems as though Room 5 did serve as the official entrance into the baptistery, however, since there is a formal doorway, with columns and decorated lintel, leading from Room 5 to Room 6. Another entrance (or exit) runs between the baptistery and the courtyard, but it is much smaller and undecorated. While the ritual of baptism was not secret, the exact nature of the preparations and individual purification involved would certainly benefit from a private (or at least limited) space.[31] Overall, the baptistery is important for a number of reasons: it is the first space dedicated to the ritual of baptism; the wall paintings indicate the development of non-funerary Christian art in the third century;

and the baptistery forms an essential part of an axis of sacred space which likely includes Room 5.

In addition to the construction of the baptistery, another major structural renovation was the creation of an assembly hall. The rectangular hall was formed in the suite of rooms located on the south side of the building. The three rooms that formed this suite are designated as Room 3, Room 4A, and Room 4B. Room 3 was originally a storeroom, and likely kept its function after renovation. Rooms 4A and 4B, however, were combined into one room by knocking down the wall between them. The field reports indicate that, in the original dwelling, Room 4A was the dining room (*triclinium* or *diwan*), which is obvious for two reasons. The first is that access to the room is gained via a formal doorway, consistent with *triclinia* in the area.[32] The second is that there is evidence of paving (or rubble) in accordance with a *triclinium* formation, located beneath the final floor level.[33] The room's walls were given a light coating of plaster, presumably to cover the ragged areas where the wall had been torn out. Small windows were added on the courtyard side of the room, in order to provide light and ventilation to the large group which must have met there. Nothing of an altar or table remains. At the front of the room, however, on the eastern side, was a raised platform or *bema*.[34] This platform is likely where preaching and teaching took place.[35] There is no evidence of permanent seating arrangements in the assembly hall, but it has been suggested that congregants could have sat on portable benches or reed mats.[36] Since the *triclinium* formation was removed, and the two rooms put together, it can be safely assumed that the *agape* meal was no longer practised here.[37] A lack of kitchen facilities confirm that this meeting place was no longer a dining room, but an assembly hall.

The structure of the assembly hall at Dura Europos was modified carefully, but its decor seems not to have received the same level of attention. In the opposite corner of the house, the community saw fit to decorate the baptistery with extensive wall paintings, relevant to Christianity and the ritual practised there. The assembly hall, on the other hand, was not painted with figural or biblical scenes. Rather, like all other areas of the house, it was covered over with a simple layer of whitewashed plaster. The only modification to this overall scheme was the patching of the plaster where the wall separating rooms 4A and 4B was removed, and an additional coating of plaster all over 4A and 4B to cover the scars of renovation.[38]

What is interesting, however, is that there was found on the northern wall of the excavated assembly hall a section of plaster molding, once part of an ornamental frieze, which wound around the wall of Room 4A while it was still a dining room.[39] The content of this frieze was bacchic; it was decorated with satyr masks, cymbals, animals, and other symbols associated with the worship of Bacchus (Dionysus).[40] The frieze is not cultic in function; it likely served as decoration in the dining room of the private house. There is no indication that the house was specially connected to bacchic worship; indeed, bacchic decoration is common elsewhere at Dura, functioning in a similar capacity.[41] At the same time, given the extensive renovation undertaken in order to modify the private dwelling into a place used exclusively for Christian worship, it is suggestive that the frieze was allowed to stay. In fact, the frieze was not even kept in its complete form, meaning that the preservation of the work as an artistic whole was clearly not the motivating factor for its continued presence. Since the wall between 4A and 4B was taken down, the portions of the frieze on the western and southern portions of 4A would have been removed entirely, leaving only two sides of the frieze on the eastern and northern walls after the assembly hall was created.[42] It is not clear whether the frieze remained on both these walls, or whether it was also removed from the eastern wall, but there was clearly an inconsistent arrangement of the frieze in the new assembly hall. Despite this aesthetic inconsistency, the frieze remained.

More important than an aesthetic inconsistency is what might be deemed an ideological inconsistency. While the function of the frieze could not be argued as cultic, it does feature subject matter pertaining to a Roman deity. In general, the frieze and its continued presence in the Durene assembly hall has been largely ignored by scholars who write on the Christian building, and little has been provided by way of analysis. In fact, a detailed image of the frieze has not been published.[43] The paintings in the baptistery, on the other hand, have been analyzed extensively, and often a "programmatic" quality has been assigned to them.[44] The bacchic frieze in the assembly hall is certainly not programmatic, and obviously not Christian in character, but it is worth asking what kind of impact the frieze might have had on an attendee at the Dura church.

Those few scholars who have mentioned the bacchic frieze have suggested a few possible interpretations. Jeanne Halgren Kilde, in her discussion of Christian sacred space, discusses the frieze in conjunction with the space of the baptistery and the assembly hall at Dura. Her overall view of the Durene building is that it both accommodated and reflected a growing hierarchical arrangement of community members, accompanied by an "increasing formality" of ritual.[45] According to Kilde, renovation and decoration in the *domus ecclesiae* would have helped to "concentrate viewers' attention on Christ and worship."[46] In other words, in the Durene building, images had power, with the ability to instruct, focus, and shift the attentions of the worshippers onto the task at hand. The specifically Christian paintings in the baptistery, then, would have had a recognizable function in the performance of the baptismal ritual.[47] At the same time, this power is not recognized in reference to the bacchic frieze in the assembly hall. Kilde suggests that the retention of the frieze could reflect "a certain level of tolerance for other religious views or a level of comfort with the syncretistic blending of symbols from other religious perspectives."[48] She does not suggest, however, that the frieze was engaged in the ritual practice of the assembly hall, as she does with the paintings in the baptistery.

Kilde does not offer reasons for the frieze's continued presence in the assembly hall. The bacchic frieze is almost entirely ignored as she puts forth potential reasons for leaving the assembly hall undecorated.[49] She suggests that "ornament was considered inappropriate to the hall, or of less importance there than in the baptistery," and, giving the baptistery pride of place, alternatively speculates that the Christian community here "had simply not gotten around to decorating the assembly hall" before the building was destroyed in 256.[50] While the discrepancy of ornamentation between the baptistery and the assembly hall is certainly intriguing, it cannot be said that the assembly hall was left entirely unadorned, given the presence of the bacchic frieze. As for rules of appropriate and inappropriate ornamentation, if ornamentation in general was not considered appropriate for the assembly hall, then surely ornamentation associated with the cult of a traditional Roman god would be even less appropriate. Kilde's final suggestion, that the community simply had not yet decorated the hall, makes good sense, although it raises interesting questions about gradations of sanctity in the *domus ecclesiae.* Kilde suggests that the community may have perceived the baptistery as "the more significant, more holy space."[51] Do the paintings in the baptistery, for example, indicate its status as a place of greater sanctity than the assembly hall, and if so, did the ritual of baptism demand greater sanctity than the ritual of the eucharist?[52] The difficulty of Kilde's analysis speaks volumes about the problematic nature of a bacchic frieze in the assembly hall of what is the only demonstrable, pre-Constantinian *domus ecclesiae* in the archaeological record.

It is not only Kilde's analysis that does not provide adequate explanation for the presence of such an object in the main assembly hall. John Pfordresher argues that the "pagan frieze with its allusions to Bacchus had not been obliterated when the room was remodeled because it was quite easy for early Christians to see in the pagan god of wine a symbolic anticipation of their Savior [*sic*], who shared wine with his followers on their last night together and who transformed wine into his own saving blood."[53] While David Balch has also argued for interaction between domestic art with polytheistic subjects and Christian viewers in the house church, that this interpretation could have been performed as easily or as naturally as Pfordresher suggests is difficult to believe.[54] Balch, for example, claims that Paul (and other teachers) would have delivered lengthy sermons and homilies explaining the ideological links between the known tales of traditional Roman gods and the message of the new tradition. Balch explores popular subjects of domestic art that depict suffering, noting that their presence and the general knowledge of their stories would have provided a context in which to understand the voluntary suffering of Jesus Christ, as presented by Paul.[55]

The suggestion that domestic art provided a rich context for a new narrative of resurrection is certainly more convincing than the notion that Bacchus would simply be understood as a symbol for Christ, but this interpretation seems laboured when applied to the Durene building. While the domestic art in a house church could not have been removed easily, the frieze in the *domus ecclesiae* surely could have been removed along with the other extensive renovations, should the community have demanded it. In addition, the frieze would hardly have been necessary as comparative material for a community already well positioned and longstanding enough to afford its own private building for worship. The fact that explanations of, and engagement with, the frieze would have been necessary also presupposes that the community would have recognized the problem outright and demanded an explanation – or, that they would have actively felt the dissonance between a partial bacchic frieze and the rituals of Christianity.

Kraeling also offers very little by way of explanation of the frieze. Indeed, he spends a good deal of time musing about the relative lack of decoration in the assembly hall, as compared to the baptistery. He suggests that the assembly hall may have been simply plastered in order to avoid distracting from the speaker's message, noting the importance of the "charismatic gifts" among the congregants at this time.[56] He wonders, therefore, whether "Christian assembly halls were not decorated at this time because the oral *praedicatio Verbi* by the ordained teacher still had a special force such as would have made it seem unnecessary or undesirable to add or interpose any other medium for the communication of substance of the divine revelation."[57] He extrapolates from the assembly hall at Dura the possibility that all Christian assembly halls – in contrast to contemporary synagogues – were left without decoration because of the *charisma* of the teacher.[58] His comment that the charisma of the preacher or teacher *still* had force in this period implies that it was a necessary function of earlier spaces. In earlier house churches, of course, many walls would have been heavily decorated with wall paintings. The implication here is that biblical narrative paintings (such as those in the baptistery) could have distracted from the words of the teacher, but how much more of an issue might distraction have been with wall paintings of polytheistic subjects? In any case, the presence of the bacchic frieze, as noted above with reference to Kilde's argument, means that the assembly hall was not free from decoration.

Other commentators ignore the frieze almost entirely. Graydon Snyder mentions the frieze in passing, noting that the assembly hall "remained decorated as before with a bacchic plaster frieze and a new coat of plaster."[59] No attempt to explain the presence of the frieze is made, although Snyder's discussion of the entire building is quite brief. David Balch and Carolyn Osiek have stated that, "while the wall decoration of the assembly hall remained *traditional*, the walls of the baptistery room were adorned with biblical scenes."[60] It is unclear whether the descriptor "traditional" is meant to refer to the frieze or to the whitewashed walls.

White, too, mentions the frieze in his analysis of the building, but does not venture a guess as to the reason for its lingering presence. He does discuss the paintings in the baptistery, drawing attention to their "programmatic quality."[61] Like Kraeling, White notes the possibility that the baptistery paintings were actually incorporated into the ritual itself, and suggests that there "may have been a conscious design of the artistic program of the room to conform to some liturgical pattern of usage in conjunction with baptismal ritual."[62] Wharton also discusses the paintings in the baptistery, claiming that they served a participatory function. She states that they "occupied the privileged core of the shrine's religious space; they were not ornamental additions to peripheral arenas of ritual."[63] Although she does not mention the bacchic frieze explicitly here, one wonders whether it is what she is referring to when she discusses "ornamental additions." Again, the art of the baptistery is understood to have a powerful function, while the bacchic frieze is simply regarded as unimportant.

In all of these discussions, there is very little conversation about sacred space as it pertains to the assembly hall. Clearly, the baptistery is seen as a centre of ritual, and therefore a sacred space. It is obvious that the baptistery was chosen as a special place in order to perform the baptismal ritual, and it was decorated as no other room seems to have been. As for the assembly hall, its character is less obvious, and the discussion of the bacchic frieze on its walls points to that lack of clarity. For the foregoing commentators, it seems that the hall itself is less significant, and perhaps less of a sacred space, than the baptistery. This view is shared by Kraeling, who sees the baptistery as the most important room in the modified space. Indeed, Kraeling asserts that the space of the hall is not "ritual in character, for the assembly rooms do not have installations serving such purposes. Instead it must be religious."[64] What is meant by religious here soon becomes clear, as he goes on to explain that the religious character of the assembly hall is "in the case of the Christian community the divine 'call' enunciated on God's behalf by Christ which constituted the company of those 'called' (*keklemenoi*) … thereby creating the Church (*ekklesia*)."[65] Kraeling is here adopting the well-worn argument that the hall is not itself a place of importance, but rather, that it serves only as the gathering place for the true church, the "ones called," or the body of believers.

The production of sacred space is linked to ritual performance.[66] If commentators on the Durene building hierarchize the space – that is, if they prioritize the baptistery as more sacred or holy than the assembly hall – they are, by extension, implying that the rituals taking place in the assembly hall are less important than the rite of baptism. At the same time, however, the assembly hall was the locus for the gathering of the believers – arguably an essential ritual – as well as for the eucharist. Implicit in the prioritization of the baptistery over the assembly hall, then, is that the rituals of gathering and eucharist, as well as prayer and teaching, are less significant than the ritual of baptism. Further, the lack of engagement with the bacchic frieze, along with the suggestion that the assembly hall did not demand ornament, seems to suggest that the assembly hall is not sacred space at all. Yet, given the dynamic relationship between ritual performance and the production of sacred space, even the gathering of the believers – while perhaps a less obviously sacred ritual of the community than the initiatory rite of baptism – would produce sacred space. Further, the structural modifications, including a *bema* at one end, indicate the centrality of this room to the Durene community. Indeed, it would have been the room in which all members were allowed to meet, unlike the baptistery, which was used only sporadically and for specific purpose.

In chapter 5, the rituals of the Christian community will be discussed, including baptism, the eucharist, prayer, and teaching. Baptism is undoubtedly a central ritual in early Christianity, functioning as it does as the initiatory, binding ritual of a catechumen to his or her new "family." One therefore expects a sacred space for the ritual of baptism, and indeed, this sacred space is exactly what is found at Dura Europos. But the eucharist is also a sacred ritual – one which few would argue is less central, sacred, or important to the Christian community than baptism. It is worth asking, then, why the space set apart at Dura for baptism is understood to be "more sacred" than the space set apart for assembly, where the sacred ritual of the eucharist undoubtedly occurred.

Later, in chapter 6, it will be argued that preexistent sacred space is not necessary for the sanctity of ritual. Instead, in house churches, the ritual itself, through its performance and enactment, served to create the sacred space in which the ritual took place. However, when the shift toward uninhabited space came, as it did at Dura Europos, the choice was made to delineate the sacred space for ritual in architectural terms. A room was set aside and decorated extravagantly for the ritual of baptism (Room 6), and separated from other areas of the *domus ecclesiae*. That this room had special status is clear. At the same time, it is not only for baptism that rooms were set apart and given specific functions at Dura Europos. A room was also set aside for the hall of assembly, in which prayer and teaching, as well as the eucharist, took place. In addition, a room was likely set aside for the preparation of baptizands (Room 5), or for the teaching of the uninitiated catechumenate before they embarked on the initiation ritual of baptism. There is no reason to assume that the space that housed the rite of the eucharist was any less sacred than the baptistery. Certainly, this raises the question of why paintings were not also set up in the assembly hall (as indeed they were in the neighbouring synagogue), but the default assumption need not be that the assembly hall was less sacred, or even neutral. Indeed, as Kilde noted, the assembly hall shows distinctive signs of reflecting changes in the community, including the separation and hierarchization of clergy, which itself has been argued as a major factor in the later development of sacred space in purpose-built architecture. Thus, the assembly hall ought to be considered sacred space, while also recognizing that it was not necessary for that sacred space to be "cleansed" of problematic elements, such as the bacchic frieze.[67]

Moving beyond the assembly hall and baptistery, it is important to note a few smaller finds of interest in the building. Among these smaller finds are two terracotta plaques, found in the excavation of the Christian building. Both are reliefs, and both depict female figures; one is a small medallion and the other is a larger plaque.[68] In the plaque, a special female figure is clearly depicted. A woman stands before a small temple with her right hand outstretched, potentially in a gesture of blessing. She has been identified as Atargatis, the great protective and fertility goddess of Syria.[69] The presence of these terracotta small finds in the Christian building is something of a riddle, and worth discussing briefly here. Based on stylistic comparison, the two terracottas have been dated to around the mid-second century; they are themselves older than the building, even when it was a private dwelling.[70] It could be suggested that they were the property of the original owner, who left them there upon giving the building over to the church, and that they were perhaps adopted by the Christians "as a symbol of the blessing of the church or its apostles."[71] Kraeling discourages this interpretation, suggesting instead that the two terracottas were part of backfill, deposited after the house was destroyed.[72] Indeed, the findspot of the smaller medallion (embedded in mud brick) indicates rather that it was deposited by workmen who were filling the structures after the destruction of the city; that is, the findspot seems to demonstrate that the medallion came from elsewhere, and was never part of the functioning Christian building at all.[73] As for the plaque, no findspot was recorded, and therefore, it is impossible to say whether it was part of the same cache, used as backfill, or whether it was a separate piece, existing throughout the tenure of the Christian building. On the one hand, it may seem ridiculous to suggest that the terracotta plaque of Atargatis would have been allowed to remain in the Christian building, but operating purely on anti-polytheistic assumptions, the bacchic frieze in the assembly hall should also have been removed. Without a recorded findspot, the default assumption for its use ought not to be predicated on a view of the space as incompatible with polytheistic elements.

Other items of note also contribute to the overall understanding of the Christian building at Dura and the coexistence of seemingly disparate practices or artistic subjects. Of interest is the presence of small circles of green-blue glass (likely the bottom of a vessel or bottle), embedded in the wall, just above the lintel, between Rooms 4B and 5, between Room 5 and the courtyard, and between Rooms 5 and 6. Kraeling has argued that Room 5 was originally the *gunaikon* of the private dwelling, and that these glass circles had probable apotropaic functions, such as warding off the "evil eye."[74] Such apotropaic devices were common in Dura, as elsewhere.[75] That they were originally connected to the *gunaikon* of the private dwelling is possible, but they were still present in the adapted structure. In fact, Kraeling later connects the apotropaic devices to the importance of Room 5, in support of his suggestion that Room 5 was used as a preparatory room for the baptismal ritual; he points out that all three access points to Room 5 have an apotropaic device associated with them.[76] Again, a traditionally polytheistic item is maintained in the Christian building, either through a lack of concern about its presence or through continued use.

Other noteworthy items include two niches: one located in the courtyard, and another in Room 6, the baptistery. The niche in the courtyard was, as Kraeling argues, placed too high on the wall to have been of purely practical function (for example, as a niche for a lamp), which associates it with the domestic cult practice of the inhabitants of the private dwelling.[77] While there is nothing to suggest the niche's continued cultic use during the period of the *domus ecclesiae*, it was also not filled in. It is unclear whether the niche may have acquired a new function, or whether it would have been left empty. As for the niche in Room 6, it underwent modification during the transformation into a baptistery; its rectangular shape was changed to an arcuated one. The function of this niche is not known, but on the basis of the attention paid to its modification, as well as its location in the baptistery, it is likely that it related in some way to the new ritual. These two niches, along with the other artifacts discussed, are vestigial yet visually striking reminders of the cultic practice of the pre-Christian building.

THE CHRISTIAN BUILDING AT DURA AND THE HOUSE CHURCH

In general, it is true that the Christian building at Dura reflects a very different stage from the one espoused during the era of the unrenovated house church. Structural and aesthetic modifications meant that the Christians in this community were thoughtful and active in reference to their space. While it can be problematic to retroject patterns and practices of later models onto earlier models, the adaptation of the private dwelling at Dura reflects dissatisfaction with the unmodified house church. Dura is the only extant pre-Constantinian dwelling that was modified in this way, but other examples soon followed, both in the provinces and at Rome.[78] It is clear that the Christians wanted a place of their own in which to worship their god. At some point, this community decided that the space of the house church was no longer sufficient for their needs.

It is less clear, however, what the motivation behind this new kind of worship space would have been. Surely, the size of the community would have been a factor, as inhabited domiciles were populated heavily and would have limited the number of outsiders who could have been accommodated. It has been suggested that these adaptations and renovations, followed by purpose-built structures, reflect a growing preoccupation with sacred space.[79] What this suggestion implies is the absence of sacred space in the house-church model, an implication based on a prioritization of the so-called "body of believers" over the space, and a failure to recognize the power of ritual in the construction of sacred space. A lack of materially articulated space does not necessarily indicate a lack of concern with sacred space, nor the impossibility of its having been present.

While again being conscious of the danger of retrojection or teleology, it is probable that the presence of polytheistic imagery, as at Dura, would have been even more prevalent in an unmodified domestic space.[80] In unmodified spaces, worshippers of Christ may also have continued to practise the domestic cult, and they may have had a number of reactions to polytheistic imagery in their worship space, ranging from indifference to confusion to reinterpretation. In modified spaces where polytheistic artifacts were allowed to remain, this same range of responses ought to be expected.

At the same time, the inhabited house surely presented difficult challenges for worship in a monotheistic religion, and it is important to question whether Dura presented a solution to the issue of Roman polytheist and Christian coexistence in the house church. Certainly the absence of daily activity (such as bodily practices and so forth) that dominated the inhabited household would immediately have contributed to a different conception of space. Further, the practice of the domestic cult, so habitual and ubiquitous, would no longer need to be performed, being tied up as it was with the life of the *familia*. Whether Dura offered a space completely set apart from polytheistic belief and experience, however, is not immediately apparent. It would be foolish, of course, to argue that the domestic cult continued at Dura Europos, or that the plaque, an *ex voto* from a shrine of Atargatis, meant that members of the community at Dura continued to worship Atargatis, and did so in the same place where Christians gathered to worship Christ. Nonetheless, the presence of a bacchic frieze in the main assembly hall, as well as the retention of the apotropaic device in Room 5, both indicate a certain level of comfort with some vestiges of traditional Roman life.

As discussed above, much of the scholarship on the Christian building at Dura has focused predominantly on the baptistery, finding there, rather than in the assembly hall, the locus of sanctity for Durene Christians. The whitewashed walls and the portion of a frieze with bacchic subject matter seems to indicate to some scholars that the assembly hall was not considered sacred space, or that its space was at least *less* sacred than the baptistery. The eucharist, however, is arguably as important a ritual as baptism, and the act of gathering should also be viewed as creating sacred space. Acknowledging and honouring the assembly hall as sacred space means that the bacchic frieze must be engaged, rather than ignored. The bacchic frieze should suggest a continued tolerance or comfort with Roman polytheistic imagery, if not with its practice.

It is possible that the Christians at Dura could have reinterpreted the bacchic frieze as belonging to a god reminiscent of their own. While perhaps initially tempting, this argument is ultimately unconvincing, especially given the contents of the frieze: satyrs, cymbals, and pan pipes. These objects are references to the bacchic frenzy of the maenads and the satyrs, of the drunken revelry that accompanies worship of the god. It is not as though the frieze depicted narrative scenes of the myth of the dying and rising Bacchus. Early teachers may well have pointed to the images of myths whose characteristics resonated with that of Jesus Christ, in order to clarify ideas about the new movement. Alternatively, they may have pointed to the images as representative of all that was wrong with the world, which Christ came to redeem. By the mid-third century, when Christianity had moved far beyond self-justification and was well established as a growing, flourishing movement, these comparative examples would hardly have been necessary. Indeed, a community that was capable of purchasing and renovating a large house for their exclusive use had already reached a point where comparison to other gods was no longer required, where Isis and Dionysus and Mithras were competition, rather than explanatory examples for teachers of the gospel. Therefore, the argument that the bacchic frieze was retained for didactic purposes remains unconvincing.

The view that the bacchic frieze was simply neutral decoration is also problematic. Anyone who came into the assembly hall would have recognized the accoutrements of the god Bacchus in the frieze. Perhaps a frieze, even one honouring Bacchus, was preferable to no decoration at all. The fact that the frieze was retained, even after the wall had been knocked down and it had gained what would have been a somewhat off-balanced appearance, likely meant that the community thought it was better than a blank wall. It may have demonstrated wealth and status, in much the same way that it must have during the period of the private dwelling. For whatever reason, it is clear that the bacchic decoration was preferable to a blank wall in the ten to fifteen years during which the building was in use by Christians. In other words, even if there were financial limitations that prevented an overall programme in the building that matched that of the baptistery, the projection of an image of health, wealth, and status was more desirable than a space that was entirely plain.

Thus, the vestiges of some polytheistic elements clearly did not interfere with the use or conception of the Christian building as sacred space. Given the material articulation of the structure, with its thoughtfully organized rooms, dedicated to ritual preparation and performance, it is clear that the Christian building at Dura is sacred space. At the same time, it is impossible to argue that the sacred space of the Christian building at Dura was the product of a wholesale rejection of polytheistic motifs and practices. The two coexisted, each not precluding the other. A bacchic frieze remained in the assembly hall while specifically Christian rituals were performed, and would not have interfered with the conception of the assembly hall as sacred space. Other artifacts also indicate the coexistence of polytheistic and Christian motifs and practices, and raise questions about what undiscovered artifacts may also have existed. Fundamentally, the example of Dura, with its clearly articulated sacred space, demonstrates that sacred space in early Christianity did not demand a "purification" or cleansing of inconsistent elements from worship space. Much more than at Dura, then, it ought to be expected that Christian and traditionally polytheistic elements – and sometimes practices – coexisted in unrenovated house-church spaces.

In sum, the *domus ecclesiae* at Dura Europos has demonstrated that, while this particular community had the ability to create permanent worship space, it cannot be argued that it was merely a lack of opportunity that would have forced Christians into constant dialogue with their polytheistic pasts (and presents). Even their worship space was not free from polytheistic elements. The ongoing practice of ritual, even in the presence of a bacchic frieze, was enough to cement the place as sacred space.

CASE STUDY TWO: THE ROMAN VILLA AT LULLINGSTONE

A second – and perhaps more powerful – example of polytheistic and Christian coexistence in early Christian meeting space can be found at Lullingstone, in Roman Britain. The site of the Roman villa at Lullingstone was built on the banks of the Darent River, located in modern-day Kent. The site was excavated by G.W. Meates, who published three volumes on the site, including the final field reports.[81] Meates's dating of the stages of occupation and renovation are generally still used, though there have been some modifications suggested since the death of Meates and the publication of the second volume of field reports.[82] The villa has received surprisingly little attention outside of scholars working

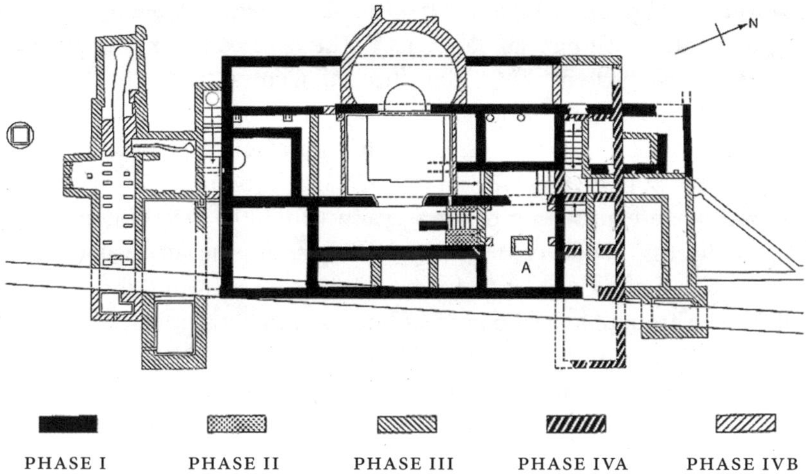

4.2 Floor plan, Lullingstone Roman villa

specifically on Roman Britain, with only a few exceptions. It is rarely discussed by scholars of early Christianity, and tends, due to its post-Constantinian date, not to factor at all into the conversation about the earliest Christian meeting places.[83]

In the first phase of occupation (between 80–90), a simple house was built, which conformed to humble proportions, and likely served the needs of a local farmer.[84] Around 180 CE, a new owner expanded the house into a villa, worthy of a wealthy Roman. A number of changes were made at this time, including the addition of a bath complex, kitchen complexes, and various so-called cult rooms. It is the consensus view that the owner of the villa at this stage was likely a wealthy Roman, of Mediterranean birth, rather than a Briton.[85] In the late second or early third century, the villa was abandoned, seemingly in some haste, and was left to fall into dereliction until around 280. At this time, the next phase began, when the villa was acquired by a new owner, again a person of some wealth. In the subsequent century, many more changes took place.

In the mid-fourth century (330–360), the central area of the house was expanded into an apsidal dining room and grand reception room (both decorated with mosaic pavements). Shortly after this period (360–385), the Christian rooms were constructed. In the late fourth or early fifth century, possibly as late as 420 CE, the villa was consumed by fire, and was never rebuilt. Immediately before this destruction, the domestic quarters of the villa were falling into disrepair, either because they were no longer inhabited, or because of financial concerns.[86] The bath complex was filled in, and one of the kitchens was no longer used. Central to the discussion of the villa as Christian meeting place are two areas: first, the so-called Deep Room, a basement cellar; and second, the Christian chapel and its neighbouring rooms. In the next section, the Christian rooms will be described, followed by an explanation of the ways in which the Deep Room enters into the discussion of sacred space at Lullingstone. The surprising coexistence of polytheistic and Christian practices evident from this discussion will then be brought to bear on earlier house-church material.

The set of rooms dedicated to Christian worship includes a chapel, a vestibule, an antechamber, and a bedroom or storeroom. These four rooms are situated on the north and east sides of the villa. The main room, often called a chapel, was positioned directly over the cellar, or Deep Room. When the villa was destroyed by fire, the collapse of the chapel into the Deep Room saved much of the wall painting that had decorated it. The chapel was unquestionably Christian, being decorated with obvious Christian symbolism. The wall paintings in the chapel depicted figures in the *orans* position, which commonly depicts prayer.[87] A number of painted chi-rho monograms were also discovered, which reconstructions have placed in the chapel and the antechamber.[88]

The question of access to these rooms is something of a puzzle, as exact dates for renovations and changes in the latest phases are unclear. Initially, access to this part of the house was gained via the corridor north of the apsidal dining room. Eventually, however, this was sealed, and a new opening was placed on the northernmost end of the house. This meant that the only access to the rooms was from outside the villa, and that those wishing to enter the chapel would have had to first pass through two rooms (the vestibule and the antechamber). The points of access will be discussed further below, but at this stage it is important to note that the outside entrance indicates use of the chapel not only by the inhabitants of the villa, but also by people outside.

The Deep Room is the key to much of the conversation that follows, and a detailed explanation of its history is necessary.[89] The Deep Room began as a cellar and loading dock facility.[90] In the late second century, under the new and wealthy owner, a well was installed in the Deep Room, which became the central source of water for the villa until the end of its occupation. At this time, the room was also transformed into a cult room (or nymphaeum), possibly dedicated to water spirits. A niche, featuring a painting of three water nymphs, was the focal point of the south wall.[91] Wide, tiled stairs led from the upper floor of the house down to the nymphaeum on the northwest wall of the house. After this period, as discussed above, the house was abandoned, and lay vacant for a time.

In the late third century, in the third stage of occupation, the Deep Room would undergo the changes that are most interesting for this discussion. The house itself was reestablished around 280–90.[92] During this period, the stairs that led down to the onetime nymphaeum were blocked off. As for the niche and what Meates terms "the Cult of the Water Spirits," these had likely long fallen out of use, and the room was not restored by its new owners to cult room status.[93] These new owners did, however, deposit two marble busts in the Deep Room during the period of their renovation and occupation. It is clear from the excavation reports that these busts were deposited in an already damaged condition, meaning that they likely belonged to the previous owner or owners of the villa. It seems then, that the new, third century owners, when moving into the house, found these marble busts and, not wanting to get rid of them, chose to place them in the Deep Room.

These busts were not simply tossed into the cellar, however; they were placed carefully on the stairs, which had been blocked off. The steps now functioned as a makeshift display shelf for these unknown souls. The room was then freshly plastered and painted, in a simple but deliberate fashion. The third-century owners also deposited in the concrete floor two votive pots, the necks of which projected from the floor, "open to receive libations."[94] As Meates points out, it seems that the new owners interpreted the busts as ancestors, and therefore did not wish to dispose of them, lest the *manes* of the dead return to wreak havoc on the new occupants of the house.[95] When the floor of the Deep Room was later redone in the mid-to-late-fourth century, the pots were covered over. Two more pots were then inserted in the new floor, in a direct line with the proposed position of the busts.[96] The busts remained in the Deep Room, positioned on the stairs in this way, until the villa was destroyed by fire in the early fifth century. It is clear that the practice of offering libations to ancestors continued right up until the villa was destroyed.[97] That is, while the Christian chapel was fully functioning directly above, polytheistic ritual practice continued below.[98]

The most puzzling problems at Lullingstone are related to access, both to the Christian rooms and to the Deep Room. As mentioned above, the main stairway to the Deep Room was sealed off by the third set of owners. There are no other clear markers of doorways or staircases in the Deep Room, with the exception of a possible opening on the east side of the house, high up in the Deep Room's east wall.[99] It is difficult to see how anyone from the house could have accessed this room. Meates suggests a trapdoor in the floor of the room above.[100] If such a trapdoor existed, it would have opened up in the floor of the chapel itself. While there is no extant evidence of a trapdoor, it is a plausible solution, especially in the absence of other possibilities. That the room was completely sealed off from the rest of the house is not a possibility, since the well, which served as the villa's main source of water in this period, was located in the Deep Room. There is evidence that the well was used and repaired right up to the end of the fourth century.[101] Thus, regardless of the fact that the entry point is not clear in the archaeological record, the upkeep and continued use of the well means that access to the Deep Room, along with the marble busts, continued up until the end.

A further puzzle presents itself in relation to the occupation of the house. It is not clear whether the rest of the house (that is, the wing south of the Christian complex) was still occupied in the final stages. General decline throughout these areas of the house, including the filling in of the baths and at least one of the kitchen pits, suggests either vacancy or perhaps a lessened financial position. It has been argued, as above, that the house was no longer inhabited in its final stages, and that the house in this late stage had been completely given over to Christian worship. The general state of disrepair in the grandest rooms of the house – the reception and apsidal dining room – as well as in the baths and one of the kitchens seems to indicate a change in circumstance. In addition, the southwest corridor seems to have been used as a depository of refuse in the latest period.[102]

The data suggesting the abandonment of the domestic wing is far from conclusive, however. Artifacts of daily life, including pottery, spindle whorls, pins, nails, and jewelry, were found throughout the domestic wing, many dating to the late fourth century.[103] The refuse found in the domestic wing included animal bones and other kitchen scraps, indicating ongoing culinary practice in the villa. Most interestingly, an infant burial, dated to the late fourth century, was also found in the floor of the southern wing of the house. This infant was buried on the opposite end of the suite of Christian rooms. The bones of the infant were accompanied by a number of articles, including some coins, a "fragment of figured bronze from a large vessel," a shard of pottery, "and a handful of carbonized wheat."[104] Meates notes that this burial was typically "pagan" in character, which raises questions again about the occupants of the house. Was this infant a member of the household? Was the infant, as Meates suggests, the child of estate workers?[105] As for the occupation of the house, the presence of a family burial seems to indicate continued inhabitation. In any case, the burial reflects ongoing polytheistic sensibilities alongside the renovated chapel and its suite of rooms.

Even if the house were no longer occupied, however, the busts in the Deep Room remain problematic. In fact, it would be more difficult to explain the continued presence of the ancestor busts if the rest of the house were no longer inhabited. Why would the busts have remained? The ancestor cult was, after all, predominantly a practice of the *familia*. Kim Bowes has suggested that the continuation of "pagan" practice in the Deep Room is merely a possibility, rather than a certainty.[106] While it is of course impossible to prove that someone poured libations to the ancestors up until the last day, it is clear that the busts were not moved from their votive position. It also cannot be argued that occupants or caretakers of the villa were ignorant of the presence of the busts in the Deep Room, since the well continued to be the source of water up to the end. Water would have been necessary whether the domestic wing had been closed off or not.[107] If the busts of the ancestors were truly problematic to the occupants of the house or the caretakers of the church, they would have been removed.

A strong case can be made for the continued occupation of the domestic wing up until the destruction of the house. Regardless of whether it was still occupied in the final stages of the villa, however, the domestic wing was certainly occupied when the Christian rooms were first constructed. Thus, both the Christian rooms and the domestic rooms were in use contemporaneously, at least for a time.

This very brief sketch of the Deep Room and the chapel above, which only begins to investigate the features of the villa, offers a great deal towards the discussion of Christian sacred space in late antiquity. In particular, it raises serious questions about the construction of sacred space in the house church, and the potential for coexistent elements of polytheistic and Christian life. The villa at Lullingstone was not a house church proper, at least in its final years. Lullingstone, like Dura Europos, reflects a slightly later stage, which involves the renovation and demarcation of space for use specifically by the Christian community.

There are, however, a number of reasons why Lullingstone provides a valuable comparison to house churches, and one perhaps more powerful than that of Dura Europos. At Lullingstone, there are indications that, for a time, Christian rooms and domestic rooms functioned side by side. At Dura, it cannot be said with certainty that the house was ever occupied at the same time that it was used by the Christians. Lullingstone, then, provides material evidence of the joint use of space for both Christian worship and domestic life.[108]

It is therefore necessary to ask whether the chapel complex in the villa at Lullingstone was considered sacred space. There are a few points to consider. First, the closing off of the Christian rooms from the rest of the house, and the creation of a new entrance from the outside, seem to point towards sanctity. Sacred space is, of course, first and foremost separate space. Second, the complex of Christian rooms also suggests a move toward sanctity. The vestibule and antechamber would have held and controlled the flow of bodies into the chapel. Control, by way of small rooms and narrow openings, was built into this Christian complex. It would only have been members of the community, and perhaps initiated members at that, who would have been allowed to pass through this series of controlled entrances and exits. Whether or not there were accompanying purification rituals, such as the removal of shoes or the washing of feet or hands, is impossible to say; but the space was certainly available to accommodate it. Both the controlled rooms and the separation of the complex from the rest of the villa point toward an interest in materially articulated sanctity. As at Dura, the extensive renovations of the Lullingstone villa indicate a preoccupation with separate worship space for the practice of early Christian rituals.

At the same time, it cannot be assumed that pollution from domestic life, including the domestic cult, would have provided the impetus for this separation of space. If these factors were considered dangerous, a conscious effort would have been made to separate Christian practices from polytheistic ones. Yet someone continued to access the well in the Deep Room, where the shrine to the busts had not been removed. Thus, even after renovations, ritual practice of a polytheistic nature continued, despite a conscious preoccupation with creating space for worship. A similar situation would have arisen in unrenovated house churches, where domestic practices almost certainly continued alongside Christian worship.

IMPLICATIONS FOR HOUSE CHURCH WORSHIP

That these third- and fourth-century spaces exhibit signs of continued polytheistic ritual, even though they were clearly adapted for Christian use, indicates a certain level of comfort with the coexistence of polytheistic imagery and Christian practice. It stands to reason, then, that house-church spaces, being unrenovated and unadapted, would also have exhibited signs of continued polytheistic ritual (and iconography), in the form of domestic cult practice. The material presence of, for example, the ancestor cult, seems not to have interfered with the ability of the Lullingstone community to create and nurture a specifically Christian meeting place upstairs. The presence of a bacchic frieze in the main meeting room of the Christian building at Dura was also clearly unproblematic for the community that gathered there. Thus, while it is not possible to say that all house churches would have been loci of both Christ-centred ritual and polytheistic cult practice, it is clear that the initiation of the former did not automatically lead to the cessation of the latter. Indeed, the shared character of domestic space makes it much more likely that these practices would have continued alongside each other.

Looking at the spaces in this way – as shared ritual spaces – resolves a number of practical issues. If some converts to the Jesus movement did not see the accoutrements of the domestic cult and its associated iconography as problematic, then there would have been no need to renovate, erase their identity as Roman, or, perhaps more prosaically, change the course of their daily household affairs. Without a strong impetus to renovate, the lack of identifiable house churches in the early period is also better explained; they simply look identical to houses *not* used by early Christians as meeting places. That being said, looking at the spaces in this way also raises a number of issues concerning our perception of the earliest Christian communities and the ways in which they understood themselves and their rituals. How did the house-church Christians practise their new rituals in a space already understood as a ritual space dedicated to the domestic cult? Indeed, how did the house-church Christians make space for their rituals at all, and in what ways did they or could they consider that space sacred? The chapters that follow will explore these questions. First, I will explore the rituals practised by the house-church communities, including the most basic, practical necessities of their practice, and the contemporary understanding of those rituals as sacred, at least insofar as it can be determined. Second, I will discuss ways in which the house-church Christians may have overcome the difficulties of coexisting, conflicting rituals, via the construction of a model of sacred space that allows for multiple uses and possibilities.

CHAPTER FIVE

Placing Ritual: Christians in the Roman House

In this chapter, the composition of the house-church meeting will be presented, including a description of the rituals known to have been practised. These rituals always will be discussed with a view to understanding where they might have been placed in the spaces of the houses used for worship. That is, rather than a lengthy excursus on the origins and meaning of particular rituals, there will instead be a focus on their placement, at least insofar as it can be known according to available textual evidence. In many cases, there is a good deal of attention paid to the practice of a given ritual, including preparation, proper ordering, and in some cases, purification. In most of these examples, however, it is apparent that placement is not at the fore. That is, while the rituals of the house-church Christians were both powerful and sacred, there seemed to have been little accompanying recognition of the power of the space in which they took place. This seeming incongruity will be further explored in the coming pages.

RITUALS OF THE HOUSE CHURCH COMMUNITIES

In house churches, the basic rituals of meeting included the following: first and foremost, a gathering of the believers; a shared meal; preaching or teaching; testimonials; prayer; and singing. The initiatory act of baptism was central to the formation of the community from its earliest days, though it likely did not occur every time the community met. Of these acts of worship, some are relatively easy to place in the canvas of domestic space, while others present difficulties, both in terms of physical space (accommodation) and ritual space (sanctity or purity). Preaching and teaching, prayer and singing could and likely did occur anywhere; any place where a group of believers could assemble would be space enough for the singing of songs and sharing of words. In very large congregations, it is possible that the group could have been too large to facilitate easily hearing the teaching, but no specific places or ritual implements were required.[1] The rituals most likely to cause difficulty in terms of space are the shared meal and baptism. Issues with eucharistic meals include concerns over adequate space for dining, as well as the size and organization of the members.[2] If members of the community were arriving to a banquet, like the ones they would have been accustomed to through membership in other groups or associations, it is necessary to explore what kind of space would have been demanded. As for baptism, the obvious problem that presents itself is access to water. There are conflicting references to the importance of baptismal accoutrements in the literary evidence, which ought to be examined in order to determine baptismal space in the house church communities. In the cases of the eucharistic meals and of baptism, there is an implicit and sometimes verbalized association with sanctity. Thus, the conversation that follows will focus on these two rituals. They are chosen in particular because of their ability to shed light on the following issues: the necessity of specific or particular space; a demand (or lack thereof) of formality or systematization; and the size of the groups which would have met in house churches. With these three issues in mind, I will give a brief survey of the rituals themselves, discuss any literary references pertaining to their placement in early church communities, and consider any material evidence for the placement of these rituals.[3] Before doing so, however, the discussion will turn briefly to an exploration of the ritual of gathering.

THE BODY OF BELIEVERS AND THE GATHERING OF SPACE

As stated above, the rituals of gathering, preaching, teaching, and giving testimonials or singing present little in the way of spatial demands. Indeed, a group could meet anywhere, gather anywhere. At the same time, the gathering of the house-church Christians is the first and arguably most important ritual.[4] It also featured prominently in the literary evidence, especially in the Pauline corpus. This gathering was what formed the "body of believers," the new temple, and the substitution of flesh and spirit for bricks and mortar.[5] Despite this ideological conception of gathering, however, the physical gathering of the believers was also essential, both in terms of carrying out other rituals, and, of course, establishing the identity of the community as a whole. While on the one hand, the argument is consistently presented that the body of believers negated the need for sacred space, on the other hand, that body of believers is the very construct that both formed and maintained sacred space. Further, regardless of any esoteric conception of the body of believers as separate or beyond such earthly concerns as space or place, it must be recognized that spaces and places needed to be made accessible to this body, in its collective formation, as well as to individual bodies, living, breathing, and in need of physical location. Thus, the need for space, and the construction of sacred space, should be understood as paramount from the moment the believers congregated.

EUCHARISTIC MEALS: BREAKING BREAD AND SHARING A TABLE

In order to discuss the shared meal, it is necessary also to discuss the terms *agape* and eucharist. The former is sometimes taken to mean a full meal, shared by the community members. The latter, by contrast, is usually taken to mean accepting bread and wine, symbolizing the body and blood of Christ. Recent scholarship concerning the *agape* and the eucharist, however, discourages stark distinctions between these two acts (or rather, these two descriptors), noting that the *agape* and the eucharist may well have been indistinguishable in many communities.[6] Further, a false distinction between a shared meal and a eucharist has led to problematic conclusions about space, especially sacred space. The view of the eucharist as a later development, which grew out of the *agape* meal, has sometimes been read as a growing preoccupation with sanctity on the part of the developing community. This preoccupation has also been tied to the assumption that the house was no longer suitable as a place for worship. David Balch and Carolyn Osiek, for example, argue that Justin Martyr's *Apology*, wherein he discusses baptism, assembly practices, and the eucharist, indicates a stage of Christianity that was moving away from typical house-church practices.[7] The eucharist on its own (that is, without the accompanying *agape* meal) is also sometimes seen as the product of accommodation for larger numbers of community members. If the church swelled beyond domestic capacity – at least in terms of a shared, full meal – then the eucharist could have solved the problem of accommodation at the table. Balch and Osiek, for example, state: "The first phase of Christian worship lasted until the middle or end of the second century, by which time numbers had grown considerably and liturgy was evolving beyond the capacity of domestic architecture to support it. No longer was Eucharist [*sic*] celebrated at a common meal, but at a ritual commemoration that retained only the stylized structure of a meal."[8] Balch and Osiek seem to be arguing that the ritual aspects of a formalized eucharist reflect a liturgy that demanded a space the domestic arena could not provide. What is not clear is whether it is the size of the space that is insufficient (numbers), or whether it is the space's degree of sanctity (or lack thereof) that is insufficient. If the former, the shortcomings of the domestic arena would be predicated on the size of the groups wishing to share a full meal; if the latter, much larger questions about the sanctity of the space are raised.

In the texts discussed below, commentators refer sometimes to the *agape* and sometimes to the eucharist, and outline differing descriptions and proscriptions.[9] These differences reflect a broad range of conceptual thinking about eucharistic meals. Rather than attempting to set a trajectory from *agape* to eucharist, I will operate on the understanding that eucharistic meals, in all of their forms, were understood to be symbolic by participants, and that they carried elements of ritual importance whether they were formalized or casual, token or substantial. Further, it is clear that the eucharistic meal was the central act of early Christian meetings. The eucharistic meal demanded both space to perform it and ritual utterances to differentiate it from other meals. Here, then, will be an exploration of some of the elements that call to light the need for space – both in a basic sense (physical accommodation) and a conceptual sense (ritual space). Thus, the examples provided below will focus on these two types of accommodation, regardless of the terminology used by the original authors.

The eucharistic meal is referenced in Christian writings very early, including the Pauline correspondence. It is clear in some cases that the food being shared is not *only* symbolic, but in fact a full meal, meant to feed the diners. Because the social makeup of the house-church congregations was mixed, it is likely that some members of the community enjoyed this meal as the best and most complete that they would have all week. It could perhaps be compared to an invitation to dinner at a patron's home, or, more likely, to the shared meal common to other groups in the Empire. This meal was meant to bring together the members of the community in common purpose. The act of a shared meal was neither original nor unique to the Christian movement. Cult associations and guild membership groups are examples of other groups whose central act of meeting was a banquet.[10] This rich banqueting tradition carried with it a number of rules and expectations, both social and cultic. Banqueting in Roman tradition was a highly stylized, hierarchized affair; poorer invitees, such as clients or freed slaves, would not have expected the same treatment as guests of honour, including wealthy business associates or members of the aristocratic elite.[11] It is likely that this Roman model of dining would have continued in Christian dining traditions as well. Roman convention dictated that domestic banquets be held in the *triclinium*, and that the diners recline, each one placed in hierarchical order according his or her status.[12] To what extent the Christians also espoused these Roman banqueting conventions during their shared meal deserves close attention.

Perhaps the most well-known example of the eucharistic meal in the New Testament is found in 1 Corinthians 11:17–34. In this passage, Paul is admonishing the Corinthians for their mismanagement of the communal meal. He alludes to and conflates the breaking of bread, or the "Lord's Supper," with the fulfillment of hunger. It can be difficult to determine exactly what Paul means when he discusses the eating and drinking habits of this particular community. Certainly 1 Cor 11:23–6 is an excursus on and reminder of the so-called Lord's Supper, taken by Jesus and his disciples on their last night together. Jesus and his disciples were sharing a complete meal, but it is from this meal, and the words attributed to Jesus during this meal, that the eucharist would eventually come. Paul says, "When you come together, it is not really to eat the Lord's Supper. For when the time comes to eat, each of you goes ahead with your own supper, and one goes hungry and another becomes drunk" (1 Cor 11:20–1).

Even though only bread and wine are specifically mentioned in this passage, it is clear from the dispute taking place that the meal they are sharing is a complete one. Paul is likely using the images of bread and wine rhetorically, in order to remind his readers (or hearers) of the true reason for their gathering. He attempts to convince them that the communal meal is to be equated – at least ideologically – with the Lord's Supper, which represents the sacrifice of Christ. Paul says: "Whoever, therefore, eats the bread or drinks the cup of the Lord in an unworthy manner will be answerable for the body and blood of the Lord. Examine yourselves, and only then eat of the bread and drink of the cup" (1 Cor 11:25–6). In 1 Cor 11:33, Paul reminds the brothers and sisters to wait for one another, that the meal is important as a communal experience, and not simply as a dinner. He admonishes the offenders among them, saying: "when you come together to eat, wait for one another. If you are hungry, eat at home, so that when you come together, it will not be for your condemnation." Implicit in these instructions, as well as the offences which led to them, is the notion that these Corinthians are coming together to share in a banquet. This community has erred, concentrating more on the enjoyment of a banquet than the practice of worship. Paul, then, needs to remind them that this meal was meant for communal edification and the commemoration of Christ's sacrifice. It was a ritual that bound the believers in Christ together as a community.

Because this meal would have felt, to the Corinthians, much like the communal banquets of Graeco-Roman society at large, they would have been accustomed to acting in ways familiar to them, which would have included hierarchical organization and, certainly, a lack of compunction about eating before the poorer members of the community arrived. There is, perhaps, a tendency to see the Christians as celebrating their love feast in an "egalitarian" manner, as would befit the theology of this new, radical group.[13] As the discussion of 1 Corinthians 11 reveals, however, the egalitarian ideal was all too easily violated.[14]

Meals are also discussed in detail in Tertullian's *Apologia*, a late second-century work (197/8 CE) aimed at correcting public opinion. The Christians were often accused of indiscretions and vile behaviour during their meetings. While on the one hand, it is obvious that these accusations, levelled by unsympathetic Roman polytheists, reflect misunderstandings of Christian meal practices, it is clear that the meals shared by the Christians are perceived as banquets. Indeed, when Tertullian defends the Christian meetings against popular opinion, he reveals that, although the Christian ideal he presents may be a more austere form of banquet than the typical Roman affair, it remains, in effect, a banquet.[15]

In addition to the outlandish accusations of cannibalism and incest that were levelled against the Christians' "love-feasts," general accusations of extravagance were also common (Tertullian, *Apol.* 39.14). Tertullian defends his group, saying that their extravagance is singled out unfairly: not only are they not extravagant in the least, but other groups in the Empire are exceptionally so (39.15).[16] Implicit in his defense is that the Christians, while much less extravagant, participate in banquets, as do other groups in the Empire.

Tertullian then goes on to explain the nature of the eucharistic meal, here referred to as "*agape*," correcting the apparently widespread notion that the *agape* is an orgy by explaining the word's root in the Greek tradition of love.[17] He also delineates the purpose of the meeting, which is partly to come together for refreshment, but also to provide for those who cannot afford it (39.16). He draws an explicit contrast between the treatment of the needy in the church versus the treatment of the parasite in the Empire at large (ibid.). Tertullian's *agape*, then, is about sustenance and community, rather than entertainment and indulgence.

As Tertullian says, the meeting is modest compared to other shared meals of the Empire: "It allows nothing vile, nothing immodest" (39.17). He also tells us that the members of the church pray before eating, and that even when eating and drinking, "only so much is eaten as satisfies hunger; only so much drunk as meets the need of the modest" (39.18).[18] Tertullian is here presenting the community in the best light possible; this ideal was clearly violated many years earlier at Corinth, as discussed above. Still, the message is clear: the meal is much more about fellowship with Christ and each other than it is about having a dinner party, as is common in most other banquets held by his contemporaries. He goes on to claim that, since their doings are modest, appropriate, and chaste, they are more like a gathering of the Senate than an illegal gathering, and that they should not be singled out for persecution (39.21). Overall, despite Tertullian's correctives, the *agape* as described here is indeed a banquet, if a relatively tame one.[19] Thus, there would need to be room enough in the gathering places of Tertullian's contemporaries to host this banquet. Despite his descriptions of the purpose and overall plan of the *agape*, Tertullian does not specify where it would have taken place.

Other references to eucharistic meals are found in Ignatius's *Epistle to the Smyrneans* 8, where he lays out the rules of order for Christian assembly:

> Let no one do anything pertaining to the church without the bishop. Let that be considered a proper eucharist which is held by the bishop or by one whom he should appoint ... Without the bishop it is permitted neither to baptize nor to hold a meal [*agape*]. (1–2)[20]

Here, the eucharistic meal has important ritual connotations, and the demanded presence of the bishop indicates the preoccupation with its right practice. As with the foregoing examples, however, there is no mention of the necessary space needed to host this ritual.

Concerning eucharistic meals, the *Didache* 14.1–2 enjoins:

> On the Lord's Day of the Lord come together, break bread, and give thanks, having confessed your transgressions so that your sacrifice may be pure. But if anyone has a quarrel with his fellow let him not participate until they be reconciled lest your sacrifice be defiled.[21]

The notions of sacrifice and purity are central to this description of a eucharistic meal; the commensality associated with the meal is supplanted by the concern for purity over defilement. The time of the meal is here denoted (the "Lord's Day of the Lord"), but place, again, is notably absent from the discussion.

In his *Apology*, Justin says of the eucharistic meal:

> For not as common bread and common drink do we receive these; but in like manner as Jesus Christ our Saviour, having been made flesh by the Word of God, had both flesh and blood for our salvation, so likewise have we been taught that the food which is blessed by the prayer of His word, and from which our blood and flesh by transmutation are nourished, is the flesh and blood of that Jesus who was made flesh. (*Apology* 1.66)[22]

Justin's conception of the eucharist is certainly that it is symbolic and sacred. It is clear from elsewhere in the text that the meetings attended by Justin took place in a domestic space above a bath complex. The sanctity described by Justin, implicit in the blessing of the food, is not accompanied by ritual injunctions concerning space. To return briefly to the argument of Balch and Osiek – which states that the formalization of the eucharist contributed to the eventual unsuitability of domestic space as ritual space – it is worth noting that here there is no apparent difficulty with the coexistence of sacred ritual and domestic space. Balch and Osiek rightly note that the numbers in the house churches were growing, and they give Dura Europos as an example of the new type of church, the *domus ecclesiae*, in which full meals would not have taken place.[23] It is true that Dura Europos does not have space for a full meal, lacking dining or cooking facilities after its renovation, but this single example ought not to be used to extrapolate similar conclusions for other regions and communities. The idea that domestic spaces would not have been sufficient in the time of Justin seems especially incongruous, given that Justin himself provides one of the few examples available of the use of a specific domestic space (the apartment above the Baths of Myrtinus) by a specific community (a group in Rome).[24] Because Justin does not specifically include the description of a full meal or banquet in his discussion of the weekly meetings, it is possible that this community did not practise the eucharistic meal in this way. There is no evidence, however, literary or material, to suggest that the formalization of the eucharist brought about or demanded a shift away from domestic spaces, or from inhabited house churches to renovated *domus ecclesiae*, for reasons of sanctity or purity of place.

In the *Traditio Apostolica*, there are some interesting points to note concerning the eucharistic meals in Christianity of the late second and early third centuries. The description in the *Traditio Apostolica* reports that, before dining on actual food, a small piece of the blessed bread is taken by the faithful, so that those present will "eat and drink in purity" (26.2). It is also clear in the *Traditio Apostolica* that the meal and assembly is still taking place in someone's house. It is not clear whether the house used by the assembly is always the same one, but there is a host and a domestic space on offer. The assembled people are told to refrain from eating and drinking to excess, making it apparent that a full meal is on the menu (28.2). One of the reasons for avoiding gluttony is so that the host of the assembly will be able to distribute the leftovers to others, it being the "food of the saints" (28.3). Thus, two points are made clear in this late-second/early third century text: first, that at this late date, the communal meal is still viewed as central to the act of meeting; and second, that the communal meal is taking place in someone's house, a fact made evident by the mention of a host.[25] Even more interesting are the overtones of purity that pervade this discussion of the eucharistic meal. The blessed bread purifies the diners before they partake, and the food that has been served to them seems to carry with it a kind of sanctity, which is then passed on to those absent believers who consume the leftovers. The meal is perceived here as being sacred ritual, at least in conjunction with the blessing of the bread and its purification of the diners. This being the case, one might expect more attention to have been paid to the method and placement of the act of dining itself. Instead, there is a preoccupation with correct behaviour both during the meal (not overindulging) and afterwards (distributing the blessed leftovers to the needy in the community). In addition to the lack of attention paid to particular place, it is unclear how this sanctity might have been achieved during the meal, and how the group might have demarcated the difference between a regular meal and a eucharistic meal, with its regulations and associated purity or sanctity.[26]

The eucharistic meal, then, is a key ritual that must be explored in determining the ways that house-church Christians negotiated their meeting space. The brief discussion outlined above has demonstrated that the communal meal was an important ritual, which bound the community of believers together, much as meals did for cult associations and occupational guilds. It has also indicated that, while at times the literary sources seem muddled concerning the distinction between full eucharistic meals and the eucharist as the blessing of bread and wine, it is clear that, at least some of the time, these practices coexisted in some communities. Indeed, as in the case of the *Traditio Apostolica*, the eucharistic blessing seems to have acted as the ritual that signified the beginning of the meal. Imagining banquets in house church meetings also raises questions about facilities, numbers, hierarchy, and accommodation. This point will be addressed further below, in the discussion of the size of house churches. Further, while the eucharistic blessing is symbolic and seemingly sacred in nature, there is nothing to suggest that the house church was automatically considered to be too impure to act as a locus for this ritual's enactment, a point to which the discussion will return in chapter 6.

EUCHARISTIC MEALS AND THE SIZE OF HOUSE CHURCH MEETINGS

As discussed in chapter 1, there is a debate about the number of churches in a given city in the earliest days of the Jesus movement. Connected to this debate is one concerning the number of people who could have met in the house churches of earliest Christianity, especially those house churches associated with Pauline communities. This debate is centred on the size of the dwelling, of course, but even if a space is agreed upon, the number of people who could have met in that space is not always obvious. Of all of the rituals of house churches, the eucharistic meal raises the most intriguing questions about the size of the meeting, bringing with it issues of hierarchy and space.

The issue of the meal and the size of house-church communities is twofold. First, there is the question of reasonable accommodation: how many people could have dined together in the spaces available to the house-church Christians? Second, there is the much more complicated issue of whether these meals conformed to typical Graeco-Roman dining traditions, and whether this conformity would have extended to the distribution of seating, food, and wine according to social status. The former question is predicated on the latter, and it is therefore necessary to unpack these issues, in order to attempt to answer the question of size in the house churches.

It is often said that very large numbers of people could have met in the houses of the Christian patrons.[27] Hypotheses with such large numbers demand a situation wherein bodies are crammed into spaces, without regard for the rituals being enacted. There are two issues with these large numbers: first, the number of participants would have varied, depending on the socio-economic status of the group; and second, the number should be estimated while always keeping the performance of the meal in mind. That is, not all groups would have had access to a large atrium house, but all groups needed a space in which to share a meal.

To return once more to 1 Corinthians 11, it is clear in this text that the Corinthians were celebrating a full meal. The Corinthians were engaging in behaviour similar to what one might expect at a "typical" Graeco-Roman banquet. That is, the richer members of the community would have arrived first, would have had the best food, and would have consumed the best wine, while the poorer members would have been left with the scraps. This text is exemplary of the many issues and boundaries the house-church Christians would have negotiated in their practice of the *agape* meal.

The organization of dining and banqueting in the house-church communities is not the focus of this study. Nonetheless, it should be clear, from even a cursory look at the spaces available to the Christians for eating shared meals, as well as from the evidence for the meal as the central act of meeting in the earliest house-church communities, that accommodating all of the members of the community would not have been easy. As discussed in chapter 2, dinner parties and domestic banquets would have been held in the *triclinium*, if such a room were available. Smaller spaces, such as tenements or shops, or even small *medianum* apartments, would not have been used for banqueting anyway, whether Christian or otherwise, and so alternate arrangements for dining would have to have been made.

Early Christian communities have often been likened to cult associations and guild groups.[28] Among these groups, the common denominator was the practice of shared meals as markers of belonging and community identity.[29] The Christians, however, were the only ones who did not have a space dedicated to their banquet meetings. Associations had halls of meeting, often with multiple *triclinia* (see, for example, the Schola del Traiano and the Caseggiato dei Triclinii at Ostia), which could accommodate a large number of reclining diners at one time. In some cases, *triclinia* would have been enlarged and extended, and in many cases, multiple *triclinia* were present.[30] These semi-public buildings, used by association and guild members, provided a space for large-scale banqueting which was quite different from the smaller, single-family unit spaces available to the house-church Christians. Even these public places had systems of hierarchy in place, though, including seating plans.[31] It is likely that some members reclined while others sat, and that the meal was served by slaves.

In Christian communities that used a *triclinium* for meeting, then, some kind of hierarchical organization must have taken place. This organization may have included the seating of some and the reclining of others, and the continuation of slave service during meals. Of course, this hierarchical organization does not correspond with the idealistic claims of Paul, or of Tertullian (*Apol.* 39), who claim that all members of the church were treated equally. Modern scholarship, too, has suggested that the earliest Christians were egalitarian in their approach to dining, or at least relatively so in comparison with their contemporaries.[32] How, exactly, would this equality have played out? If there were all the space imaginable available to the house-church Christians, with multiple *triclinia* and multiple couches, then this equality might have permitted all the members to recline. It has already been established, however, that even in the most sumptuous of houses, space for dining would have been at a premium. *Triclinia*, in general, could reasonably accommodate nine reclining diners, or twelve at the outside.[33] The act of Roman banqueting also demanded table service; slaves were trained not only to perform entertainment, but also to cook the food, mix the wine, serve the courses on offer, and clean up afterward.

There are, therefore, two possible solutions to the problem of the eucharistic meal. The communities may have allowed their numbers to grow past the point where all members could recline, and simply espoused the same dining traditions and hierarchies that were practised in other, similar groups. In other words, the "ideal" of egalitarian community would not have been possible.[34] Another possible solution is that house-church cells were kept very small, but in order to practise equality at the *agape,* the cells would have to have been very small indeed. As discussed above, the usual number of diners accommodated was nine, and twelve at the outside; is it truly worth suggesting that only twelve members made up a house church? This number would barely cover the number of people in a household, especially a wealthy household. The arguments of Robert Jewett, as discussed in chapter 1, presume that a radical egalitarianism was performed.[35] This position only works, however, if it is assumed that all members of the community were poor; that is, that there were no leaders or members with money. In these cases, the meal may well have been shared in a communal area of a *medianum* apartment. It is important, as ever, to acknowledge that there was no one set rule for participation in the house church, and different spaces would demand different behaviours from those who met in them.

At the very least, it should not be blithely suggested that large groups of fifty or sixty Christians could have met easily for the *agape* meal; the space simply does not allow for easy accommodation of this many diners.[36] Balch and Osiek's suggestion of the eucharist supplanting the *agape* is also of little help here, given the evidence for contemporary practice of the *agape* well beyond the first (and smallest) generation of Christianity. It seems most likely, then, that the house churches were capped at reasonable numbers, depending on the size of the space available to them, and that the number of people able to participate in the *agape* was increased by the practice of hierarchical organization.

BAPTISM: INITIATION AND RESURRECTION

The rite of baptism is among the more difficult rituals to place in the earliest house churches. It is clear from the example at Dura Europos that, in at least one community, this rite of initiation demanded a separate place for its enactment. Theories about the performance of baptism abound, with loci including public baths (especially when considering the testimony of Justin and his meeting place above the baths), rivers or streams, the *impluvia* of atrium houses, basins, and sprinkling rather than immersion.[37] There is no clear textual evidence that provides a standard or even typical location for the practice of this ritual. There are many instances of liturgical guidance, of prayers and sacraments to be taken and administered in the rite of baptism, and excurses on the theology and symbolism of the baptismal rite. None of these, however, demands a specific location or type of location for the performance of the act. Even as the liturgy grows, there is no concomitant growth in the importance of *place*. A brief examination of baptism from the first to the third centuries will demonstrate the varied approach to baptism and the lack of clarity concerning its placement.

Paul of course discusses baptism and its importance for the binding of the new community in the spirit. Romans 6:3–5 outlines the symbolic importance of the act of baptism, signifying death with Christ as well as resurrection with him. He states:

> Do you not know that all of us who have been baptized into Christ Jesus were baptized into his death? Therefore we have been buried with him by baptism into death, so that, just as Christ was raised from the dead by the glory of the Father, so we too might walk in newness of life. For if we have been united with him in a death like his, we will certainly be united with him in a resurrection like his.

Paul's conception of baptism is related to the all-important confession of sin and subsequent freedom from its enslavement. His focus is on the confession, rather than the rite. Certainly, Paul is referring to a ritual known to the community; it is not necessary for him to explain the process of the rite to his audience. Yet it is clear that the symbolic side of baptism is the major point of concern for Paul, rather than the act of baptism, or the locus of its performance.

The author of 1 Peter discusses baptism in conjunction with the flood, noting that this salvation through water is echoed in the rite of baptism:

> God waited patiently in the days of Noah, during the building of the ark, in which a few, that is, eight persons were saved through water. And baptism, which this prefigured, now saves you – not as a removal of dirt from the body, but as an appeal to God for a good conscience, through the resurrection of Jesus Christ. (1 Pet 3:20–1)

Here, the distinction between flesh and spirit is made explicit. The water is used not to cleanse the body but to provide the believer with a new conscience and resurrection in Christ. Again, the theology of baptism is well thought out and negotiated, without even passing reference to the act itself, and without reference to the locus for its enactment.

It is passages like these which compel readers to assume that the place of worship and the place of ritual was unimportant to the earliest Christians. Certainly, if Paul had his way, the spirit would cast off the difficulties of the flesh in all ways, rather than be fettered by it; but this ideal mode of living only in the spirit is not possible, and indeed, the rituals of the church, including baptism, cater to a fleshly existence. It must be remembered, however, that whether or not Paul acknowledges the importance of the rite of baptism (and its placement in worship space), the fact remains that a place for baptism would always need to be found.

In other documents, the enactment of the rite is often accompanied by a preoccupation with proper practice. In the *Didache*, which is usually seen as a manual for proper practice in the early church community of Syria, the rite itself is discussed. The *Didache* is generally dated between the last decades of the first century and the first decades of the second century, and considered to be original to a group of Jewish Christians in Antioch.[38] The document is brief, and thus the description of baptism also; there is little here concerning the symbolism of the ritual, or any explicit reference to baptism as an initiatory ritual.[39] The treatise concerning baptism in the *Didache* is as follows:

> And on the subject of baptism, baptize thus: after having taught all that precedes, baptize in the name of the Father, and of the Son,

> and of the Holy Spirit, in living water. If for some reason you do not have living water, baptize in other water; and if you are not able to in cold water, in warm water. If you do not have (enough) of one or the other, pour out water three times on the head, in the name of the Father and Son and Holy Spirit. Before the baptism, let the baptizer, the baptized, and others who can, observe first a fast; as for the baptized, you must enforce a fast before-hand for two days. (7)[40]

Because of the Jewish background of this Christ-confessing community, the focus on purity during (and preceding) the baptismal ritual is perhaps more obvious than in gentile Christian documents of the same period.[41] In addition, the hierarchy of waters seems to follow the guidelines as set out in the Mishnah (*Mikva'oth* 8.36), where living waters are the waters deemed most pure. Also found in this section of the *Didache*, there are distinct rules about fasting, for the one performing the baptism as well as for the other members of the community.

The injunctions about the use of "living water" likely indicate a spring or a river of flowing water. Even these references to living water, however, seem more like suggestions than requirements. If there is no living water, any water will do; if there is no cold water, warm water will do; in the absence of either of these, pouring out water over the baptizand's head will suffice, so long as it is done three times, and in the name of the triune God. The implication here is that those Christ-confessors reading the document would likely seek out rivers or springs in which to baptize, and that these locations were seen as ideal, but if they were not available, there would be no decreased efficiency (or sanctity) in the performance elsewhere of this all-important rite. Thus, here too is an absence of specific place for the ritual.

In Tertullian's lengthy treatise, *On Baptism*, he discusses the idea of baptism, describing water as the "vehicle of divine operation" and comparing it to the hovering of God over the primeval waters (3). He also describes the ritual itself, including creeds spoken and prayers uttered, the laying on of hands, and the anointing of the faithful after they have "issued from the font" (6–8).[42] That baptism is performed in a font (*lavacro*) is mentioned, but a font is not deemed necessary for the ritual. It seems clear that, in Tertullian's community at least, baptismal fonts were used for the ritual. At the same time, it is equally clear that a font is not a requirement, and that any place where water is available is suitable for the performance of the rite, as Tertullian states: "Accordingly it makes no difference whether a man be washed in a sea or a pool, a stream or a fount, a lake or a trough" (4). Thus, on the one hand, there were fonts in at least some churches in the late second or early third century; on the other hand, there seems not to have been any particular demand for them, and certainly no demand for a sacred construction in which to house them.

Eucharistic meals also seem to be a part of the baptismal ritual, at least in some communities. After the *catechumens*, or initiates, have been anointed with oil and cleansed in water through baptism, they are finally able to enjoy their first eucharist, which would have been denied to them prior to their initiation. This post-baptismal eucharist is described in detail by Justin Martyr (d. 164):

> After thus washing the one who has been persuaded and who has assented, then we lead him to those who are called brothers, in the place where they regularly assemble … We finish the prayers and salute one another with a kiss. Then bread and a cup containing water and wine are brought to the president of the brethren. And taking them he offers praise and glory to the Father of all through the name of the Son and of the Holy Spirit … When the president has given thanks and the whole congregation has assented, those who are called deacons by us give to each one present a portion of the bread and of the water mixed with wine for which the thanksgiving had been made. Then, they take it to those who were not present. (*Apology* 1.65)[43]

From this text, it is clear that baptism seems to have been sealed by the taking of food, shared with the community of which the initiates were finally a part. It is also suggested, in this particular text, that the place of baptism is in fact separate from the place generally used for assembly. In Justin's community, it seems not to have been the case that a font or basin was in the regular assembly space, or brought in especially for the rite. Rather, the baptism took place elsewhere, and the initiates returned afterwards in order to be welcomed into the community through the sharing of a eucharist.[44] Certainly, the partnering of these two rites indicates their mutually affirming role, and the sanctity of their enactment.

Another conversion and baptism tale is preserved in the *Apocryphal Acts of Thomas* (third century, Syriac). The apostle Judas (Thomas) proselytizes Siphor, a high-ranking official, and his teaching culminates in the rituals of baptism and eucharist for Siphor and his family. Here, the dining room is the location of this activity, as Siphor himself points out in the text: "I will prepare for Judas (my) dining room (*triclinium*) in which he may teach" (*Acta Thomae*, 131).[45] Judas anoints the new believers in oil (132), baptises them in a basin, which he requests to be brought for that purpose. It seems as though any basin will serve, since they are in the house of Siphor, and clearly, he would not have had a baptismal basin ready to hand. Again, the locus of baptism is less important than the rite itself. Here too, the eucharist serves as a seal for the initiation of the new converts. Judas prepares bread for consumption by Siphor, his wife, and his daughter: "He placed bread upon the table and blessed it saying, 'Bread of life, of which those who eat remain incorruptible, bread which fills hungry souls with its blessing, you are the one worthy to receive the gift so that you might become forgiveness of sins for us and so that the ones eating you might become immortal'" (133).[46] Thus, it is again clear that the locus for baptism is not important, nor, for that matter, is the locus for the meal, which follows immediately after the baptism. Despite these acts clearly having transformative, sacred qualities, there is a complete absence of concern for a separate (or sacred) place dedicated to their performance.[47]

Overall, then, even the briefest examination of a selection of ritual texts from the first three centuries of Christianity indicate the broad range of approaches and practices associated with the key rituals of eucharistic meals and baptism. There seems also to be a lack of clarity concerning the conception of these rites as sacred, or whether they demand purity. What is surprisingly consistent, however, is the almost complete lack of engagement with the issue of place for these rituals. That these rituals were performed is certain; where they would have been performed (in the house, or in the case of baptism, perhaps outside the house) is less so. Because of the nature of the house church – that is, its unmodified and unrenovated state – one would not expect to find material articulation of the location of these rituals. A brief exploration of the textual evidence also provides little in terms of material or permanent placement of these sacred rituals. Given the lack of material articulation in this period, then, it may seem simpler to suggest that the house-church Christians did not have sacred space in which they performed their rituals. A lack of articulated place, however, does not necessarily indicate a lack of sanctity. Despite the seeming lack of concern over specific ritual places, there is still a preoccupation with right practice. Thus, an attempt to understand the possibilities of sacred space ought to be explored. Before undertaking some of the ways that house-church Christians may have constructed sacred space, it will be necessary to discern early Christian opinions about and attitudes toward sacred space.

EARLY CHRISTIAN ATTITUDES TOWARD SACRED SPACE

A number of texts have already been explored in reference to early Christian meeting places. In these texts, there is very little explicit reference to Christian sacred space. Further, those texts which do mention space are frequently unclear and often contradictory. Far from being descriptive or prescriptive of existing sacred space, they instead explore theological and ideological approaches to the new community's sense of place in the broader context of a polytheistic world. Therefore, these texts tend to reflect an ideal, rather than a real, situation.

It is interesting to note that there is not a clear trajectory that moves from rejection to acceptance of sacred space. The texts overlap, contradict, and double back on one another throughout the three centuries leading up to Constantine. Characterizations of sacred space range from a utopic understanding of space – wherein holiness or sanctity resides in the bodies of the Christians, rather than in their meeting places – to a blatant rejection of sacred space. On the other hand, there are numerous texts that name specific places of meeting, and further, which incorporate rules of behaviour, attire, and other place-based prohibitions. In order to better understand the spectrum of Christian approaches to Christian sacred space, a selection of these texts will be discussed here, before broadening the discussion to more theoretical aspects of sacred space. The data presented will be representative, rather than exhaustive, and reveal conflicting views and approaches. In this section, the approaches to sacred space will be divided into three categories: first, approaches that consider the sacred to be housed not in physical structures, but in bodies; second, approaches that acknowledge but reject sacred space; and third, approaches that concern themselves with specific meeting places and the ordering or purification of space, whether or not sanctity is explicitly mentioned.

BODIES AS TEMPLES

The first approach, concerning the body as locus of sanctity, is clearly articulated in the Pauline correspondence. Paul's letters focus predominantly on the assembly (that is, the gathered bodies of the believers, who form the *ekklesia*), rather than the physical places in which the assembly would have met. Frequently, Paul refers to the believers as a temple of God, as in 1 Cor 3:16–17: "Do you not know that you are God's temple, and that God's spirit dwells in you? If anyone destroys God's temple, God will destroy that person. For God's temple is holy, and you are that temple." Here, the body is specifically understood to be the locus of sanctity or holiness. Throughout his letters, Paul uses the metaphor of temple (*naos*) to clarify the importance of right behaviour.[48] At the same time, there is no indication that this metaphor of temple is or ought to be extended into a discussion of materially articulated worship space.[49]

The temple metaphor is also employed elsewhere. In Ephesians 2:21–2, the author says, "In him the whole structure is joined together and grows into a holy temple in the Lord; in whom you also are built together spiritually into a dwelling place for God." Here the author locates sanctity in the believers themselves, rather than in a specific building. In this passage, the subject concerns the relationship of Jews and gentiles to one another. The author uses the metaphor of the temple to indicate the fixity of their connection to each other, despite having come from different places and experiences. The language of the temple certainly emphasizes the collectivity and sanctity of the body of believers, but it is not really about the understanding of temple space at all. Rather, it is about the relationship between the subjects of the Jewish and gentile missions. Thus, despite the fact that the author refers to the people of God as the temple of God, thereby negating the need for a physical temple, it cannot be read as a blanket injunction against sacred space.[50]

Even in Paul's letters, however, there is a recognition of different types of space. At times, there is a distinction made between the ordinary space of the house (*oikia*) and the space of the house church (*ekklesia*). The most obvious example of this distinction in Paul's thought can be found in 1 Corinthians 11, wherein he admonishes the Corinthians for eating the Lord's Supper as though it were their everyday meal. It is clear that, in this instance, there is a perceivable difference between a meal taken by the *familia* and a meal taken by the Christian family group – a difference the Corinthians all too readily violate.[51] Both the family meal and the Lord's Supper would have taken place in a domestic setting, however, meaning that some other action would have been needed to signify the shift from *oikia* to *ekklesia*. Thus, despite the fact that Paul repeatedly focuses holiness in the body of believers, even here there is a necessary distinction between – for lack of a better term – *oikia* bodies and *ekklesia* bodies.

Tertullian, writing in the late second century, also understood the locus of sanctity to reside in the body. In his work *de Spectaculis*, he discusses the defilement of the Christian body through presence in popular places of polytheistic worship, including the *ludi* and the civic celebration of sacrifice. In a manner consistent with most of Tertullian's work, his admonitions reflect the wholesale rejection of polytheistic influence as ideal behaviour. Tertullian's ultimate goal is to discourage Christians from going to the circuses or from attending public sacrifices, and ideally, to avoid those places even when the games or sacrifices are not occurring. Interestingly, however, he notes that it is not the places themselves that transfer pollution to the Christian body; rather, it is participating in the rites performed in these places that is problematic. Tertullian says, "Why, even the streets and the market-place, and the baths, and the taverns, and our very dwelling-places, are not altogether free from idols" (*de Spectaculis* 8).[52] That is, if it were possible to accrue pollution simply by being present, there would be nowhere that a Christian could go, so ubiquitous was the worship of these deities. He goes on: "it is not by merely being in the world … that we lapse from God, but by touching and tainting ourselves with the world's sins … The places in themselves do not contaminate, but what is done in them" (ibid.). Thus, while the ideal is to reject entirely those places of polytheistic activity, it is through the practices of the body that holiness or defilement occurs. By the same token, it is not the place but the body that houses sanctity or holiness.

EARLY CHRISTIAN REJECTION OF "SACRED SPACE"

Other Christian texts not only utilize the metaphor of the body as holy place, but couple it with a rejection of sacred space. In Clement of Alexandria's *Stromata* (ca. 180–203), he sees the assembly as the locus of sanctity:[53]

> But if 'the sacred' is understood in two ways – both as God himself and as the structure built in his honour – how shall we not rightly call the church, made through knowledge for the honour of God, sacred to God – of great value, neither constructed by mechanical skill nor embellished by the hand of a vagabond priest, but by the will of God made into a temple? For I call not the place but the assembly of the elect the church. This is the better temple for receiving the great dignities of God. (7.5)[54]

Here is an obvious rejection of the built environment; the place is rejected in favour of the people. In the broader context of the work, Clement of Alexandria asserts that there can be no holiness in something made by human hands, nor can humans make holiness; instead, only that which is made by God can be holy.[55]

A similar argument is made in the *Octavius* of Minucius Felix, discussed briefly above.[56] The relevant sections of this document note the opposition between polytheistic and Christian conceptions of ideal worship space.

Minucius Felix argues with his polytheistic interlocutor, Caecilius, about the reason for the lack of articulated worship space among Christian groups. It is not because the Christians are hiding away, as Caecilius suggests, that they do not have temples or altars that can be seen by everyone. Instead, it is because temples, as Minucius Felix claims, cannot contain God (*Octavius* 32.1–2). He says, "Shall I shut up the might of so great a majesty within one little building?" (32.2) He rejects the idea that statues or temples could ever be appropriate for his god. He then denounces the rite of sacrifice, completing his rejection of polytheistic ritual practice and worship. The dialogue is clearly an apologetic, providing reasons why the Christian community is superior to and worthy of respect from the broader community. It is not a catalogue of acceptable worship spaces or a blueprint for architectural models. At the same time, the vehemence with which Minucius Felix rejects the temple model is quite telling; there is an explicit association between polytheism and temple architecture. The mind and heart act as loci for the dwelling place of God, and the spirit acts as the substitute for the sacrifices and libations of polytheistic worship (32.2–3). Thus, like Clement in the *Stromata*, Minucius Felix also adopts the physical body (both individually and collectively) as the locus of sanctity, and rejects sacred space as it is understood in the surrounding community.

A similar view is expressed by Origen in his work, *Contra Celsum* (ca. 248). Like Minucius Felix, the argument against temple architecture has at least partially to do with its containment of the deity. Origen asserts that one of the reasons why Christians do not need temples is because their god is omnipresent: "Even an uneducated Christian is convinced that every place in the world is a part of the whole, since the whole world is a temple of God" (*Contra Celsum*, 7.44).[57] Like the argument that a temple is inferior because it is made by human hands, the argument for the omnipresence of God is predicated on the belief that the Christian god cannot be manipulated or contained by human action.

There are, in the foregoing texts, explicit rejections of temple architecture, but it should be questioned whether these texts are representative of contemporary practice. Minucius Felix's diatribe, for example, is a valuable response to the criticism that Christians did not build temples, but it ought not to be read as a rejection of place altogether. The same is true of Origen. Indeed, there were certainly specific places for worship by the time Minucius Felix and Origen were writing their texts, whether they were purpose-built or not.[58] Justin Martyr's claim, about the meeting place above the baths, is an indication that there were known places of meeting even in the second century.[59] One could also argue that Paul's letters demonstrate the knowability of Christian meeting places as early as the first century; his naming of patrons in Romans 16, 1 Corinthians 16, and Philemon 1–2, for example, demonstrates an ongoing relationship between hosts and their communities. Clement of Alexandria, Minucius Felix, and Origen all clearly reject worship space, but only a specific type: the specifically polytheistic, traditional temple model. The rejection of the temple model should not be read as a rejection of sacred space altogether. Indeed, the temple as model of worship space was rejected even after the peace of Constantine; a new type of Christian architecture emerged out of the desire for the community to differentiate itself from its contemporaries.[60]

What these texts reveal is not the practical experience of the Christian community, but an expression of difference between Christian and polytheistic Roman identity, expressed through the tangible medium of temple architecture. There is a valuable sense of identity through difference being cultivated in these texts which reject the purpose-built sacred space of temple architecture. It would seem, given the material evidence of Dura, and the known places discussed in Paul's letters (houses of hosts) and the Acts of Justin, that there was indeed a collection of known places, which housed an increasingly systematized ritual practice.

SPECIAL SPACE?

In addition to the texts expressing a utopic understanding of the body as temple, and those texts which reject the built environment of the temple, there are also texts that indicate – if not sacred space – a kind of special space used by Christians. Returning to Tertullian, it is clear that, despite his rejection of polytheistic or idolatrous spaces and his understanding of the body as locus of holiness, he recognizes the meeting places of Christians to be separate from ordinary space. In his work *de Idolatria* (ca. 196/7), he expresses frustration at those members of the Christian community who believe that they can make idols and still be a part of the church. He asks, "Does a Christian come from idols into the church [*in ecclesiam*], from the workshops of the adversary into the house of God [*in domum dei*]?" (7.1)[61] A number of interesting features emerge from the study of this excerpt. First, it is clear that a structure is implied. Tertullian refers to the *ekklesia*, which could of course refer to the assembly of believers, as in the Pauline literature. When contrasting the idol-maker's workshop with the church, however, he refers to the Christian meeting place as the house of God (*domus dei*). There is a linguistic distinction between the assembly and the church building. Second, that the meeting place is called the house of God indicates its importance and significance to the community. The title *domus dei* also implies a known place of meeting. Third, the fact that Tertullian calls attention to this potential act indicates a fear of pollution or defilement. The issue is of course one of faith; the Christians ought not to be engaging with polytheistic practices at all. At the same time, there is a sense that the *ekklesia* and the *domus dei* ought to be kept free from the polluting agents of idol-makers. The church building was not necessarily a place with purity and pollution regulations, as was the Jerusalem Temple, but it is clear that there is some anxiety surrounding the mixing of polytheistic and Christian practices in the same space.[62]

A similar attitude can be found in Tertullian's work, *de Pudicitia* (ca. 210/11), wherein Tertullian rails against adulterers who dare to attend the Christian meetings, despite being sinful. He says of the adulterers that they ought to be driven away "not only from the threshold [*limine*] but in fact from the shelter of the entire church building [*omni ecclesiae*]" (4.5).[63] Here, Tertullian uses the term *ekklesia*, but the reference to a threshold (*limen*) implies an actual structure. Earlier in the same text, he also refers to the sinful ones prostrating themselves before the doors of the church (*pro foribus eius*), again implying a built environment. Like the passage from *de Idolatria*, while there are no specific purity regulations in play here, there is a sense that the structure of the church is no place for sinfulness. Therefore, just as Tertullian is concerned with the defilement of Christian bodies, so too is he concerned with the defilement of their meeting places.

Clement of Alexandria also makes a distinction between assembly space and other types of space in the *Paedagogus* (180–203). He discusses appropriate behaviour and attire for members of the church, saying, "Women and men should go to church [*ekklesia*] decently attired, with natural step, clinging to silence" (3.2).[64] White points out that this use of *ekklesia* not only specifically refers to an actual church building, but it is the "earliest clear usage of the phrase so as to indicate a recognized place of assembly."[65] Indeed, the entire passage is about those hypocrites who behave appropriately when in the church building, but who return to their polytheistic ways when outside its walls. It is clear that here, there is a specific place of meeting, and that it has associated modes of behaviour. While Clement's purpose is to encourage Christians to behave properly at all times, there are already social expectations among members of the church that encourage them to behave righteously when in church, even if they are less than perfect outside of their meeting places.

A more explicit example of special place can be found in the *Acts of Peter* (ca. 190), as discussed earlier.[66] In this text, the owner of the house, Marcellus, purifies it through sweeping, sprinkling water, and invoking the name of Jesus Christ before allowing the apostle to come in and teach the assembly (*Acts of Peter* 19). Here, it seems that the polluting work of Simon Magus must be exorcised from the space before the true apostle is able to work. While purification is not necessarily a requirement of sacred space, the act of purification by Marcellus does signal a separation from ordinary space.

SOME CONCLUSIONS

Early Christian approaches to sacred space are not straightforward. The body-centred locus of sanctity, with its utopian trappings, seemed to dominate the ideological view of space. Temples, associated with idol worship and polytheistic practice, were rejected out of hand. At the same time, it is clear that some places were understood to be important or significant to the community, and in some cases, they had associated rules of behaviour or purity. In no case is there an indication that earlier Christians rejected space while later Christians embraced it.

It could be argued that, as the formalization and significance of ritual grew, so too did the importance of the space in which it was enacted. It should be noted, however, that ritual was always a key element of early Christian meetings, and therefore, one should expect to find sacred space well before it became materially articulated. Indeed, it will be argued below that the places used by the earliest Christians – that is, the house churches – were in fact sacred spaces in their own right. Finding sacred space in the house church is no easy task, given the lack of material boundaries between Christian and domestic space. In general, perhaps the biggest roadblock to conceiving the house church as sacred space comes from the recognition that the house itself was a polytheistic, cultic space. How, then, could the house church create or maintain sacred space in the face of domestic cult practice? The characterization of sacred space in the house church presented below will argue that, rather than a cessation of the domestic cult, the ritual formulation of sacred space in the house church would have allowed life in the house to continue as it always had. In the following sections, an attempt will be made to flesh out the nature of house-church sacred space, beginning with a general conversation about sacred space, and then moving into a discussion of ritual and its relationship to sacred space.

Chapter Six

Sacred Space and the House Church

The foregoing chapters have laid the groundwork for the conversation about early Christian sacred space in the house church. Given the variety of domestic spaces available for house-church meetings, the rituals that would have taken place in them, and the occupation of those spaces by family members and domestic cult practitioners, the domestic arena raises a number of sometimes troubling questions concerning the perception, production, and use of sacred space by the house-church Christians. Still, having established *that* domestic spaces were used as meeting places, the following chapter will discuss *how* these domestic spaces might have been understood by the groups that met in them. To be precise, I will argue here that, despite the myriad issues of conflict, coexistence, and cognitive dissonance that were inevitable in a mixed space like a house church, the house-church Christians perceived their meeting space to be sacred.

As discussed in the introduction, there is a popular view that Christians met in houses in order to avoid pollution from polytheistic sacred places, choosing instead the "neutral" territory of the house. It is also sometimes asserted that the choice of house as neutral meeting place was a conscious rejection of sacred space, and that this rejection represented a purer form of Christianity in the period before Constantine.[1] In tandem with these views is the frequently touted "body of believers" argument, which presents the church not as a structure, but as a locus of sanctity formed in the bodies of the Christ followers. In each of these views, it is either implicitly or explicitly asserted that house churches were not sacred space.

These views, while supported somewhat in the textual evidence, do not present a complete or accurate picture of house-church space. First, the Roman house was not a neutral space, and therefore could not have provided Christians with a neutral place of meeting. Second, the so-called body of believers, formed in union with Christ, represents an ideological space, not a physical one, and allows no room for the essential categories of embodiment and emplacement. Ignoring these essential categories creates a false or "disembodied" picture of early Christian worship, and discounts the relationship between space, place, and the body. The discussion that follows, then, will attempt to find sacred space in the house church while honouring both the populated space of the Roman house and the embodiment of the members of the house-church communities.

UNDERSTANDING SACRED SPACE: WHAT IS SACRED SPACE?

What, then, is sacred space? How is sacred space made, discovered, or maintained? What function does sacred space perform in the development of religious and ritual identities? There are many different models of sacred space geared toward addressing these questions, among others. Most theories of sacred space tend to prioritize purpose-built environments, such as temples, churches, or cathedrals, focusing on the use of these places by established communities. Other theories of sacred space expand the definition to include natural environments, such as groves, mountains, bodies of water, and springs. Applying these models can be difficult in the case of adaptive or non-purpose-built environments, however. In the first case, the buildings are constructed to facilitate belief and practice in their specific system of ritual. In the second case, while the natural environment is not constructed by humans, the relationship between humans and the natural environment is emphasized. The house church, on the other hand, is a place within a place; the Roman house is constructed for the business of daily life and preexisting domestic ritual, not for the facilitation of early Christian ritual. Therefore, the sacred space used by Christians must be found within the already existing sacred space of the home in its Roman context.

Early Christian sacred space can be read in conjunction with Jewish and polytheistic views of sacred space, since there was clearly an influence on early Christianity from both traditions. The Jerusalem Temple and the many temples of the polytheistic world offer immediate and contemporary comparisons to the Christian development of sacred space. At the same time, early Christian sacred space presents unique issues. The house church challenges preconceived notions of sacred space, since it tends to defy standard categories of built environments. The house church is without a sacred precinct or clearly demarcated boundaries, without priests or priestesses assigned to tend it, without clear and obvious guidelines for its construction and maintenance. One might understandably suggest, on the basis of the texts discussed above and the lack of physical boundaries, that there could be no sacred space in the house church. On the other hand, there are indications that there was some effort undertaken to preserve the integrity of the house-church meeting place. This took place either through purification or through the introduction of the household or domestic codes in the new Christian communities, as discussed in the third set of texts in the previous chapter.[2] Rituals occurring in the Christian meetings were also clearly recognized as sacred acts. Further, the movement toward renovated spaces in some communities reflected an ongoing concern with sacred space. The process of permanent, purpose-built place-making was a gradual one, rather than a sea change brought about by the advent of the Constantinian building program. Preoccupations with sacred space or appropriate space would have been part of the communities' concerns from the earliest days. Thus, rather than rejecting the notion of sacred space in the house church outright, it is necessary to determine the type and nature of sacred space found in the house church, and ask how it conforms, or not, with some of the longstanding definitions of sacred space.

Sacred space is usually understood first and foremost as a place set apart. It carries with it, however, many other implications, including those of being: central (in the community, the world, or the cosmos); a meeting point (between human and divine); differentiated space (as opposed to "profane" or "neutral" space); powerful or holy space (associated often with transcendence, healing, or mysticism); and pure space (free from defiling elements, including processes of the body). Sacred space is often understood to be the locus for power or for something beyond the ordinary, because of its perceived ability to negotiate between earthly and heavenly or transcendent activity.

The following discussion will focus on three sets of theories of sacred space, each set delineated by the central question it is designed to answer. The first set of theories asks whether sacred space is heterogeneous with profane space; the second, whether sacred space is produced by human action; and the third, what features can be said to be common to most theories or conceptions of sacred space. The discussion will then move to embodiment, including the relationship between human beings and their environment, and most importantly, human beings and ritual, and the role played by the ritual in marshalling the body through space and negotiating (and producing) sacred space. The examination of these key models of sacred space will reveal the interrelated character of emplacement and of ritual, and demonstrate the need for a model of house-church space that incorporates both of these elements.

SACRED/PROFANE DICHOTOMIES AND ELIADE

The character of sacred space is, in its simplest terms, space "set apart." The definition of the term sacred can be somewhat problematic, however, and it is necessary to investigate possible interpretations. The word finds its origins in the Latin word *sacer*, which itself carries a number of meanings. It is clear that *sacer* pertains to the gods; for example, in Roman ritual practice, the word was frequently applied as a descriptor of a sacrificial victim. An animal deemed *sacer* was devoted or consecrated to the gods, which provided a state of "specialness." At the same time, this belonging to the gods also set the animal apart, meaning that it was no longer part of the natural world. This setting apart meant that the animal acquired the additional burden of being "accursed" or "horrible," as it was "devoted to a divinity for destruction."[3] It was accursed because its life was now forfeited, despite also acquiring the character of holiness or sanctity.[4] Fundamentally, however, the meaning of *sacer* pertains predominantly to a belonging to, or ownership by, the gods. *Profanus*, on the other hand, is defined as "unholy, not sacred, common, profane."[5] Its basic definition is solely that which is not *sacer*, that which does not belong to the gods – that is, everything else. Like *sacer*, *profanus* can also acquire darker meaning, including "wicked, impious," or "ill-boding."[6] Despite these potentially sinister connotations, in Roman culture the sacred and profane tended to be defined as what belonged to the gods, and what did not. The sacred and the profane represented fundamentally different categories.[7]

In his famous work, *The Elementary Forms of Religious Life*, Émile Durkheim focused on this distinction between the sacred and the profane, claiming that their absolute "heterogeneity" is what drives all systems of religion.[8] While the term "sacred" can sometimes conjure up holiness or purity, and the term "profane" can sometimes be associated with dirt or impurity, Durkheim points out that the fundamental meaning behind both of these words is that one is set apart, or forbidden (sacred, belonging to the gods), while the other is mundane (profane, belonging to the everyday, or to everything else). As Durkheim argues, "Sacred beings are, by definition, separate beings."[9] For Durkheim, there is nothing inherently sacred in the space set apart; it is sacred only *because* it is set apart. The decision to demarcate space in this way is made by the community, and is sometimes the manifestation of what Durkheim terms a "collective consciousness."[10] This collective consciousness, according to Durkheim, needs an outlet for the transcendent, and community members therefore project a notion of the sacred onto a specific place, which then serves to orient itself as a community. The exact places where communities are established are irrelevant for Durkheim. What matters is that the society collectively chooses a place (and a model of spatialization) to orient themselves and their notions of the divine, their worldview, and their ethos as a community.[11] That place is then sacred, belonging as it does to the transcendent, or to that which the collective has determined to be transcendent.

According to Durkheim, the distinction between the sacred and the profane also sets rules of differentiation, and eventually, of access and exclusion.[12] The radical or absolute heterogeneity of the sacred and the profane creates a heterogeneity of sacred and profane space. Durkheim argues that "religious life and profane life cannot coexist in the same space. For religious life to flourish, a special place must be arranged from which profane life is excluded."[13] While this model could work when applied to purpose-built structures, it creates problems in the reading of adapted spaces, like the house church. According to this dichotomy, it would be impossible for religious life to flourish in the house church. Daily life, with all of its profane concerns, would be constantly encroaching on the space used for meeting. As has already been established, no specific place was set apart in the house churches.

A similar sacred/profane dichotomy was embraced by Mircea Eliade, who can perhaps be called the father of modern theories of sacred space. His approach to finding the sacred is very different from Durkheim's, focusing on the manifestation of the divine in the natural world and its connection to the cosmogony. The sacred and the profane, however, retain their heterogeneous nature in his discussion of sacred space. While much of Eliade's theory has now been rejected, his work contributed to the formulation of many other key theories of sacred space, and will therefore be briefly outlined here.[14] In his work, *The Sacred and the Profane: The Nature of Religion*, Eliade describes the difference between space and sacred space.[15] Like Durkheim, Eliade places sacred and profane in oppositional categories; sacred space is ontologically different from profane space. He notes from the outset that, "for religious man, space is not homogeneous; he experiences interruptions, breaks in it."[16] These breaks, according to Eliade, are brought about by what he terms "a hierophany, an irruption of the sacred,"[17] and they are usually understood to be the actions of the gods.[18] The irruptions provide the point of contact, the break wherein a fissure between earth and heaven can be opened up, allowing for communication but also, transcendence.[19] Eliade claims that this "real" space is what provides orientation for the rest of the world. The rest of space orients itself around or in opposition to this point.[20] Further, this is not only a space of orientation, but also of founding, or of existing. By contrast, profane space has no orientation; it is simply formless space, or as Eliade describes it, "homogeneous and neutral."[21]

For Eliade, theophanies and hierophanies provide more than just necessary breaks in otherwise homogeneous space; they also act as signs that there is something beyond this world.[22] Where there are no obvious signs, signs must be created or discovered, thereby providing another mode of consecrating space. He argues that human beings must have sacred space, since it provides orientation and founding, but the consecration of space where hierophanies are absent is not purely the work of society. He continues: "But we must not suppose that human work is in question here, that it is through his own efforts that man can consecrate a space. In reality the ritual by which he constructs a sacred space is efficacious in the measure in which it reproduces the work of the gods."[23] Thus, while he acknowledges the work of ritual as being a human endeavour, he denies the actual production or construction of space by human beings *de novo*; instead, the human beings are repeating the primordial hierophanies of sacred space and, therefore, of orientation. Further, Eliade draws connections between this repetition and the sacred, claiming that "the cosmicization of unknown territories is always a consecration."[24]

Eliade's notion of cosmicization and hierophany is predicated on the idea of the centre. Because of the orienting and fixing power of the hierophany, the location of the hierophany is the "Center of the World," where the *axis mundi* runs through.[25] Ritual repetition of the cosmogony, or of the primordial "First Thing," maintains the space set apart by hierophany as sacred. This sacred space is wholly other from profane space. Eliade sees the sacred/profane dichotomy as comparable to the idea of chaos versus cosmos. Chaos represents profane, homogeneous space, and cosmos, sacred, real space.[26]

Eliade's theory of sacred space is not without its problems, including the focus on hierophany and irruption. While Eliade does allow for other ways of consecration (where signs or hierophanies fail to appear), it is unclear how this consecration would actually be carried out. As with the work of Durkheim, however, it is the sacred/profane dichotomy that creates the most problems in application. Both Durkheim and Eliade argue for the absolute separation or heterogeneity of the sacred and the profane. Durkheim holds that it is society that sets the boundaries between the sacred and the profane, while Eliade points to hierophanies and irruptions as causing the break between them. Despite the gulf between Durkheim's social-constructivist view and Eliade's ontological view, they share a fundamental assertion: in these models, there can be no blending or mixing of the two types of space and their associated behaviour.

CRITICISMS OF THE SACRED/PROFANE DICHOTOMY

Jonathan Z. Smith has levelled a series of criticisms against the notion of a sacred/profane dichotomy, and against Eliade's work in particular. Smith draws attention to one of the key issues with this dichotomy: in the attempt to categorize sacred and profane as radically other, there is no recognition of the difference between ideology and practice. In other words, while sacred things and profane things may be in opposition to each other in an ideal or ideological sense, there may often be a mingling of those things in lived experience. As Smith notes, "the tribe as observed need not correspond in fact to their own systematic statements about themselves."[27] There is understandably a difference between what a community says about itself – or indeed, what a community's elite members say about themselves – and what the practice of the community actually looks like. This difference, which Smith terms a "cognitive gap," can be both consciously and unconsciously enacted.[28] Far from being evidence for a lack of belief, this cognitive dissonance is to be expected, especially when all of the complications of lived experience and embodiment come into play. For example, while the early Christian community was ostensibly concerned with issues of equality under Christ, the habits and external factors of lived experience would have amounted to something very different. It is exactly this cognitive gap that Paul is addressing in 1 Corinthians 11, for example, when he admonishes the Corinthians for behaving normally – or profanely – rather than in a manner befitting the ritual of the Lord's Supper. This cognitive gap can also be applied to sacred space. As discussed above, many early Christian writers rejected the idea of sacred space. Space was necessary for the practice of ritual, however, and in many cases, that space needed to be shared with profane life in all its forms.[29] Rather than arguing that there could be no sacred space in the house church, or that sacred space would be impossible if profane experience were allowed within it, recognizing a cognitive gap allows for a more nuanced reading of sacred space.[30]

Smith goes on to assert that the key issue is one of "discrepancy: the perception of a gap between the 'socially ideal' and the 'socially real.' A more active and political name for such an essentially cognitive gap is conflict."[31] Smith's argument highlights the complex nature of the relationship between ideology and practice; the greater the complexity, the more likely that aberrations from the ideal will occur. In the house church, the potential for conflict was extensive, given the commingling of domestic life with ritual practice, or of believers with unbelievers (in mixed households, for example). The blurring of ideological boundaries would have occurred as a matter of course, since there would have been few controls set in place.

It is mainly the enforcement of rules, predominantly political and hierarchical in nature, that is most likely to close this cognitive gap.[32] The more controlled the community, the less likely it is that practices would occur that exist in that space of conflict. The early church did eventually grow into a political, hierarchical arrangement (with the development of the monoepiscopate), which in turn enforced orthodoxy, as well as liturgy, ritual practice, and communal behaviour. With the advent of renovated spaces and, later, of purpose-built structures, the enforcement of right practice (as an accompaniment to right doctrine or belief) could finally have been achieved, or at least, could have been made to adhere more closely to the ideal. Before purpose-built structures, however, it would have been difficult, if not impossible, to enforce ideal practice.

It is clear, therefore, that the sacred/profane dichotomy cannot be made to apply consistently to space, and certainly not to house-church space. Given the tendency for sacred and profane space to overlap in practice, then, how might sacred space be better defined or described?

THE ROLE OF SACRED SPACE IN SOCIETY

Other models of sacred space do not emphasize a radical dichotomy of sacred and profane, but instead attempt to define sacred space by its function or its role in society. In their edited volume, *American Sacred Space*, David Chidester and Edward T. Linenthal question how one determines whether sacred space is substantial (that is, reflecting the "real," as Eliade might argue) or situational (that is, reflecting a specific culture or community). They term this distinction the "poetics" and the "politics" of sacred space.[33] The poetics and the politics of space work together to produce and maintain sacred space, creating a framework that is more readily applicable to different types of communities.[34] Chidester and Linenthal also discuss the production of sacred space, recognizing that it is not preexistent or "revealed," as in Eliade's model. They instead define sacred space as "ritual space, a location for formalized, repeatable symbolic performances."[35] They note that, "as sacred space, a ritual site is set apart from or carved out of an 'ordinary' environment to provide an arena for the performance of controlled, 'extraordinary' patterns of action."[36] Implicit in this definition are a number of defining features of sacred space. First, it is, as one might expect, a space set apart. Second, sacred space is ritual space; it is the locus for the ritual activity of a given community. Rather than being the dwelling place of a deity, or space that is essentially different from profane space, there is nothing inherently different about sacred space in comparison with "ordinary" space. It is "carved out" in order to provide an arena for ritual, which in turn consecrates and differentiates the space. Third, because of this carving out, there are boundaries put in place to set apart sacred space.

Perhaps most importantly, there is a fundamental relationship between ritual practice and the production of sacred space. On the one hand, a site where ritual is performed is sacred space; on the other hand, sacred space gives ritual its essential character. The meaning and function of ritual and its relationship to sacred space is fundamental to the production of sacred space. How sacred space and ritual relate to each other, however, is not always straightforward, and so this relationship will be discussed in detail below.

Like Durkheim and Eliade, Chidester and Linenthal also note the importance of sacred space in the identity formation of a given community. It is for this reason that sacred space is so often subject to interpretation. Sacred space "focuses crucial questions about what it means to be a human being in a meaning-filled world."[37] While for Chidester and Linenthal, sacred space is the labour of human action and specifically, of ritual, it serves the same purpose of orienting human life, and of providing a framework of ordered spaces and places. This orienting is especially true of built environments, since the location of meaning and significance is deliberately placed and deliberately maintained.

Sacred sites are also sites of conflict. They are places where ritual is performed, which causes a conflict between purity and defilement, consecration and profanation. They can also be places that belong to or are used by more than one community. In *American Sacred Space*, Chidester and Linenthal discuss examples of native land claims versus the manifest destiny ideology of American law to demonstrate two very different interpretations of a single space.[38] These warring ideologies, fundamentally incompatible with each other, serve to heighten the tension and power of a sacred site. Ritual sites with more than one role, or more than one community staking claim to them, tend also to be sites of what Chidester and Linenthal term "contested meaning."[39] A place, then, fosters and affords different meaning to different groups at different times, which in turn leads to the danger of multiple interpretations. But this contested meaning does not negate the sanctity of the space; indeed, as Chidester and Linenthal argue, it can strengthen it. Like Smith's cognitive gap, this tension can heighten focus and attention during the enactment of ritual.[40]

Ownership and power, then, are paramount in the making of sacred space. At the same time, this ownership and power must be continually asserted, remade, and reconstituted through the practice of ritual. The importance of ritual in the production of sacred space is clear. It is possible for more than one group to stake a claim on a given site, so long as they are able to perform rituals within it. In the same way, a given site may even be used by the same group for different sets of rituals; or two sets of rituals may have overlapping participants. The house church was certainly a place of conflict, where ritual and domestic life were forced to coexist, however uneasy the relationship. Some members of a Roman *familia*, for example, might have been members both of the house-church group and of the practising domestic cult group. Those who were only members of the house-church group – that is, people who were not members of the host *familia* – would have been participants in a single manifestation of the space, present only during meetings of the house church. Thus, different types of house-church members, depending on their access to the space, would have had different views of it. Some members would have had more complicated relationships with the space, and may have constituted that space differently at different times. Further, Chidester and Linenthal note, "Since no sacred space is merely 'given' in the world, its ownership will always be at stake."[41] While legal ownership might always have belonged to the host of the house church, ownership of the house *as sacred space* would have changed, depending on whether the house-church group or the family group were using it.[42]

Building on the notion of ownership and contested space, it is also important to recognize that sacred space can be found anywhere. This conception of sacred space is described by what van Gennep has termed the "pivoting of the sacred."[43] This pivoting of the sacred, or the recognition that sacred space is sometimes *not* sacred, means that sacred space "can coalesce in any place that becomes, even if only temporarily, a site for intensive interpretation."[44] Here, the focus is on "interpretation" (that is, the conversation of a community about itself and its space) rather than ontology (that is, a site where the sacred is understood to exist), and it is for this reason that the sacred can in fact move, change, be produced or erased. Thus, permanence is not necessarily a requirement of sacred space. Whether for reasons of conflict, coexistence, or simply the passage of time, the space may acquire or efface its sacred status. The recognition of temporal factors, as well as conflict and the cognitive gap, will contribute to building a valuable interpretive framework for house-church sacred space, below.

BOUNDARIES AND SACRED SPACE

Implicit in all of the models of sacred space thus far is the notion of bounded space. For a space to be set apart, it must have boundaries. Space cannot be differentiated without demarcation. While it is not necessary to have physical or architectural demarcation, most sacred precincts do in fact demarcate space in this way. Temples in Greece and Rome, for example, as well as the Jerusalem Temple, were surrounded by walls, fences, or vegetal boundaries in order to separate them from the surrounding space. Progressive levels of sanctity were also enforced via access barriers and further boundaries within the precinct.[45] Access and control, marshalled by power brokers in a given community, are maintained by boundaries. These boundaries are of course more easily negotiated when the sacred site is architecturally differentiated from the space around it. As Chidester and Linenthal note, "Built environments are more obviously constructed as cultural locations of religious meaning and significance."[46]

Sometimes, boundaries also indicate which actions must be taken by bodies. For example, purity regulations, such as the exclusion of menstruants, recent mothers, and ejaculants, were controlled in the Jerusalem Temple via the enforcement of physical boundaries.[47] In addition, the Jerusalem Temple restricted access according to gender; women were not permitted to go beyond the court of the women, and non-priestly members of the male community were restricted from the sanctuary. Of course, the Holy of Holies was restricted yet further; only the high priest could enter, and even then, only on a particular day of the Jewish calendar. The Jerusalem Temple offers a clear picture of bounded space and graded sanctity, with accompanying regulations restricting access and demanding purity.[48] Greek and Roman temples, too, were strictly bounded; precincts were often marked by walls of stone or foliage, and while some temples were accessible to worshippers, many had inner chambers which were accessible only to the priesthood.[49]

Here again, the house church provides challenges, especially if the traditional understanding of boundaries is implemented. Converts to Christianity out of polytheistic tradition as well as the Second Temple tradition would have found much that was different about the house-church setting. Rather than a monumental civic building with an associated precinct, boundary markers, and access barriers, members of the house churches would have encountered domestic space. As is evident from the discussion in chapter 2, it is not that the Roman house would have been without boundaries. Indeed, there were rooms that were kept private in the Roman house and to which visitors, including members of the house-church community, would not have been allowed access. These boundaries, however, were those pertaining to public and private life, or to civic and domestic life, rather than boundaries between sacred and profane, or pure and impure.[50] Ritual performance, in the previous experience of these converts, would have been practised in a place with articulated boundaries. In the house church, for ritual to have been performed in a manner congruent with its powerful role, other modes of establishing boundaries would have been demanded. How, then, might these boundaries have been formed? Two key elements will guide the discussion of boundary-making in the house church: *embodiment*, or the physicality of the believers, and *ritual*, the sacred acts, utterances, and practices around which the meeting revolved.

EMBODIMENT AND EMPLACEMENT

Embodiment holds the key to understanding the way that ritual operates within and upon space, and will therefore be discussed first. As embodied beings, humans necessarily cultivate a relationship between their bodies and the world in which they live. Edward Casey argues that human beings are "always already in a place, never not emplaced in one way or another."[51] It is because human beings are embodied that they are "never without emplaced experiences."[52] In other words, there is no such thing as a purely intellectual or purely emotional or purely ideological experience. Experience is always sensed by, developed in, and marshalled through the lived experience of the body. In order to discuss house-church Christian space, it is essential to first understand the ways that bodies exist in and are conditioned by places, what places are, and what places do. The bodies of the house-church Christians were present in the already-existing place of the Roman house, and were therefore conditioned by it, whether conscious of that conditioning or not. It is for this reason that bodies cannot be divorced from the collective ideology of the "body of believers." The body of believers is not *only* an ideological construct; it is also the gathering together of physical bodies in a particular place.

Bodies, in conjunction with place, have an impact on human experience in a number of different ways. First, and perhaps most obviously, the senses formulate basic human experience. They demand and enable the body's survival, sending messages concerning the need for food, drink, and shelter. These senses are then ordered by and processed through the body, which creates perception. Bodily perceiving is essential to the construction of experience. Yi-Fu Tuan, humanistic geographer, draws attention to the importance of the body in the construction of perception; the senses create a complicated framework of data to which the conscious and unconscious mind necessarily respond. Certainly the work of culture is also at play here; as Tuan argues, perceptions of high versus low, left versus right, front versus back, are all important spatial perceptions which can be dictated by the collective and sedimented culture.[53] Because the body is emplaced, the body is also the locus for the understanding and experience of space. Second, the body orients the person, dictating the way that a person interacts with his or her space through what Michel de Certeau has called the "spatial practices" of the body.[54] A body, through movement and pause, perceives and interacts with its environment. As de Certeau argues, these spatial practices are unconsciously enacted, but are no less powerful for being so.[55]

In general, bodies, far from being afterthoughts or unwieldy obstacles to the life of the mind, actually do the work of emplacement. As Casey asks, "Could it be that the body is *essentially*, and not just contingently, involved in emplacement?"[56] Casey's answer is yes; the body is essential in the human experience and constitution of place. At the same time, the environment establishes some order through which the body moves. The body can then impose its own will on the environment, now acting in keeping with the environment, now in opposition to it. There is, therefore, a complicated relationship between the body and its environment. It is not always clear how or whether they might work together, or which of them is more important in the production of sacred space. There are a number of ways in which this relationship can be understood. Three models will be discussed here in relatively broad terms, in order to demonstrate that the relationship between body and place must necessarily be both dynamic and dialectic.

Among the earliest theories of human interaction with place is the theory usually referred to as environmental determinism. This model of place, grounded in the classical tradition, indicates the direction of influence as moving from place to people. That is, places, including climate and topography, have an impact on humans, rather than the other way around, and act upon the body as well as the personality. What formulates human experience of a place is the place itself. According to environmental determinists, not only are human *experiences* formulated by place; a human's very nature is formed in this way as well. An example of this view is touted by Vitruvius, when he asserts that Romans have their glorious climate to thank for their superiority (6.1.11).[57] In general, this model puts humans at the mercy of the place in which they find themselves, and not only their bodies, but their dispositions, their identities, and their likelihood of success are all formulated by their physical location.

The second model lies in fundamental opposition to the first. Human geography (another term for humanistic geography) always positions the human mind and body as primary over place. The human mind acts upon place to create it, to imbue it with meaning, and to encode it with further signifiers, which are dictated by cultural and social cues. As Tuan argues, human beings make places, creating them as manifestations of their desire to embody their experiences in "tangible material."[58] For human geographers, human beings are the centre of the cosmos, and place-making is an act of anthropocentrism.[59] For example, the wide open space of the Canadian Prairies might seem hostile to some, especially as the winds blow across the plains in winter; but to someone who grew up in Saskatchewan, the Prairies are "home." Thus, even the most inhospitable environment can be transformed via human action and the work of culture. Here, human beings not only control place, but create it. The same holds true for sacred places; a human geographer would reject the notion of hierophany in favour of a culturally constructed place of power or importance.[60]

The third model lies somewhere between the two, and is a dialectical one, wherein the bodies that inhabit places are both constituted by and constitutive of those places. The dialogue between body and place can be conscious or unconscious. Fixed factors, such as climate and topography, are in constant play with non-fixed variables (technology, for example) and cultural variables (political or religious structures).[61] The former belongs to place, while the latter belongs to the body, expressed both individually and collectively, as culture or society.

Edward Casey argues that "*lived bodies belong to places* and help to constitute them."[62] Implicit in this notion is the dual nature of the relationship between them. On the one hand, lived bodies belong to place, seemingly indicating the preexistence or preeminence of place over against the body. On the other hand, lived bodies also constitute place, suggesting that, if place is preexistent, it is never complete. As Casey argues, "A given place may certainly be perduring and consistent, but this does not mean that it is simply something inactive and at rest."[63] The constitution of place can be active or obvious, through the construction of roads, buildings, and so forth. It can also be passive or less obvious, by trespassing, or transgressing boundaries such as fences and sidewalks.[64] More dramatic examples include the eroding of shoreline or the destruction of fragile ecosystems through human activity. This human action, especially if enacted over long periods of time, can actually change a place into something other than its original state. On a micro level, the same outcome can occur; if members of a household always choose to eat in front of the television instead of the dining room, the couch, rather than the dining table, becomes the "eating place."

Despite the ability of the body to constitute place, it must be acknowledged that, "just as there are no places without the bodies that sustain and vivify them, so there are no lived bodies without the places they inhabit and traverse."[65] A body, by virtue of its physicality, can never be in no-place; it is always emplaced, and therefore, subject to influence from various factors in that place. In addition, as Casey argues, "places actively solicit bodily motions."[66] Built and natural environments dictate activity patterns and function, both in public and private places. Inhospitable environments, like bedrock, swamp, or desert, inhibit the success of human life. A city dictates walking patterns through the construction of grids, sidewalks, and green spaces. Public buildings restrict access through doorways, passages, and locked rooms. The layout of houses determines public and private space, as well as sleeping space, cooking space, and lounging space.[67] The body may move around within place, or move from place to place, but in every case, the body is always and only existing in place. Thus, place is affected by the body, but the body will also be affected by its place, if only by virtue of being there.

This dialectical formation means that places are dynamic, never static. It also allows for the impact of place (as in environmental determinism) without negating the power of the human body to change its surroundings (as in human geography). Over time, the use of a place can dictate its value, but places can themselves limit or expand functional boundaries as well. In other words, humans are in a constant conversation with place in order to determine its meaning as well as their own. Accepting, then, this dialectical model of the relationship between humans and their environment, it should follow that: first, humans are affected by their interactions with places; second, places are never static, because they are affected by human activity; and third, no place can be characterized as "neutral," since it is already imbued with meaning, and it is a repository of further meaning through the continued actions of its inhabitants.

Having understood the dialectical relationship between embodiment and emplacement, one might ask how this relationship might have played out in the house church. Certainly, the work of emplacement is not performed only by the body; nor is it performed only by individual bodies. Instead, the work of emplacement is achieved through individual embodiment in conjunction with individual experience, which is in turn shared with other individual bodies and experiences, thereby forming a collective experience.

As mentioned above, Jorunn Økland has convincingly argued for a "collective body" in the Pauline community, which constitutes a kind of collective rule whereby perception is constituted.[68] This body of believers ought to be understood in terms of a dialectical relationship between embodiment and emplacement, which is predicated on a few factors. First, the body of believers is itself composed of individually emplaced bodies. Second, the body of believers creates a place for worship, collectively, through the act of gathering together. Third, the bodies, both individually and collectively, find themselves already emplaced in a house, which is a place in its own right. The place of the house, however, like all places, is dynamic, not static; it is multivalent and able to respond to the work of embodiment and movement, both conscious and unconscious. Thus, while the Roman house (for example) is already a place specifically geared toward Roman domestic experience, the gathering of the bodies of Christians and the forming of a collective body (the body of believers or *ekklesia*) acts upon the place to create new place: that of Christian worship. At the same time, this new place does not negate the preexisting place of the house, which continues to act upon the body (and bodies) of believers.[69] The body, then, individually and collectively, acts both as recipient of place and emplacement, and as actor and constitutor of place. Thus, in order for the collective body to perceive sacred space within domestic space, there must be a dialectical and dynamic relationship between space and the body, between emplacement and embodiment. The way this collective perception and constitution of place is enacted is through the practice of ritual.

Before moving into a discussion of ritual and its relationship to sacred space, it would do well here to supply a working definition of sacred space. Scholarship on sacred space after Eliade has tended to reject an ontological or theological model of sacred space, and has favoured instead those models which focus on the social construction and interpretation of space. The social construction of sacred space allows for the interaction between place and body, which has already been argued as fundamental to the human experience. The social construction of sacred space also underscores the outcome of this production, including identity formation, political power and hierarchy, and, of course, Smith's reminder of the cognitive gap between ideology and practice. The models most useful for the discussion of the house-church community are those which reflect the dynamic and dialectical relationship between ritual and space. Thus, the model of sacred space most useful for the discussion of house-church Christianity is one that is set apart (either permanently or temporarily), socially constructed and maintained (either consciously or unconsciously), bounded (either through architecture or through the actions of the community), and which serves as the locus for ritual practice. This model will be expanded further through the investigation of ritual.

RITUAL PRACTICE AND THE PRODUCTION OF SACRED SPACE

Like sacred space, ritual is also the subject of numerous theories, some functioning in opposition to each other. The breadth of the theoretical response to ritual is testament to its complexity, ranging from the attempt to discover the origins of ritual to determining the meaning and function of ritual. Theorists have tended to focus more on the role of ritual in society, rather than the relationship between ritual and the production of sacred space.[70] Here, however, the focus will naturally be placed on the relationship between ritual and sacred space. It is clear that ritual was a fundamental part of the house-church community and, as will be argued below, that it was instrumental in the production of house-church sacred space. Since house-church Christians did not have access to purpose-built structures, with materially articulated, bounded worship space, they depended on ritual to demarcate their meeting places from their living places. That ritual is an agent in the production of sacred space will become apparent in the discussion which follows.

Ritual theorists have demonstrated the fundamental relationship between ritual and many social factors, including identity formation, community, worldview, and political or hierarchical organization. The ways in which early Christian ritual served to bind its members as a community, as well as both subvert and uphold hierarchical structures, has been discussed at length elsewhere.[71] Thus, an exhaustive review of ritual theory will be avoided here; instead, I will focus on a few particularly helpful modes of thinking about ritual in conjunction with space. In the next section, a brief overview of some key theories of ritual that are relevant to space, followed by a consideration of performance and especially practice theory, will provide a better understanding of sacred space in the house church.

THEORIES OF RITUAL: PERFORMANCE, PRACTICE, AND PLACEMENT

Catherine Bell's work on ritual has become an essential guidebook to ritual theory in contemporary scholarship.[72] Bell divides ritual theorists into three categories: those concerned with origins and essences; those concerned with the role of ritual in society; and those concerned with ritual as cultural communication and expression of cognitive categories.[73] The discussion here will be concerned predominantly with ritual theories from the latter two categories, as the question of an ontological or essential sacred reveals very little about what ritual actually does.[74]

Bell has divided rites into a number of different types, or what she calls the "basic genres of ritual action": rites of passage; calendrical and commemorative rites; exchange and communication rites; feasts and fasting; and political rites.[75] She has also outlined some of the key characteristics of ritual, including formalism, symbolism, and performance.[76] While Bell presents these categories, and attempts to slot most ritual practices into them, she also recognizes the impossibility of a universal character of ritual. As she states, "The survey of genres and ways of acting demonstrates that there is no intrinsic or universal understanding of what constitutes ritual."[77] That is, despite the value of categories in describing many kinds of ritual, it is not always true that a given ritual or set of ritual practices will conform to these categories. The reason this recognition is important is that many communities find themselves existing between the lines, or between their own categories, thereby demanding different things from ritual than a settled community might. Certainly this is true of the house church. The recognition that both communities and their rituals might find themselves between categories is another way of articulating the "cognitive gap" pointed out by Jonathan Z. Smith: lived experience demands different things from different rituals, depending on what is actually needed by the community. Awareness of this also allows for agency on the part of the practitioners.

A key theorist of ritual whose work is especially helpful in terms of spatial organization and society is Arnold van Gennep. In van Gennep's work, *The Rites of Passage*, he introduced what he called the "pivoting of the sacred."[78] Van Gennep explained the pivoting of the sacred in the following terms:

> Characteristically, the presence of the sacred (and the performance of appropriate rites) is variable. Sacredness as an attribute is not absolute; it is brought into play by the nature of particular situations.[79]

Like Durkheim and other social constructivists, van Gennep recognized the integral relationship between ritual and society, and the power of ritual to reveal the nature of society.[80] Unlike Durkheim, however, van Gennep theorized that ritual was actually responsible for creating that nature. As Bell has noted,

> What he designated as the 'pivoting of the sacred' alerted scholars to the ways in which ritual can actually define what is sacred, not simply react to the sacred as something already and for always fixed.[81]

In this way, van Gennep recognized the power of ritual as agent, rather than simply as revelator.[82]

Van Gennep is concerned predominantly with rituals that denote transition, such as birth rites, funerary rites, and initiations, but the same pivoting of the sacred can readily be applied to space. Van Gennep himself recognizes the importance of spatial frameworks and boundary markers in the enactment of ritual. He explains transitional rituals through a series of spatial metaphors, including frontier, boundary, threshold, and portal.[83] While van Gennep's focus is on the state of a human being in relation to his or her community, he makes a number of interesting, and indeed groundbreaking, remarks about space. He argues, "The categories and concepts which embody [transitional spaces] operate in such a way that whoever passes through the various positions of a lifetime one day sees the sacred where before he has seen the profane, and vice versa."[84] Taken further, van Gennep's powerful statement about the pivoting of the sacred and its lack of fixed or absolute character implies the multivalent nature of human beings, of situations, and of space. If ritual, then, is capable of bestowing sacred character onto a given entity, it stands to reason that, upon completion of the ritual, the entity would return to its profane status.[85] In other words, rather than an ontological or fixed sacred, there is instead a temporary, ritually constructed sacred.

The next two sets of theoretical engagement with ritual are usually termed performance theory and practice theory. While performance and practice theorists focus on different elements of ritual, what they share is the recognition that human activity is constructive and that this construction is enacted through the body. Embodiment and praxis are key elements to both performance and practice theory.

Bell categorizes performance theory approaches into three focus areas. First, ritual is an event "which actually effects change in people's perceptions and interpretations."[86] That is, ritual is *doing something*. Second, ritual events also provide a focus on or "appreciation of the physical and sensual aspects of ritual activity."[87] Embodiment of the ritual actors is essential to understanding the event. Third, the performance of ritual can be seen as a "framing" event, insofar as it helps to set apart the action and speech of a ritual from the mundane or quotidian.[88] The idea of framing, especially, acts as a helpful corollary to understanding sacred space and its characteristic boundaries; ritual framing serves the same purpose of setting apart as would an enclosure or structure, but without the need for physical or material separation.

Ritual as an event resonates with the conversation about sacred space. Performance theory tends to focus on the *event* of ritual, rather than the system to which it belongs. Thus, contradictions, implicit in all formulations of ritual behaviour, are not necessarily problematic. There is room in a ritual event for enactments that dwell in the "cognitive gap" between ideology and practice. Since performance is an event, it does not have to be static or consistent; as Bell states, it can and should be recognized "as a changing, processual, dramatic, and indeterminate identity."[89] Rather than inconsistencies demanding explanation, the changes and contradictions of a given event are part of what actually defines the culture and its development.[90] Further, thinking about ritual as an event contributes to an understanding of sacred space as temporally constructed.

As for embodiment, performance theories not only investigate the role of the body, but understand it as central to the ritual event. The bodies of participants are physically enacting and reenacting the rites, revealing what the rites symbolize. Bell argues that performance theory models "suggest active rather than passive roles for ritual participants who reinterpret value-laden symbols as they communicate them."[91] That is, the ritual does not happen to the participants; the participants make the ritual happen. At the same time, it is not necessarily conscious action that interprets and reinterprets the symbols presented during ritual enactment. As Bell states, the "active imagery of performance has also brought the possibility of a fuller analytical vocabulary with which to talk about the nonintellectual dimensions of what ritual does, that is, the emotive, physical, and even sensual aspects of ritual participation."[92] Ritual is perceived and interpreted through the medium of the body both consciously and unconsciously, similarly to the way in which the body perceives and interprets space and place.

In general, performance theory acknowledges the power of ritual to do something. It is not simply a repetition, a mnemonic, or a reenactment of a cosmological myth lodged deep in the collective unconscious of the community. Instead, ritual actually effects change. In the Roman world, it is clear that rituals were perceived as effecting change. An example from the domestic sphere is the transition from boyhood to manhood, the rite of passage wherein the *bulla* is exchanged for the *toga virilis*.[93] This ritual, performed by the family and attended by the domestic gods, actually effects the transition from boy to man, and he is ever after considered an adult. It is not until the ritual is performed, however, that the real change is made. Even though the timing of the ritual is predicated on cultural factors – the boy usually being at least fourteen, and the ritual sometimes being performed during the public festival period of the *Liberalia* – the ritual itself is the key element of the change. Performance is certainly an aspect of this ritual as well, given the fact that donning a toga properly was in the first place both highly formalized and standardized. Public processions of newly minted men heightened the performative aspect of the ritual, displaying the now-effected change to the rest of the community.[94] The relationship between culture and the body is therefore a dynamic one, negotiated through this ritual performance. A similar performance can be perceived in the rite of baptism, the enactment of which actually effects the change in the believer from *catechumen* to initiated member of the community.

Practice theory, like performance theory, provides helpful models for understanding house-church sacred space. Practice theory recognizes the engagement of the body, but, further, is built on the habitual and sometimes unconscious nature of physical action. According to Bell, practice theory "claims to take seriously the ways in which human activities, as formal as a religious ritual or as casual as a midday stroll, are creative strategies by which human beings continually reproduce and reshape their social and cultural environments."[95] In addition, practice theorists tend to focus on the ability of ritual to negotiate, uphold, or transgress power relationships, rather than to enact a single performance or type of performance.[96] The structures of society, especially hierarchical relationships, are evident in ritual, whether they are subverted (e.g., through ritual reversal) or maintained.[97] This connection between society and structures is especially evident in the work of Pierre Bourdieu. He focuses predominantly on a reworking of the notion of *habitus*, or the practice of the body over time.[98] The body moves and manipulates itself and its environment in ways that may be purposeful, but which are, more often than not, an unconscious enactment of structures. For Bourdieu, the *habitus* – as he calls it, "history turned into nature" – is a force that translates structures into activity, which in turn substantiates and maintains those structures.[99] Because structures are translated into activity, they are therefore enacted by the body, and the body and its practices become central to the production of culture. As Bell states, "ritual does not actually bring history and structure together since neither exists except insofar as they are embodied and reproduced in human activity as cultural values."[100] Thus, instead of ritual being a reenactment of a cosmogonic myth, it is the actual production of history, which does not exist outside of bodily enactment. Again, this enactment can be conscious, but for Bourdieu, it is predominantly unconscious. This practice is especially powerful *because* it is unconscious. The house-church Christians, then, would not necessarily be aware that they were creating sacred space through ritual enactment, but the powerful interaction between the bodies of ritual agents and their space would have done exactly that.[101]

In the same way, practices of the body also have an effect on space. Much as de Certeau argues concerning the effect of embodiment on space, Bourdieu and Bell argue for the structuring quality of the body's practice in ritual space. Indeed, part of the act of ritual involves the structuring of space. There are, Bell argues, "a series of oppositional schemes that are mobilized as the body moves through space and time; these schemes are generated by the gestures and sounds of the body and act to qualitatively structure the physical environment."[102] Thus, the body not only moves through preexistent space (and time), it also structures that space as it operates within it. Given the focused and formalized movement of ritual, it demands preexistent space for its enactment, but also creates different space through its enactment by bodies, carving sacred space out of preexistent space. Importantly, the actions of the ritual agent (the body) are constantly structuring and restructuring space, but it is not necessarily the active or stated *goal* of the ritual. Rather, the restructuring is a *product* of the ritual.[103]

The negotiation between the goal (stated or otherwise) and the product of ritual is difficult, especially in terms of sacred space. This difficulty arises predominantly out of the fact that the relationship between ritual and space is fundamentally circular. On the one hand, ritual demands space; on the other hand, it creates it. This inherent circularity confirms the dynamism of place, as discussed above. No place can be static in itself, especially in conjunction with embodied inhabitants. Thus, the labour of ritual is the formal, standardized mode of bodily practice that constructs, reconstructs, and reformulates space.

This connection between ritual and space – or to be precise, place – is brought into focus with the work of Jonathan Z. Smith.[104] For Smith, ritual only makes sense when taken in conjunction with its most fundamental element: emplacement. It is important, then, to understand what Smith means when he says "place." He weighs the theories of human geography and environmental determinism, eventually asserting that "place is not best conceived as a particular location within an idiosyncratic physiognomy or as a uniquely individualistic node of sentiment, but rather as a *social position within a hierarchical system*."[105] While recognizing the impact of place on personality, as in environmental determinism, and the impact of human beings on their surroundings, as in human geography, Smith's fundamental assertion about place is that it is socially dictated, organized, and maintained. It is a social configuration, based on hierarchical power relationships. Therefore, places that are meaningful (or sacred) in a given cultural system are chosen arbitrarily by those who hold political power.[106] This meaningful place then confers meaning on practices that occur within it.

Smith's key example is the Jerusalem Temple. He notes that the plot of land where the temple was constructed was chosen by those members of the community who held social power. By now a place layered with centuries of belief, loss, and yearning, the original location of the temple was chosen, Smith argues, in an arbitrary fashion. He argues, "There is nothing inherent in the location of the Temple in Jerusalem. Its location was simply where it happened to be built."[107] Smith notes the this-worldly influences that led to building in that particular place, including especially the wielding of political power and social control. In its original context, the temple "was the focus of a complex, self-referential system," ordering and orienting its associated community.[108] As the central place of a cultural system, it had the power to sacralize both the things and the people within it. For Smith, place – arbitrarily chosen and socially constructed – is what makes ritual sacred.

Smith defines ritual in a number of ways, but as he states, "Ritual is, first and foremost, a mode of paying attention."[109] The primary function of ritual is to direct attention in a specific manner among a specific group of people. Smith goes on to write that "it is this characteristic, as well, that explains the role of place as a fundamental component of ritual: place directs attention."[110] On this view, there is a dynamic relationship between ritual and place, but place seems to be preeminent, for it is place that confers meaning to ritual. As Smith asserts, "Within the temple, the ordinary ... becomes significant, becomes 'sacred,' simply by being there. A ritual object or action becomes sacred by having attention focused on it in a highly marked way."[111] The temple, as meaningful place, directs attention toward the ritual acts, which themselves acquire sanctity. In other words, there is nothing inherently sacred about ritual utterances, implements, or practices; it is only in conjunction with socially constructed place that meaning, or sanctity, can be conferred.

In addition to drawing or gathering attention, Smith notes that ritual performs important social functions. He argues that "ritual is, above all, an assertion of difference."[112] This difference is made manifest through the separation that occurs during the enactment, in place, of ritual. Emplacement creates an obvious separation from the mundane (and the profane), setting boundaries between life inside and outside of ritual behaviour. In addition, he states that ritual "is a means of performing the way things ought to be in conscious tension with the way things are."[113] It is through and during the enactment of ritual that a community can assert its ideology, whatever cognitive gaps may arise during the rest of the members' lived experience. The practice of ritual, however, does not permanently negate or remove practices in conflict with its associated ideology; it is only during the rite that the ideal can be sought.

Smith continues, saying, "Ritual relies for its power on the fact that it is concerned with quite ordinary activities placed within an extraordinary setting."[114] It is clear that Smith sees ritual as effective only when it is emplaced, that it is only in place that ordinary acts become extraordinary. At the same time, this definition breaks down when applied to a situation such as the house church, where ritual place is not only not materially constructed, but in fact shared with an entirely different cultural system. The very nature of the shared, adapted space of the house church meant that there could be no closed, self-referential system of purpose-built place. Further, the preexisting cultural system was completely at odds with the fundamental precepts of Christian belief. If the Roman house were to confer meaning on the acts of Christian ritual, it is hard to see how that meaning could be congruent with monotheistic Christian ideology, especially considering the powerful connection between the space of the house and the practice of the domestic cult. Certainly, the Roman house conferred meaning on domestic cult acts, since, as Smith points out, places are formulated through social configuration. The meaning conferred on Roman domestic cult, however, was part of a different socio-cultural system than was Christianity. It is much more likely that Christian ritual did not acquire its sanctity – separate from the sanctity of the domestic cult rituals – from the Roman house itself. Rather, it would have to formulate its sanctity in opposition to the structures of the Roman house, inextricably linked as they were to the *Lares*, *Penates*, and ancestors.

Over and over again, Smith draws our attention to the power of place to confer sanctity on ritual objects, utterances, and implements: "It is not their symbolism or their meaning that is determinative; the songs are sacred or profane sheerly by virtue of their location. A sacred text is one that is used in a sacred place – nothing more is required."[115] On the other hand, he also claims that "ritual is not an expression of or a response to 'the Sacred'; rather, something or someone is made sacred by ritual."[116] Again we are confronted with the circularity of the relationship between ritual and place. If, as Smith argues, the key to ritual effectiveness is emplacement, there must therefore be place. Place, however, is not always permanent or purpose-built, like the Jerusalem Temple.

It is worth asking, then, whether place cannot also be constructed temporarily, and in a setting that might otherwise be, in Smith's terms, "ordinary." If place is extraordinary only temporarily, it does not negate its power, nor the fundamental relationship between emplacement and ritual. Indeed, temporary place would emphasize the need for boundaries or separation from otherwise ordinary place. What it does not demand, however, is particular, *material* place which is ongoing or permanent. In addition, temporarily meaningful place demands that meaning must inhere in the act of ritual itself. Given the lack of particular place in house-church Christianity, it must be recognized that the ritual, without preexisting place dedicated to its enactment, does the work to *create* place. In the house church, the ritual creates, out of the space of the Roman house, a place for Christian worship. The place created through ritual becomes not physically or materially bounded, but ritually bounded. While the house-church Christians may not have had material places set apart for ritual worship, they were still able to "emplace" ritual through the setting of temporal boundaries.

Smith himself recognizes the power of temporal placemaking when discussing the post-Constantinian Christian liturgy. He discusses the fourth-century Christian appropriation of Jerusalem and its transformation into the Holy Land, followed by the development of "stational liturgy."[117] In this period, the places where Jesus and his disciples walked became important markers of Christian faith, and through the appropriation of previously Jewish places of sanctity, Christianity was able to build its own meaningful place. Pilgrimage rose in popularity, and with it, a formalized liturgy. Smith states, "It is at this point that formal, liturgical ordering takes hold, establishing a hierarchy of significance that focuses the devout attention, chiefly achieved by adding a temporal dimension to the locative experience."[118] This temporal dimension is achieved by taking the pilgrims through the life and death of Jesus and the creation of the liturgical year. The Holy Land, therefore, became the key "place" for Christianity, as "the overlaying of a temporal system and a spatial system."[119]

This formulation of place coincided, of course, with the advent of purpose-built structures for Christian worship, and the beginning of a new mode of ritual practice in Christianity – one, in fact, which corresponds much more closely to Smith's model of the Jerusalem Temple and the preeminence of place. What is essential here, however, is the recognition of the role that *temporality* plays in the formation of place. Once Smith has set up the development of the place of the Holy Land, he notes the problems that could have arisen when liturgy was moved out of the pilgrimage context, and away from its original location. These problems were solved through the formation of the liturgical year. The temporality of the liturgical year is what "guaranteed replicability" even outside of the Holy Land.[120] Because the prayers, hymns, and scriptures were adapted to a festal calendar (dictated by the progression from Nativity to the Passion), they could then be replicated elsewhere. The ideal place may still have been Jerusalem, but the power of the rites could be transported to any place. As Smith says, "The sequence of time, the story, the festal calendar, have allowed a supersession of place."[121] Smith's argument, then, is not one of placelessness superseding place; rather, it is a recognition of the power of ritual, in a temporal context, to overcome "the divisiveness and particularity of space."[122]

While this argument of Smith's is constructed to explain the post-Constantinian mode of practising Christianity, the recognition of temporal elements in placemaking and ritual practice is one which can readily be applied to house churches. House churches, of course, suffered from a particular divisiveness, being situated as they were in the heart of both "ordinary" life and ritual life. In the house church, multiple ritual traditions and practices would have had to coexist under one roof. In the same way that Smith proposes that the stational liturgy of Jerusalem provided a mode of being meaningfully emplaced without physically being there, so too could the rites of the house-church Christians have provided a solution for the divisiveness and polytheistic particularity of the house. It is not necessary for ritual to be formalized, universal, or canonized in order to provide a solution to the problems of adapted space. While there was not yet a stational liturgy, certain elements of the Christian story were in fact being replicated already, such as the Last Supper, the baptism of Jesus, and so forth. In this way, the theories that work to clarify the relationship between dedicated sacred places and ritual practice can also be applied to places that were neither purpose-built nor dedicated solely to Christian ritual practice.

Performance and practice theories work well together with the theory of emplaced ritual proposed by Smith. All of these theories recognize the importance of embodiment, which in turn emphasizes the importance of emplacement. Ritual is powerful *because* it is emplaced and embodied. While place is fundamental (and for Smith, perhaps preeminent), ritual is not passive; it plays the role of agent in the creation of place for its own enactment. Ritual is conditioned by but also conditions place. Rather than a circularity between the two elements, they ought to be seen as being in a dialectical relationship, where neither is static and both are mutually reinforcing. What this relationship means, however, is that ritual does not make place out of neutral space; it is always already emplaced, just as bodies are.[123]

In the house-church context, this place is one that presents particular difficulties, namely the practice of the domestic cult. Because of the social and material power of the domestic cult, it likely would have continued to be practised. To assert otherwise demands persuasive evidence, since to assume that the cult would have ceased is to fail to recognize the power of the relationship between place and ritual. Recognizing the power of temporal placemaking, on the other hand, means that there is no need to imagine a cessation of the domestic cult in order for the house church to have sacred space; space for the Christian rituals could be carved out from preexistent domestic space through ritual enactment. This means that both the domestic cult and the Christian rituals could use the same space, that space being made sacred for each set of rituals at different times. Indeed, the Roman house on its most basic level already functioned on a temporal model of spatial organization, and was thus particularly suited to this kind of temporal boundary-making.

Therefore, when characterizing the domestic life that could have – and likely would have – continued in the houses used by Christians for worship, one must include domestic cult practice. On the one hand, the continuation of domestic cult practice is at odds with the ideology of monotheistic Christianity. On the other hand, it is an essential part of placemaking in the Roman house, and not easily cast aside. Bearing in mind also the "cognitive gap" between ideology and practice, as discussed above, the idea that the domestic cult may have continued in some houses used by Christians should not be difficult to believe.

The foregoing discussion of ritual theory demonstrates that, when attempting to find sacred space where material boundaries do not exist, practice theory, and to some extent, performance theory, provides a valuable reading of the production of sacred space. Understanding the fundamental role that temporality plays in the setting apart of place as sacred raises a number of compelling issues. First, if place for worship is ritually produced and maintained, it ought to be understood as sacred space. The conception of house-church Christians as utopic, placeless, or defined only as the body of believers, without engagement with the places they utilize, is untenable. Second, since house-church place could be made sacred only through ritual practice – not having material articulation – it would acquire, by virtue of its creation through ritual, only a temporary sanctity. Thus, the houses used by Christians did not become permanent sacred places.[124] Third, given that the sacred places carved out by Christian ritual were temporary in nature, one ought to expect that life in the house continued as it normally did when ritual was not being performed (that is, the rest of the time). Normal life, in the case of the Roman house, included the domestic cult. These two sets of ritual, at odds with each other ideologically, may well have coexisted.

In order to understand how the domestic cult could have been practised by Christians or by non-Christians in Christian meeting places, it will be necessary to also examine the domestic cult with a theoretical lens. Applying practice and ritual theory to its enactment provides a way of understanding how this may have occurred. In the next section, the domestic cult will be examined with a lens provided by Pierre Bourdieu's interpretation of the *habitus*. The combination of the "cognitive gap" present in ritual communities and the practice of embodied, emplaced ritual will demonstrate that it is not only possible, but probable that domestic cult practice continued in Roman houses used by house-church Christians – all without negating the space as sacred for the house-church Christians.

BOURDIEU, DOMESTIC CULT, AND THE PRODUCTION OF SACRED SPACE

As discussed in chapter 3, for a Roman family, the practice of the domestic cult was an essential part of daily life. It was a constant practice, with rites for all important events and experiences of a *familia*. In many cases, it is clear from the material evidence that the presence of the domestic cult was physically articulated and therefore not easily removed or replaced, especially in large, aristocratic homes. As already mentioned, the relationship between the domestic cult and the house-church Christians has been largely ignored in the study of early Christianity. This lacuna may be the product of the assumption that the two simply could not have coexisted, given the conflict between Christian and polytheistic ideologies. Further, this assumption is related to a common view that Christianity represented something more, something better than what popular rituals had to offer. With the advent of this new religious movement, the emptiness of polytheistic ritual, both public and private, could be swept away.[125] Given the integral role of ritual in the formation of culture and identity, however, it is worth asking whether the domestic cult might have been tossed aside so readily. As Bell, Smith, and Bourdieu argue, ritual practice is bound up with social structures and hierarchies. They also highlight the fundamental relationship between practice and place. If the Roman house is understood as a place, and if place is understood as having a dialectical relationship with its inhabitants, then it must also be recognized that there could be no easy transition from one set of rituals to another, especially in a place already steeped in ritual practice of another kind, namely: the Roman domestic cult.

One might easily assume that a true believer would immediately recognize the inherent problem with worshipping the domestic gods, and simply stop doing so. In a "placeless" reconstruction of the house church, this might make sense. As has already been demonstrated, however, this reconstruction would be a negation of place. In addition, ritual action is not always conscious, but rather, it can be performed habitually by the body.

To return briefly to Bourdieu, the *habitus* is a force that translates structures into activity.[126] Ritual activity, then, upholds structures in a formalized context. When speaking of the Roman domestic cult, one can see the structure as being twofold: first, and most obviously, it is the structure of the *familia*, in which the *pater* acts as priest and head. This structure is borne out by his arbitration of the family rituals. Second, it is the structure of Rome herself, and by extension, her Empire; the *pax deorum* of the civic sphere is repeated in the domestic sphere, protecting the citizens of Rome en masse by demanding their individual propitiation. The private worship of the elite Roman household then becomes a microcosm of the civic worship of the public festivals and feasts of Rome, and the *pater* is rendered the microcosmic equivalent of the *pontifex maximus* or Emperor. Far from being an individualized practice of a particular *familia*, the domestic cult – while taking place predominantly in the private sphere – was part of a much larger and more highly systematized set of structures.

The *habitus* of the *pater familias* was learned through the lived, practical experience of his action in the home, first as son and then as father. Bourdieu notes that, more often than not, the enactment of the *habitus* has an unconscious quality.[127] Furthermore, this "unconscious" action is itself a performance of "objective intention"; that is, the objective structures of history and society are present in the action, whether the agent is aware of them or not.[128] For example, the *pater* would not, in most cases, have been conscious of the fact that his daily ritual action substantiated both his own authority and that of the emperor – but this is exactly what it did. Indeed, Bourdieu holds that "it is because subjects do not, strictly speaking, know what they are doing that what they do has more meaning than they know."[129] The key element of praxis, like performance, is recognizing its ability to effect some sort of change without overtly stating its objective. Catherine Bell has also written that "most symbolic action, even the basic symbols of a community's ritual life, can be very unclear to participants or interpreted by them in very dissimilar ways."[130] That is, through practice of a ritual, participants can be doing something without knowing that they are doing it. Depending on the ritual and the community, what is done will vary, but it cannot be assumed that participants are always cognizant of the outcome of their ritual practices. Thus, praxis has an effect, whether or not it is immediately recognizable or interpreted, on the culture of a given community.

Bourdieu also states that "the habitus is the universalizing mediation which causes an individual agent's practices, without either explicit reason or signifying intent, to be nonetheless 'sensible' and 'reasonable.'"[131] Thus, even when an agent is performing ritual "unconsciously," the ritual still makes sense, because it has been internalized as part of the *habitus* of the agent. The *habitus* ensures that the agent will continue to act whether or not he or she consciously engages with its meaning. A *pater*'s *habitus* demands that he perform the protective rituals of the household cult, which serve to bind and protect his family (and by extension, the Empire). He is to ensure that the busts of his ancestors receive their libation of wine on the assigned days. The meaning beyond the immediate action is not constantly in play; the *habitus* of the *pater* demands particular practices, and so the *pater* does them. The structures of Roman society are upheld through constant enactment of the domestic cult rituals.

Returning to the discussion of place, it is clear that the Roman house is a place in its own right, replete with particularity, habitual action, and the sedimentation of history, memory, and ritual. The ritual action of the family creates a place that upholds the structures of Roman society, which in turn continues to act upon the inhabitants of the house to ensure their appropriate behaviour within this structure. The dialectical relationship between ritual and the locus for its practice is constantly in play. The place of the home constitutes the *pater*'s *habitus*, and the home itself – including any shrines, the atrium where ancestor masks are kept, the hearth – acts as a trigger for the continued enactment of this *habitus*.

According to Bourdieu's *habitus*, one does things *because they are done*. An example of this in the Roman house might be the pouring out of a libation before a meal. In the present day, it might be compared to the dipping of one's finger into water and crossing oneself before entering the nave of a Catholic church. It is a practice imbued with meaning, to be sure; it serves to substantiate the sanctity of the place, the authority of the church, and the holiness of the ritual about to occur within it. Its enactment by a lifelong member of the Catholic church, however, might not reflect conscious meaning beyond the remembered injunction that one is to cross oneself before entering a holy Catholic church. By the same token, while the pouring out of a libation before a Roman meal is *actually* substantiating a structure in which domestic gods exist and demand propitiation, it need not be done with this structure in mind. Indeed, it has far more to do with the *habitus* of the *pater*, who himself may be remembering an injunction of his own father: "one pours out a little of the wine before one serves a meal." Other members of the *familia*, of course, would have their own habitual roles to play in the family practice of the domestic cult.

Thus, it is not an obvious conclusion that domestic cult practices would have stopped altogether in houses used by Christians.[132] If the *habitus* of the *pater* were enacted unconsciously, it would be all the more difficult to eradicate. The Roman house is a place that is both structured by and structuring of Roman culture, which is itself based upon the *pax deorum*. Not only, then, were the Christians not meeting in neutral space; they were in fact meeting in powerful place, encoded with meaning completely at odds with their new beliefs. It would have taken time, first, to recognize this dissonance as problematic, and second, to find a solution for it. When Christians finally began to build and renovate places of their own, they were likely moving out of Roman houses not only because their numbers were growing, but also because they had begun to recognize the Roman house as a site of conflict. That is, it would have been easier to move worship practices out of the house than to attempt to reorganize the structure of the Roman house itself. That being said, however, the case studies of Dura Europos and Lullingstone demonstrate that even these adapted, renovated places would not be entirely free from polytheistic influence and practice.

The foregoing argument is, of course, a theoretical one, but it provides a framework that allows for more fluid interpretations of space and identity in communities still finding their footing. Bourdieu's conception of the *habitus* also underscores the fact that preexistent cultic practice would have been internalized as an essential part of dwelling in a Roman house. The argument also recognizes the key elements of the interaction between human beings and their space, since the *habitus* model depends heavily on both embodiment and emplacement. It also allows for an organic, slower-moving development of early Christian sacred space, rather than reading a sea change into the building of the Lateran in Rome. In fact, given that polytheistic elements would not need to be absent in order to create sacred space, conceptions of sacred space can be imagined much earlier than the advent of monumental building programmes under Constantine. This framework also honours the available material evidence for an ongoing adaptation of buildings for Christian worship, without demanding a consistent typology of architecture.

Conclusion

Towards a Theory of Sacred Space in House-Church Christianity

The foregoing work has asserted that the meeting places of house-church Christians were sacred spaces. In order to demonstrate this assertion, it was necessary first to situate the house-church Christians in their meeting places. To do so, a series of available models of housing in the Roman Empire were presented, each as potential spaces for meeting. Rather than focusing solely on one model or another – such as a *domus*, reflective of wealthy members, or a tenement, reflective of subsistence-level members – a mix of housing was discussed. This mix corresponds with the mixed social structure and demographics that made up the Christian communities in the first three centuries.

In addition to this discussion of Roman domestic space, the population of the Roman house, including its inhabitants and their rituals, were presented. Understanding the domestic space available for Christians, on its own terms, raised key questions about the coexistence of polytheistic domestic life and Christian worship practice. The cult practice and material presence of the domestic gods were explored, demonstrating the ubiquitous nature of the domestic cult. Further, it was asserted that the domestic cult was not only a common or normative set of rituals, but also a fundamental expression of Roman identity. Given its fundamental nature, then, the characterization of house-church sacred space ought to allow for the possibility that the domestic cult would have continued in at least some of the meeting places of these Christians.

The rituals of house-church Christianity, imagined in their domestic context, also raised a series of questions about the size of the groups, the social organization of the groups, and the accessibility of spaces for the groups in general. It was made apparent that, while some early Christian writers rejected the idea of sacred space, others recognized the special nature of ritual and its accompanying performative space. Further, the description of the rituals clarified the types of spaces that would have been necessary for their enactment.

Theories of sacred space were then explored, with a view to applying relevant theoretical concepts to fill in the gaps – areas, that is, where material and literary data were silent concerning house-church sacred space. The discussion of ritual practice, especially its role as both constituted by and constitutive of sacred space, emphasized the importance of practice and performance in the construction of sacred space. The essential categories of embodiment and emplacement, so frequently ignored in the imagining of the earliest Christian communities, made clear the need to engage space and place in the discussion of house churches.

It was argued that bodies can act as powerful agents, constructing sacred space through the practice of ritual. The power of place and its impact on these bodies is also an essential part of this construction of sacred space. Recognizing the dialectical relationship between bodies and place means that the place of the Roman house can be acknowledged in its own right, rather than presented as a neutral canvas upon which the new rites of the nascent Christian movement could be exercised. Indeed, the mutually reinforcing elements of bodies and places means that, just as Christian space would have been produced through ritual, so too would polytheistic space have been created through domestic rituals, as discussed via Bourdieu's *habitus*. Thus, domestic cult practices cannot be easily imagined away, especially without suitable Christian replacements. This messy state of affairs would eventually have been addressed (though not necessarily resolved) through the renovation of houses into uninhabited buildings, but so long as a space had to function both as home to a Roman *familia* and home to the house-church rituals, the coexistence of seemingly divergent practices ought to be expected.

Perhaps most importantly, the case studies of Dura Europos and Lullingstone revealed that, even after renovation and adaptation in some Christian communities, the polytheistic practices of the domestic sphere continued to flourish, despite being ostensibly incompatible with Christian ritual and sacred space. It was asserted that, given the continued presence of polytheistic ritual in these renovated spaces, one might expect to find yet more presence of the domestic cult in those spaces that continued to be uninhabited, and which were not yet subject to renovation or adaptation – in other words, the house churches.

Overall, I propose here a model of sacred space that is temporary in nature, rather than permanent. I suggest that a framework of multivalent space, dictated by ritual performance, would not have demanded that everyday life in the house necessarily change. The temporally structured boundaries of house-church sacred space could allow both the production of Christian ritual space and the continuation of Roman domestic life, including domestic cult practice.

If one were to imagine the cessation of the domestic cult, on the other hand, a series of problematic assertions would need to be made. For example, a house that no longer hosted the practices of the domestic cult would demand the wholesale conversion of an entire household or *familia* of a domestic space used by Christians, including the extended family and slaves. It would also demand a conscious recognition of the dissonance between domestic cult practice and the ritual practice of Christians on the part of all hosts and their families, a recognition that is not supported by the mid-third- and early fourth-century evidence of Dura and Lullingstone. There would have to have been a conscious recognition by hosts, families, and congregants of the need for a space free from polytheistic cult practices or material presence of any kind. Finally, this claim assumes that domestic cult rituals could have been stopped easily, including those practices surrounding the dangerous life-cycle events of childbirth and death.

If, however, a conceptual framework of the house church allows for the possibility of coexistence between polytheistic and Christian cult practices, a more realistic view of the house church emerges. Mixed households could play host to the church, patrons or patronesses could host the church whether or not their entire *familia* belonged to the movement, and an immediate rejection of Roman life for the entire family would not be demanded upon the point of a host's conversion. A multivalent, temporally constructed sanctity provides a compelling model for house churches, because it allows for nuanced conceptions of mixed family life. In addition, the material evidence for the coexistence of mixed rituals, despite their seeming incongruity, is clearly present at both Dura and Lullingstone.

The notion of a multivalent, temporally constructed sanctity also honours the need for sanctity in house-church ritual practice while recognizing the lack of purpose-built architecture or house-church-specific modification in the archaeological record. The model of sanctity proposed here means that one would not expect to find any material evidence for house-church practice in the period before adaptation began in earnest. Indeed, if one were to be certain that a house church existed in a specific Roman town, one ought to expect that there would be no traces of house-church practice in the foundation, organization, or decoration of the house itself. Nor would it necessarily be absent of typically polytheistic domestic life, including the material presence of the domestic cult. The creation of sacred space in the house church did not demand special altars, rooms, or accoutrements (or the removal of polytheistic elements); it depended instead on the enactment of ritual by member bodies, gathered together for specific purpose at specific times.

In sum, this work presents an imaginative framework that accounts for the eventualities of mixed social groups, mixed ideologies and identities, and the development of new identities, both individual and communal. It also affords preexistent domestic space its due; no longer is the Roman house understood as a place without its own encoded ideologies, practices, and rituals. Embodiment, fundamental to the human experience, is also here honoured rather than negated, as it would be by esoteric and theological characterizations of a body of believers. The house-church Christians, then, can be imagined to have been participants in sacred rituals, performed in sacred space, while also engaged in a constant process of negotiation – of their bodies, their spaces, and of course, their identities.

Notes

INTRODUCTION

1 Hereafter, all dates refer to the Common Era, unless otherwise specified.

2 Beyond domestic spaces, other spaces, such as baths, rented rooms, warehouses, and workshops were also likely used as meeting space for Christians. For an excellent and recent discussion of possible spaces used by Christians outside of exclusively domestic space, see Adams, *Earliest Christian Meeting Places*. In some cases, these alternative spaces may also have included domestic space; workshops, for example, were often inhabited by the owner or proprietor of the shop, as will be discussed below, in chapter 2.

3 Harold Turner, in his work *From Temple to Meeting House*, argues just that; he claims not only that the spaces used by the Christians were not sacred, but that the lack of sanctity inherent in domestic spaces was in fact "the essence of this new form," and that the house was "free from bondage to holy places" (156). He argues also that the pre-purpose-built meeting place was not a "holy place, but a holy people, sanctified through union with … the new temple" (152). The notion of a sacred body of believers over against sacred places will be addressed more fully in chapter 6.

4 Notions and definitions of sanctity and purity will be discussed in detail in chapters 5 and 6.

5 The most influential among these works are of course Krautheimer, *Early Christian and Byzantine Architecture*, and both volumes of L. Michael White's *Social Origins of Christian Architecture*. Gregory Dix's *Shape of the Liturgy* was also influential in the early work on the development of early Christian architecture. For an excellent review of the body of literature on early Christian architectural development, see White, *Social Origins*, vol. 1, 12–25. It should be noted that White's review of theories of early Christian architecture

is predominantly concerned with the development of the space from house church (private) to basilica (public, monumental).

6 Krautheimer was the first to popularize this term in conjunction with Dura Europos. See Krautheimer, *Early Christian and Byzantine*, 27. See White, *Social Origins*, vol. 1, 154n36, for a discussion of the term's history.

7 Other sets of questions arise when negotiating questions of space in, for example, Jewish households. Concerns over purity and separation, for example, might have arisen in Jewish households in ways that they would not in (polytheistic) Roman households. The question of menstrual purity and childbirth regulations in Jewish households used by Christ-confessing communities is an especially fruitful topic for further consideration.

8 The terms "convert" and "conversion," of course, are also not without their issues. Conversion has often been seen as an ideological, personal, and psychological shift from one mode of being to another, or from one mode of thinking to another. In this context, it would be difficult to imagine "converts" to the Christian movement continuing with practices that were at odds with their new faith. At the same time, the structure of conversion in the ancient world demands a more nuanced reading. As Zeba Crook has pointed out in *Reconceptualizing Conversion*, there are complexities of social behaviours in the ancient world, especially surrounding the structure of patronage, that demand closer reading. Loyalty, for example, is highlighted by Crook as being a key element in understanding the relationships between patronage, experience, and culture. He argues that, rather than seeing "conversion" as "primarily an internal, personal and introspective experience," it is rather one predicated on externality and action or practice (*Reconceptualizing Conversion*, 255). Indeed, this focus on action, loyalty, and external structures will be central to the discussion below on Roman domestic cult practice and house-church communities. Despite the imperfect nature of (and lack of consensus on) these terms, in this work I will continue to use the term "converts" to describe those persons who formulated a particular group – namely, self-professed members of a Christ-confessing community who encountered that community with a personal history of traditional Roman piety and ritual behaviour. It is also important to reiterate here that these "converts," even narrowed to those with a polytheistic background, were hardly a monolithic group, with a shared or identical approach to experiences both inside and outside the house-church community.

CHAPTER ONE

1 For an overview of the essential literature on this subject, see 173n5.
2 See, for example, McCready, "Ecclesia and Voluntary Associations." In his review of the meeting places used by the churches of the early Jesus movement, he states that, in the period between 150 and 250 CE, "it is likely that residential buildings had their interiors changed to give secular structures a religious sanctity" (68). He is here dependent on the work of Willy Rordorf, who himself uses Dura as the primary (and only) evidence of this interior reorganization (Rordorf, "Was wissen wir," 121–2). This overemphasis on the example of Dura can provide a deceptively clear picture of second and third century Christianity, about whose meeting places very little is known.
3 See, for example, Bowes, *Private Worship*, 127; Bowes, "Christianization," 143. Earlier, W.H.C. Frend noted a similar phenomenon in his work, "Pagans, Christians, and 'The Barbarian Conspiracy,'" 131.
4 Michael White, too, sees the periods of house church, *domus ecclesiae*, *aula ecclesiae*, and basilica as being somewhat fluid, allowing for overlap to continue into the fifth and sixth centuries. See White, *Social Origins*, vol. 1, 23. See also Petersen, "House-Churches," where she has stated: "We may therefore postulate a period from the middle of the first century to the late second or early third century when Christians worshipped in ordinary private houses and when the ecclesiastical organization had not yet been set up. This was probably followed by a period from the early third century to the accession of Constantine, when rooms concealed in secular buildings were set aside for worship and appropriately decorated, but when in Rome, at any rate, there were no church buildings as such" (266).
5 Kim Bowes, for example, demonstrates the continued use of private space for worship by Christians, although in a different context than the domestic worship before Constantine (*Private Worship*; see especially 125–60, on the rural estates that hosted fourth-century rural Christianity).
6 Malherbe, *Social Aspects*, especially chapter 3.
7 Meggitt, *Paul, Poverty and Survival.*
8 Theissen, *Social Setting*, especially 99–110; Meeks, *Urban Christians.*
9 Meggitt, *Paul, Poverty and Survival*, 5–7. Meggitt argues against the "myth of Paul's affluent background" (80–96), and also claims that "what material assistance he received from *individuals* such as Phoebe and Gaius was probably also modest: there are no firm grounds for assuming that these benefactors were rich in anything but commitment" (78).
10 Meggitt, *Paul, Poverty and Survival*, 98.
11 Ibid., 99.

12 Ibid., 163.
13 For an excellent critique of Meggitt's claims, see Martin, "Review Essay," 51–64.
14 David Horrell, for example, has called Meggitt's work "a clear polemic against the new consensus view" and noted that, in many cases, his arguments privilege the data that best fits his argument. See Horrell, "Domestic Space," 358–9.
15 Jeffers, "Jewish and Christian," 130.
16 Ibid., 130–1.
17 Meeks, *Urban Christians*, 73.
18 Scheidel and Friesen, "Size of the Economy, 61–91.
19 Ibid., 83–91.
20 Bruce Longenecker, in his article, "Exposing the Economic Middle," supports the notion that a broader distribution of wealth in the Empire is preferable to a binary model of economic structure in the ancient world. At the same time, he cautions against unilaterally applying that diversified model to the early Christian groups (270). He does, however, note the value of performing new exegetical explorations of New Testament texts with the kind of model presented by Scheidel and Friesen, in order to determine its viability (271–3).
21 Indeed, in his second edition (as cited above), Malherbe contests criticisms of his earlier work, which, he claims, misinterpret his findings as assertions that the Christian community of the first century was in fact "top heavy," and claimed that he had meant only to propose that earliest Christianity had members from every stratum of society, even in the first century. See *Social Aspects*, 120–1.
22 Gerd Theissen bases his assertion that members of a higher socio-economic class were part of the Pauline communities on a few factors, including: the ability of Phoebe, Priscilla and Aquila, Erastus, Stephanas, and "Chloe's people" to travel (*Social Setting*, 91–5); and the identification of the Corinthian *aedile* Erastus as the same Erastus mentioned as "city treasurer" in Rom 16:23. Theissen states that he "can see no compelling argument against this identification of the Christian Erastus," and further, that such an identification indicates full citizenship for Erastus, and "a certain amount of private wealth" (83).
23 Bowe, *Church in Crisis*, 14–15; 20–8. 1 Corinthians 11 will be discussed further below.
24 Balch and Osiek, *Families*, 98.
25 Meeks, *First Urban Christians*, 73.
26 Lampe, "Early Christians," 24. Interestingly, Lampe also notes that "the higher we rise in the Roman social strata, the more Christian women and the fewer men we encounter" (23).

27 See Maier, *Social Setting*, 36–8; Filson, "Significance of Early House Churches," 111.

28 Generally, the model of patron or host of the church can be depended upon for the remainder of the house-church period, although regional and financial differences would have been numerous across the Empire and in specific periods. Rather than attempting to give a précis of patronage in the third and fourth centuries, the communities associated with specific case studies will be discussed in the following chapter.

29 Balch and Osiek, *Families*, 98.

30 This theme runs throughout the *Shepherd of Hermas*, but see, for example, *Vis.* 3:9.4. Maier discusses this section at length (*Social Setting*, 62–4). See also Lane, "Social Perspectives," 237. Lane discusses both the *Shepherd* and *1 Clement* as evidence for members vying for patronage or leadership status via their claims to wealth.

31 See Maier, *Social Setting*, concerning the "plurality of leaders" and the subsequent division into multiple house churches. Maier discusses *Sim.* 9 to demonstrate concerns that resonate throughout the text (65–71).

32 Maier, *Social Setting*, 71.

33 Lane, "Social Perspectives," 242; see also Bowe, *A Church in Crisis*, 76.

34 Malherbe, *Social Aspects*, 63; Jeffers, *Greco-Roman World*, 49; Meeks, *Urban Christians*, 9–50; Lampe, *Paul to Valentinus*, 10; Jewett, "Tenement Churches," 23–43.

35 As will be discussed below, other types of spaces (besides strictly domestic spaces) were likely also used by members of the early Christian communities. Workshops, *tabernae*, and perhaps rented halls would also have been available to some Christian groups. See, for example, Ascough, *Paul's Macedonian Associations*, where he claims that Paul, while in Thessalonica, may have used the workshop available to him not only for labour but for spreading the gospel (175). Note, however, that in some cases, these spaces (such as workshops) may also have doubled as domestic space. See also Adams, *Earliest Christian Meeting Places*, 137–45, for a discussion of workshops as Christian meeting places; Adams's earlier work, "Placing the Corinthian Meal," also suggests the Roman cellar building at Corinth as another type of space that may have accommodated the Corinthian Christians (32–5).

36 Jewett, "Tenement Churches," 23–43. See also Billings, "From House Church to Tenement Church," 567–79.

37 Jeffers, "Jewish and Christian," 133. This suggestion relies, of course, on the assumption that there would have been a member of the community whose economic status afforded one of these deluxe apartments. Peter Oakes's *Reading Romans* also proposes a house-church demographic that focuses on

social non-elites, noting that hosts – while perhaps socially non-elite – would have to have been solvent enough to have offered a space large enough to host the house-church community. Thus, houses of wealthy craftspersons, for example, are offered as possibilities for meeting places (70). Billings, on the other hand (using the case study of Ephesus), proposes a model of "tenement churches" that would allow for the development of a Christian space even if wealthy patrons with lavish houses were not available (or if numbers grew to large enough numbers that the patrons' houses were no longer suitable). He writes: "Having outgrown its members' houses, it would have been logical for the Christian community to seek to establish a physical presence in the context of multi-resident, high-density housing, in which the vast majority were already domiciled" ("From House Church to Tenement Church," 569).

38 Jeffers, for example, in his book *Conflict at Rome*, sees the Roman Christian community as being composed predominantly of slaves and freedpersons, rather than citizens, and puts the first-century number of Christians at somewhere between one and five thousand, as early as 64 CE (17).

39 This minority view is espoused by Green, *Christianity in Ancient Rome*, 33. Green posits that there was a single church at Rome, rather than a series of cells. He also rejects the possibility that Phoebe's role was as messenger between different cells of Roman Christianity (ibid.).

40 Meeks, *Urban Christians*, 9–10.

41 Balch and Osiek, *Families*, 99.

42 Meeks, *Urban Christians*, 143; Malherbe, *Social Aspects*, 70.

43 The first letter to the Corinthians also mentions some believers by name; "Chloe's people," for example, could be a group of people meeting in Chloe's house (1 Cor 1:11). So too could the household of Stephanas (1 Cor 1:16) be construed as a house church. Both of these cases, however, are unclear and therefore offer only possibilities, rather than probabilities, of separate meeting places.

44 John S. Kloppenborg notes that modest numbers are likely the most responsible; he discusses membership lists for cult associations and guilds to provide comparative data for the size of the Pauline Christ groups. See "Membership Practices."

45 An extensive discussion of Christian ritual practice will be undertaken below, in chapter 5.

46 Balch, "Rich Pompeiian Houses"; Wallace-Hadrill, "*Domus* and *Insulae*"; George, "Domestic Architecture"; Økland, *Women in Their Place*; and Osiek, MacDonald, and Tulloch, *A Woman's Place*.

47 See, for example, Fai, "Body/Temple Metaphor," 81–5; Balch and Osiek, *Families*, 91–102; Neyrey, "Spaces and Places"; Neyrey, "Teaching You in Public"; and Stowers, "Social Status."

48 White, *Social Origins*, vol. 1, 111.

49 See also the admonition for the Roman church to host Phoebe (Rom 16:1–3), a travelling servant or patron from Cenchreae.

50 1 Cor 11:17–22 also discusses Christian assembly in a way that indicates household worship. The Lord's Supper, and the issues of hierarchy which emerged in this community's practice of it, will be discussed in chapter 4.

51 Col 4:15, a debated Pauline epistle, can also be included here. Mentioned as a patroness is Nympha, along with the "church in her house."

52 See the discussion of apartment versus *insulae* below, 69.

53 More will be said in the next chapter concerning the types of spaces probably used by these early Christians.

54 See Lampe, *From Paul to Valentinus*, 276–8, for a discussion of the difficulties of translating various recensions of the text. These difficulties revolve mainly around the discussion of whether this place was also used as a kind of philosophical school (see n56, below); that Justin himself claimed to stay there when he was in Rome, and that it was used as a place of assembly, is not in question.

55 The question of the size of the Christian groups will be engaged below in the discussion of house-church rituals (chapter 5).

56 There is a good deal of debate surrounding this reference to a meeting place above the baths. This meeting place has been described elsewhere as a "school," of the type used by philosophers. See, for example, Snyder, "'Above the Baths of Myrtinus,'" 336. Snyder argues that the apartment above the baths where Justin resides doubles as a philosophical school, and he includes an analysis of the kinds of apartments available above regional bath complexes. Despite these arguments, however, that Justin also resided there should indicate the place's status as domestic, at least insofar as I have defined it above.

57 Trans. White, *Social Origins*, vol. 2, 44–8. It is interesting to note that, in this story, Thecla's house is near enough to that of Onesiphorus that she can sit in her own window and overhear the teaching of Paul.

58 For a discussion of the difficulties involved in naming, translating, and collating the apocryphal Acts of Peter, see Baldwin, *Whose Acts*, 4–25.

59 This particular example is especially interesting when engaged in the discussion of sacred space. It is not even clear whether this particular homeowner is a believer in the message of Christ, or whether he is rather interested in playing host to popular movements (as evidenced by his hosting of the meeting of people to hear Simon Magus). Regardless of whether this man is a believer, it is intriguing that the house must be purified before Peter agrees to speak there, a point to which the discussion will return in chapter 4.

60 Trans. White, *Social Origins*, vol. 2, 46. This text is rich with suggestions about the ways in which space could be purified for teaching and preaching

in early Christianity, and will be discussed again below. Note also that, when Peter does enter the house, he enters the "dining-hall" (*Acts Pet.* 20), which is where the believers are gathered to read (and presumably hear) the gospel. The locus of the teaching within the house is often taken to have been the dining room, or *triclinium*; the discussion of the rituals practised in the house churches will be discussed in chapter 5.

61 Accusations of cannibalism, incest, and wanton lust were commonly levelled against the Christians, as well as other minority groups (including adherents to the mystery rites of Bacchus). See, for example, the Pliny-Trajan correspondence on the Christians (*Letters* 10.96–7); Tertullian, *Apology* 7.1; Eusebius, *Ecclesiastical History* 5.1.52, 5.1.26.

62 It is also interesting to note that there is a clear connection here between the word temple and the practice of sacrifice. Since the Jews are mentioned in the accusation, it is not unreasonable to assume that the Christian rejection of sacrifice as explained by Octavius is a rejection of its use in both polytheistic and Jewish temples. This rejection of temple as model of space is explored further in chapter 6.

63 The ideology expressed by Octavius here is a common one, claiming that the reason why there are no churches is because God dwells in the mind (32.1) and that "spirit" and "conscience" are the substitutes for libations and sacrifices (32.2–3). On the impracticality of this disembodied worship, see chapter 6.

64 Trans. White, *Social Origins*, vol. 2, 51. The Latin is as follows: "*Theofilus … qui erat cunctis potentibus in civitate sublimior, domus suae ingentum basilicam ecclesiae consecraret.*" The dating of this pseudepigraphic literature is debated, with dates ranging from the first to the fourth centuries; its provenance is equally debated. Thomas Smith posits a *terminus ante quem* for the document, as the *Recognitions* are quoted by Origen in 231. See Smith, "Introductory Notice," 73–5.

65 Also of interest is that the house of Theophilus is consecrated (*consecraret*), and has set within it a chair (*cathedra*) placed for the Apostle Peter (*Recognitions*, 10.71).

66 Note also that the apostle performs the conversion and baptism of the household (or at least of the immediate family: Siphor, his wife, and his daughter) in this meeting. There is at no time any mention of leaving to go to another room; rather, it is asked that a basin be brought to the place where they are meeting (the triclinium) in order to perform the ritual (*Acts of Thomas*, 132). See also White, *Social Origins*, vol. 2, 48.

67 See White, *Social Origins*, vol. 2, 122 for a catalogue of items; most examples are discussed between 121–258. White's work is still the most exhaustive collection of literary and archaeological evidence concerning early Christian

architecture, and is used extensively in many later works. As mentioned above, White's concern is mainly with the development from house church to *domus ecclesiae*, to *aula ecclesiae* and eventually to the basilica; thus, the references to later developments are less relevant here.

68 Trans. White, *Social Origins*, vol. 2, 161.

69 While the missing text has a number of interpretations, none of them would suggest anything other than the close connection mentioned above. It is likely that what is missing simply identifies the church as belonging to someone or to a community of believers. See White, *Social Origins*, vol. 2, 162, for a discussion of the possibilities.

70 See, for example, the discussions by Balch, "Rich Pompeiian Houses"; Jewett, "Tenement Churches"; and Horrell, "Domestic Space and Christian Meetings." This sampling of the scholarship demonstrates the wide variety of imagined places for house-church Christians, including villas, shops, *insulae* or tenements, and *tabernae*.

71 For an exhaustive catalogue of these spaces, the obvious place to turn is White's *Social Origins*, vol. 2, 121–258. White's work includes a substantial bibliography and reference to both primary sources and field reports. White's focus is on architectural development and adaptation, rather than sacred space, but is an invaluable resource for anyone working in the field of early Christian architecture.

72 Lampe, *From Paul to Valentinus*, 22–3.

73 Krautheimer, *Early Christian and Byzantine*, 8–9; Petersen, "House-Churches," 266; White, *Social Origins*, vol. 2, 209–40.

74 Petersen, "House-Churches," 266. See also Bowes, *Private Worship*, 66–7. She argues here that *titulus* specifically referred to donated property.

75 For example, the *Titulus Byzantis* (ss. Giovanni e Paolo), San Clemente, and Sant'Anastasia. See Petersen, "House-Churches," 267–70. See also White, *Social Origins*, vol. 2, 3–6, 209–40; Krautheimer, *Early Christian and Byzantine*, 30; Snyder, *Ante Pacem*, 76–7; and Finney, "Early Christian Architecture."

76 It should be noted also that each of these places is known for having been inhabited by the Jewish population of first-century Rome, and so there is some inclination to attach these *tituli* to the earliest days of the Christian movement. See, for example, Lampe, *From Paul to Valentinus*, 41. On the connection between Jewish neighbourhoods in Rome and the development of the Christian community, see also Brändle and Stegemann, "Formation of the First 'Christian Congregations.'"

77 See Krautheimer, *Early Christian and Byzantine*, 9; and see White, *Social Origins*, vol. 2, 209–18 for a complete technical analysis of the foundations.

78 White, *Social Origins*, vol. 2, 210. Note that this date is contemporary to the renovation of the Christian building at Dura Europos.

79 The *confessio* was likely constructed after the initial renovations. There is some debate over the date of the confessio, though most agree that it was set up by the last quarter of the fourth century. See Petersen, "House-Churches," 269; White, *Social Origins*, vol. 2, 217 (dating of the *confessio* at "the later fourth century"); Krautheimer, *Early Christian and Byzantine*, 9.

80 White, *Social Origins*, vol. 2, 217. For an overall plan of the basilica and the buildings beneath it, see figure 3.

81 For example, the domestic spaces under the basilicas of San Clemente and San Crisogono (310 CE), among others.

82 For example, concerning the *Titulus Clementis* (San Clemente): see Jerome, *De viris illustribus (On Illustrious Men)*, 15 (392 CE); Lampe, *From Paul to Valentinus*, 21n8. A good overall treatment and list of references for major *tituli* in Rome can be found in Lampe, *From Paul to Valentinus*, 19–24. Inge Neilsen, in "Housing the Chosen," has also noted the problematic nature of assuming that later churches are automatically evidence of earlier worship spaces on the same property, although she emphasizes the lack of particular sanctity of house churches as a potential reason: "Because private houses and other meeting places were not considered holy by the early congregations, there is really no reason why they should have been maintained and later built over with a church" (184). The issue of sanctity in the house church will be addressed at length in the coming chapters.

83 Lampe, *From Paul to Valentinus*, 22.

84 The circumstantial evidence in favour of the place as related to Peter is discussed in White, *The Social Origins*, vol. 2, 154–5, and includes the testimony of the famous Pilgrim of Piacenza.

85 There is, of course, literary evidence from the Gospels that places Jesus and his followers using the house of Peter at Capernaum (Matt 8:14–15).

86 The fourth century date is assigned based on the second phase of the site's development and construction. See White, *Social Origins*, vol. 2, 158. See also Richardson, *Building Jewish*, 105–6.

87 For the Julianos Church (Umm al-Jimal), see White, *Social Origins*, vol. 2, 141–51; Richardson, *Building Jewish*, 139; for Khirbet Qana, see Richardson, *Building Jewish*, 81–2, 100–7.

88 Taylor, *Christians and the Holy Places*, 268–94. In addition to the "House of Peter" at Capernaum, Taylor explores a number of other sites with legendary (and in most cases, ultimately unsubstantiated) origin stories in the pre-Constantinian era.

89 The Christian prayer hall at Megiddo is another potential candidate for the discussion, though it has been plagued with problematic dating and resultant issues of use, ownership, and function. It is also not clear whether the building in its entirety can be understood as private domestic space, resembling as it does army barracks. A structure similar to this one might be the Caserma dei Vigili at Ostia, which had shared courtyard space, shared ritual space (dedicated to the Imperial cult), and separate living quarters. See Bakker, "Caserma dei Vigili (II,V,1–2)." For an excellent discussion on the problems associated with Megiddo, as well as suggestions of how to move forward, see Adams, "Ancient Church at Megiddo," 62–9; on the issue of dating, see especially 65–7.

90 White dates the house to 232/233 CE; see discussion in *Social Origins*, vol. 2, 124.

91 Ibid., 123.

92 Ibid., 124. White dates the renovation to 240/241 CE.

93 The building at Dura Europos will be discussed in detail in chapter 4, below.

94 It could certainly be argued that this type of adapted domestic space would have continued to be the norm for this community for an even longer period, if the town itself had not been destroyed through invasion.

95 As with the *tituli*, there were of course apartment complexes and *insulae* that were converted to Christian places of worship (including what White has termed *aula ecclesiae*). These places, however, were not necessarily inhabited in the same period that they were used for worship. See White, *Social Origins*, vol. 2, 190–9.

96 Meates, *Roman Villa*, vol. 1, 19–23; chronological table, 24.

97 The Roman villa at Lullingstone will be analyzed in detail in chapter 4.

98 See Meates, *Roman Villa*, vol.1, 41–2, for a discussion of the period during which the Christian room or chapel was used. The overlapping of habitation and worship space is not always straightforward; more time will be spent on the relationship between lived space and worship space at Lullingstone in the coming chapters.

99 The Lullingstone villa is a key piece of material evidence to which the discussion will return with regard to sacred space. It is important in that it is an example of a place that was still used as domestic space while the chapel existed, and which has a clear demarcation of space (including a separate entrance and walls separating the ritual space from the rest of the house), as well as evidence for the concurrent practice of both Christianity and the ancestor cult.

100 As above, the *domus* argument is espoused by Murphy O'Connor, *St. Paul's Corinth*; Dix, *The Shape of the Liturgy*; and Krautheimer, *Early Christian and Byzantine*. Balch allows for the possibility of *domus* worship in "Rich

Pompeian Houses," but also includes humbler spaces in his analysis of potential meeting places.

101 As above, see Horrell, "Domestic Spaces," and Jewett, "Tenement Churches" on these types of spaces.

CHAPTER TWO

1 Krautheimer, *Early Christian*, 23; White, *Social Origins*, vol. 1, 140–8.

2 The development of synagogues is also a discussion auxiliary to this one. For helpful discussions of the development of synagogues as well as early churches, see Branham, "Sacred Space Under Erasure," especially 135–209.

3 As will be discussed below, while there are clearly provincial variations in domestic architecture across the Empire, in many cases the houses built by Roman provincial elites reflected the same cultural identity and awareness as did their Italian or Roman counterparts. As will become clear in the discussion of housing types, it would be foolhardy to generalize too broadly about the layout of houses, which had many variants, even within controlled regions.

4 Early arguments for this claim of architectural continuity include: Dix, *The Shape of the Liturgy*, 19–35; Murphy O'Connor, *St. Paul's Corinth*, 177–8; and Krautheimer, *Early Christian*, 482. These arguments for architectural forerunners, including the transformation of atrium into nave, of tablinum into altar, and so forth, have been reviewed and problematized by L. Michael White. See his introduction to *Social Origins*, vol. 1, 11–20.

5 White, *Social Origins*, vol. 1, 17.

6 Some Campanian houses, such as the House of Pansa (VI.6.1), Pompeii, are consistent with the Vitruvian ideal, with axial construction (as discussed below), and constitute the notion of a "typical" *domus* or atrium house.

7 All subsequent references to Vitruvius are from his work *On Architecture*.

8 Vitruvius 6.3. It should be noted that Vitruvius's writings are the ideal, rather than the real models for domestic space. Vitruvian categories emphasize symmetry and perfection. Even the most cursory of glances at the town plan for Pompeii, Herculaneum, or Ostia reveals that such perfection in plan was rarely attainable.

9 Below, the public and private dimensions of the typical aristocratic house will be discussed in greater detail. Here, it will suffice to say that, more often than not, the house in the morning (during the ritual of *salutatio*) would be open to the public. Of course, there were particular persons who may have been denied entrance, even during these public hours, and thus it was the duty of the slave who kept the gate to keep them out.

10 There are a great many examples from Campania of the embellishments of the atria of Roman aristocratic houses. A fine – though not a typical – example is the House of the Faun, Pompeii (Regio VI, XII), which had a number of atria, each in a different order (Doric, Tuscan, Corinthian), and each heavily decorated.

11 There is a fine example of an extant table in the House of the Wooden Partition, Herculaneum (III, 11–12).

12 Bear in mind, of course, that not all atrium houses adhered strictly to this ideal vertical axis. Many wealthy *domus* had multiple atria, such as the House of the Faun (VI.12.2) or multiple courtyards/peristyles, such as the House of the Vettii (VI.15.1), both in Pompeii; houses extant in both Pompeii and Herculaneum demonstrate the necessity of floor plans that fit with the available space in their bustling neighbourhoods.

13 The Villa of Publius Fannius Synistor at Boscoreale (now housed at the Metropolitan Museum of Art, New York) provides a well-known example of the elaborate decoration that was present in some cubicula, including mosaic floor decoration and wall painting. A number of cubicula at the Villa of the Mysteries at Pompeii also bear elaborate decorative programmes.

14 See Allison, "Labels for Ladles," 58–9, for a discussion of the importance of including artifacts wherever possible in the discussion of architecture and room function.

15 Not all guests were appreciative, however, of dinner invitations. Clients, especially, may have resented the occasional invitations they received from their patrons. As Juvenal writes in the late first century CE, "But what a dinner! You get wine that fresh wool wouldn't absorb: you'll see the guests turned into Corybants" (Juvenal, *Satires* 5.24, trans. Braund, LCL 91, 217).

16 See Wallace-Hadrill, "Domus and Insulae," 3–18.

17 See Cooper, "Closely Watched Households," for a problematization of the terms "public" and "private" when associated with the Roman house. She prefers the terms "*communia*" and "*propria*," (25). See also Vitruvius, 6.5.1.

18 Wallace-Hadrill, "Rethinking," 238–40.

19 George, "Domestic Architecture and Household Relations," 12.

20 Penelope Allison's work, including the above-cited "Labels for Ladles" and her book *Pompeian Households*, is invaluable for noting the importance of including artifactual evidence in the analysis of domestic spaces. Countless loom weights, for example, have been found in the atria of Pompeii.

21 For a sampling of the debate over public and private axes, see: Grahame, "Public and Private"; and Kate Cooper's corrective to the public/private axis in "Closely Watched Households," 24–33, especially her discussion of

Vitruvian categories of *communia* and *propria*, rather than public and private. Cooper argues that the architecture and flow of people in the *domus* is not so much about access as it is about concern; that is, the actions performed in the home during the *salutatio*, for example, are really actions pertaining mainly to civic concerns. On the one hand, the ritual of salutatio is intimately concerned with the home of the *pater familias*, but on the other hand, what happens in his home has everything to do with how he is perceived by the outside world. Thus, rather than public or private axes, which tend to dichotomize these actions, Cooper proposes a paradigm of overlapping concerns, which range from position directly in the sphere of civic interest to "beyond the reach of public authority" (25).

22 The main issue discussed below, in terms of self-representation in the home, is linked to domestic cult practice.

23 It is clear that women exercised some authority in the early church. See, for example, Osiek, MacDonald, and Tulloch, *A Woman's Place*, especially 144–63, 220–43; Miller, *Women in Early Christianity*, especially 15–68; and Cohick, *Women in the World of the Earliest Christians*, especially 195–224.

24 It is important to note that the distinctions between *matrona* and *mater familias* were not always clear; see, for example, Saller, "*Pater Familias*." For the use of *mater familias* as it is used here (that is, as a woman not under *potestas* and the mistress of the household in a legal sense, as *de facto* head of the household in the absence of a *pater familias* (either husband or father), see Ulpian's assertion in *Digesta* 1.6.4, as discussed in Saller, "*Pater Familias*," 194.

25 See, for example, CIL 1.2.1211 [*ILS* 8403], an epitaph that praises the virtue of a woman, Claudia, who supposedly espouses the character of the ideal Roman wife and matron: *Hospes, quod deico paullum est, asta ac pellege. Heic est sepulcrum hau pulcrum pulcrai feminae. Nomen parentes nominarunt Claudiam. Suom mareitom corde deilexit souo. Gnatos duos creavit. Horunc alterum in terra linquit, alium sub terra locat. Sermone lepido, tum autem incessu commodo. Domum servavit. Lanam fecit. Dixi. Abei.* The Republican Roman ideal held women to the standards of chastity, modesty, homemaking or women's work, and privacy (exemplified by the Roman virtue *pudicitia*).

On the other hand, it is clear that women could and did exercise some public power, as Livy bemoans: "our ancestors would have no woman transact even private business except through her guardian; they placed them under the tutelage of parents or brothers or husbands. We suffer them now to dabble in politics and mix themselves up with the business of the Forum and public debates and election contests" (34.2; trans. Mellor, *Historians of Ancient Rome*,

235). Despite the slackening of public expectations in the Empire, however, a woman's main role was still the management of her home and family.

26 There is not space here to examine the many exceptions, inconsistencies, and legal loopholes that dictated interaction in the Roman family. For excellent overall studies of the Roman family, see: Rawson, ed., *The Family in Ancient Rome*; Rawson and Weaver, eds., *The Roman Family in Italy;* Dixon, *The Roman Family*; and George, ed., *The Roman Family in the Empire.*

27 See George's article, "Domestic Architecture." She discusses the passage in Livy (1.57) where proper matrons are said to do their weaving in the atrium, noting that "the Roman woman was not confined to this space, but moved freely in the house, probably avoiding the atrium during reception events that excluded her, such as the *salutatio*" (12).

28 There are a number of excellent discussions that emphasize the temporal or diurnal articulation of space, as opposed to the built articulation of space. Michele George, "Domestic Architecture," for example, discusses the "polyvalence" of space in the Roman household. George has also argued elsewhere against the notion that a second atrium or peristyle can sometimes be an indication of gendered space in a Roman house. See George, "Repopulating the Roman House," 307–9. She convincingly argues that many so-called secondary atria are in fact appointed in a manner befitting guests, as any atrium would (308). She states also that, "although customs in behaviour probably did occur along gender lines, they cannot be identified securely in the architectural evidence" (309).

29 See, for example, Foss, "Watchful Lares," 217. Foss argues that in the largest houses slaves would have had their own spaces. Michele George argues against this claim in her article, "*Servus* and *Domus*," noting that it is not possible to "delineate living space for [slaves] in the extant houses of Pompeii" (24).

30 Among these is, again, Michele George, who also cites Tacitus (*Germani* 25); she notes that he "finds worthy of remark the custom of the northern tribe of the Germani to have separate servile sleeping quarters, which strongly suggests that such separation was not only foreign to Roman custom but even objectionable" ("Domestic Architecture," 13).

31 See Foss, "Watchful Lares," 81. The idea is that different groups in the household would have had their own shrines, to the *Lares* or to the gods of their choice. The ritual landscape of the Roman domus is discussed in detail in chapter 3.

32 See Balch, "Rich Pompeiian Houses"; Jewett, "Tenement Churches," 25–6; Horrell, "Domestic Space and Christian Meetings."

33 Apartment complexes are often referred to in modern scholarship as *insulae*, a term that causes some confusion, since it is the same term used to describe a city block. Thus, apartment buildings are sometimes called *caseggiati*, especially at Ostia. Bakker, *Living and Working*, 44–5. At Ostia, I will follow Bakker's terminology in order to avoid confusion; elsewhere (for example, at Rome), it may be less confusing to use the term *insula*, given the history of scholarship in that area.

34 Apartment buildings are less common at Pompeii and Herculaneum, which were places more conducive to villas and country homes, rather than urban centres. An exception to this at Pompeii is the *Insula Arriana Polliana* (VI,6). See Pirson, "Rented Accommodation at Pompeii."

35 Bakker, *Living and Working*, 44–55.

36 Bakker, "Topographical Dictionary," http://www.ostia-antica.org/dict/topics/houses/houses.htm, accessed 14 June 2011. See also Hermansen, *Ostia: Aspects of Roman City Life*, 24–43, for examples of eight different apartments and types from Ostia.

37 Bakker, *Living and Working*, 44.

38 See, for example, *CIL* 4.138 [*ILS* 6035], which advertises lodging for rent in an apartment complex with streetfront shops.

39 For many excellent images of these spaces, see Bakker, "Regio III – Insula X – Case a Giardino," http://www.ostia-antica.org/regio3/9/9.htm, accessed 14 July 2011.

40 Bakker, *Living and Working*, 49–50; on the problems associated with determining room functions, especially in conjunction with *domus* terminology, see Hermansen, *Ostia*, 24; 44.

41 See Hermansen, *Ostia*, 18–24; see also Bakker, *Living and Working*, 48–9.

42 While the representation of Trimalchio in Petronius's *Satyricon*, as well as his pretensions to elite status, are not necessarily reflective of the majority of freedpersons, there are a number of extant monuments that demonstrate the desire of freedpersons in the Roman Empire to claim and to advertise their manumitted status. There is an ongoing debate concerning the level of emulation present in these funerary monuments, including the question of whether they are attempting to efface their freeborn status, or conversely, to advertise it. Regardless of the outcome of this debate, it is clear that freedpersons also contributed to the upholding and continuation of Roman values through their adoption of traditional Roman mores. That continuation of *Romanitas* was frequently employed in funerary art. See, for example, the Tomb of Marcus Vergilius Eurysaces, where the baker and his wife are attired in the garb of a Roman citizen and a chaste Roman matron. The Tomb of the Gessii also depicts a freedwoman in the traditional garb and pose of

pudicitia, while a funerary relief dedicated to the Servilii features a young boy wearing a *bulla*, a marker usually reserved for freeborn boys. For further discussion of these monuments and others, as well as the question of whether freedpersons meant to efface or advertise their status, see Mouritsen, *The Freedman in the Roman World*, 246–8, 278–83; Stewart, *Social History of Roman Art*, 62–70; and Petersen, *The Freedman in Roman Art and Roman Art History*, 84–122. Petersen argues against any specific "freedman taste" in both funerary and domestic contexts. Other remarks on freedpersons or non-elites in domestic contexts can be found in Grahame, "Material Culture and Roman Identity," 172. He argues here that, while there may not be anything quite so obvious as a formula for *Romanitas*, certainly freedpersons of the Empire emulated the elites as much as possible, especially in terms of status and wealth. In other words, while Roman identity did shift, especially from the Republic to the Empire, the elites (represented by status rather than ethnicity, as Grahame argues) still set the standard in art and architecture.

43 The first and perhaps second floors are what I mean by "lower floors" here; ground floors were generally taken over by shops and communal spaces, as at the Caseggiato di Diana.

44 Hermansen sees the *medianum* as the place where all of the occupants of apartments on a given floor would take their meals. See Hermansen, *Ostia*, 44.

45 Bakker, *Living and Working*, 47; he gives a number of examples of back or upper rooms of shops, likely inhabited by the tenant who ran the shop as well. Included among the examples are three rooms behind two shops in the Caseggiato di Diana (III,III,I). See also Ellis, *Roman Housing*, 78.

46 Ellis, *Roman Housing*, 78–9; Bakker, *Living and Working*, figure 14.

47 For example, the sprawling Villa of Poppaea at Oplontis or that of Publius Fannius Synistor at Boscoreale.

48 In villas of the late Empire, money and space afforded the ultimate modes of Roman expression. The latest fashion for architecture, decoration, and design were found in villas of the wealthy all over the Empire.

49 The Roman villa at Lullingstone, which will be discussed in detail in chapter 4, is a fine example of this rural estate model.

50 Ellis, "Power, Architecture, and Décor," 118 (see also his discussion of Ammianus Marcellinus 28.4.12, 118). On the imitation of imperial palaces, see L'Orange, *Art Forms and Civic Life*, 74–8.

51 Trimalchio, the star of Petronius's *Satyricon*, is a good (if exaggerated) example of the ways in which lower classes of Romans, including freedpersons, attempted to cultivate a "Roman" persona by emulating the aristocratic elite.

52 Grahame, "Material Culture and Roman Identity," 174–6.

53 Ibid., 163–4.

54 Wallace-Hadrill, *Houses and Society*, 10.

55 Grahame, "Material Culture," 175. Kate Cooper also notes the connection between the architecture of the house and the formation of Roman identity. Because a high-ranking person or patron would have a constant flow of visitors, his house would reflect that. She states, "To possess *vestibula*, *tabulina*, and atria was a sign not only of the wealth needed to build them but a self-fulfilling prophecy of the social standing which would make them necessary" ("Closely Watched Households," 13). See also Clarke, *Houses of Roman Italy*, 2–10.

56 The apsidal dining room is central at Lullingstone, for example. See also Ellis, "Power, Architecture, and Décor," 75–80, for a discussion of trends in later dining traditions.

57 Stewart, *Social History*, 43, italics original.

58 See, for example, Hales, *The Roman House and Social Identity*, 144; Stewart, *Social History*, 43.

59 Stewart, *Social History*, 53.

60 Scott, "The Power of Images," 54.

61 Ibid., 57.

62 Wallace-Hadrill, *Houses and Society*, 149.

63 Ibid., 173.

64 Ibid., 179. On this point see also Scott, "Power of Images," 53–67; Grahame, "Material Culture," 172–5; Ellis, "Power, Architecture, Décor," 121–4; Hales, *Roman House*, 18–21.

65 Ellis, "Power, Architecture, Décor," 123.

66 Grahame, "Material Culture," 172–5.

67 Below, a discussion of the Lullingstone Roman villa in Britain will expand on these points.

68 On this point, see the excellent discussion in Grahame, "Material Culture and Roman Identity," 163–5.

CHAPTER THREE

1 In Megiddo, for example, homes with shrines and figurines have been excavated; at Deir'Alla, Jordan, a house with niche shrines was also discovered. Beebe posits that the cults of local religion were worshipped privately after the cult of Yahweh dominated public worship. See Beebe, "Ancient Palestinian Dwellings." The Greeks also worshipped deities in their homes, as did the Etruscans.

2 Balch, "Rich Pompeian Houses."

3 Much of the discussion concerning social status and self-representation through piety *is*, it must be acknowledged, specific to the mentality of the aristocratic (male) Roman. However, characters such as Petronius's Trimalchio demonstrate that even those Romans who were not born into the practice of ancestral and household piety recognized its importance for establishing their own place in the competitive Roman class-world. Upward mobility, then – the goal of many low-born Romans – was connected to the adherence of Roman ideology and piety.

4 Much of the later literary evidence comes to us from Christian apologists, who discuss the ideal relationship between Christians and their religious past, including devotion to the domestic gods. These testimonies are discussed in chapter 4, below.

5 See Stark, "Religious Competition and Roman Piety," 19. Stark's article notes "relatively high levels of religiousness among the Romans" in the period leading up to the triumph of Christianity (24), but the majority of the article points out that this religiousness is played out to its fullest in mass movements, such as those dedicated to Isis, Cybele, Bacchus, and Mithras (as well as Judaism and Christianity) – and not "traditional" Roman religion, both private and public. The common interpretation of Roman religion as "archaic" and less spiritually fulfilling than the mysteries and Christianity was perhaps spearheaded by Franz Cumont in his work *Oriental Religions in Roman Paganism*; see especially 27–45.

6 Orr, "Roman Domestic Religion," 1559. Orr's study is still the best overview of the Roman household cult to date.

7 Ibid., 1570. The Genius also had civic implications; the Genius of the emperor, for example, was celebrated publicly in the same way that the Genius of the *pater familias* was celebrated privately. Some household cults also worshipped the emperor as one of their collection of favourite gods. See, for example, Gradel, *Emperor Worship and Roman Religion*, 198–212, for a good overview of these debates.

8 This lack of clarity seems to have been an issue in the ancient world as well; Cicero's demand to have his house and by extension, his gods, returned to him (see his *De Domo Sua*) shows that this point is one of confusion. Cicero and his house will be discussed in greater detail below.

9 It is this familial and hereditary power on which Augustus capitalized in his adoption of the divine lineage claimed by his adoptive father, Julius Caesar. A figure of Aeneas, sacrificing on an altar to his family gods, holds pride of place on the Ara Pacis Augustae.

10 See Orr, "Domestic Religion," 1570; Harmon, "Family Festivals of Rome," 1601; and Cato, *de Re Rustica*, 143.2.11.

11 Harmon, "Family Festivals," 1593.

12 Trans. Klauck, *Religious Context*, 60.

13 See, on libations to the Lares, Petronius, *Satyricon*, 60.8; Ovid, *Fasti* 2.631–34: *dis generis date tura boni (Concordia fertur illa praecipue mitis adesse die) et libate dapes, ut, grati pignus honoris, nutriat incinctos missa patella Lares.*

14 Indeed, it could be that the representation of the *pater*'s Genius is performing this type of libation in many of the paintings and statuettes of the domestic gods. There does seem to be a clear association between meals (both the preparation and consumption of meals) and the domestic gods.

15 Ovid, *Fasti* 6.310: "Even into our own days, a trace of this old custom has survived: a clean vessel bears the food that is sacrificed to Vesta" (trans. Klauck, *Religious Context*, 61).

16 See Robinson, "Domestic Burnt Offerings," 97–9. Robinson contributes a valuable analysis of the evidence of charred fruit, vegetable, and animal remains in houses destroyed by Vesuvius. He rightly distinguishes between the food that was most likely left behind and charred (or carbonized) by the eruption, and the food that was clearly organized as an offering. The most frequently represented animals in the burnt offerings are domestic fowl, especially males, which shows again a purposeful choice in this ritual process. The layering of the remains of the sacrifices is such that it was clearly an ongoing practice; this archaeological evidence is borne out by the painted *lararia* from the same area, depicting just such sacrifices.

17 The *bulla* was restricted to freeborn male children.

18 Naming seems to have occurred on the eighth day for females, and the ninth for males; there is, however, some confusion over this process. See Plutarch, *Roman Questions* 102.

19 See Bradley, "The Roman Child in Sickness," 89–92.

20 Harmon, "Family Festivals," 1596–601.

21 Ibid., 1598. For further bibliography on the *toga virilis* ceremony, see: Juvenal, *Satire* 5.165 (on the *bulla*); Statius, *Silvae* 5.3.118–20 (on the performance of the ritual in the presence of the entire household, including the domestic deities); Pliny, *Epistulae* 1.9.2 (on the fact that the ritual could take place on any day, not just the Liberalia); Seneca, *Epistulae morales* 4.2 (on the procession to Forum after private ceremony); Persius, *Satirae* 5.30–7 (on the entire event taking place in the presence of the gods); *Phaedrus* 3.10.10 (on the rite taking place in non-aristocratic families).

22 Victor Turner's notions of rites of passage, and the liminal stage as the one which is most dangerous to the practitioner fit in well here. Deities must protect the subject while in the liminal phase, and also must be there upon return to society, as indeed the Roman domestic gods are for a Roman boy. The

relationship between ritual practice, relationship to the gods, and the creation of sacred space will be discussed below. See Turner, *Forest of Symbols*.

23 Harmon, "Family Festivals," 1598. Note that the hairstyle usually called the *sex crines* is often also referred to by the term *seni crines*.

24 A young seated woman, for example (accompanied by a maid and an *eros*), in the well-known frieze from the Villa of the Mysteries, is sometimes interpreted as a bride in the process of having her hair styled and adorned in the manner of the *sex crines*.

25 Staples, *Good Goddess*, 145. See Staples, too, for a good discussion of bridal attire and its parallel in the attire of the Vestals (145–7). See also Beard, "Sexual Status of Vestal Virgins," especially 13–16. Beard's article rightly highlights the difficulty in determining the direction of influence between the attire and hairstyle of the Vestals and that of Roman brides; however, that both signify virginity – and its potent role in the maintenance of the people's safety on both a micro and a macro level – is clear.

26 See Toynbee, *Death and Burial*, 43–64. Imperial rituals, funerals, and burials were obviously more elaborate than ordinary ones, and had more public aspects. The present discussion is concerned with the rites associated with those Romans who were not necessarily in high public offices, although high-ranking aristocrats could also have public as well as private aspects to the funerary celebrations.

27 For a good discussion of the *funerarii*, professionals working in funeral preparation and arrangement, see Graham, *Burial of the Urban Poor*, 28–31; Bodel, "Dealing with the Dead," 128–52.

28 Toynbee claims that this account of the funeral couch and its placement mainly reflects the practice of wealthier Romans (*Death and Burial*, 44). See also Lindsay, "Death-Pollution," 152–72. Both Graham, above, and Lindsay ("Death-Pollution," 163–4) discuss the difficulty of applying this practice wholesale to the rest of the Roman population. Obviously not all Romans were wealthy enough to have atrium houses, and thus this practice reflects an ideal, especially of the Republican aristocratic Roman. That the body was to be displayed in the house (or other living space), is clear; the practicalities of this mandate must, however, in many cases remain unknown.

29 See, for example, the Tomb of the Haterii, which shows the deceased woman lying in state on a funeral couch with mourners or family members standing alongside. Note also the garlands, candelabra, and flute-players. Many other sarcophagi depict the particularities of Roman funerary ritual, including the *conclamatio*, processions, and mourning. The tomb at Amiternum provides another excellent visual representation of these practices.

30 See Paulus, *Opinions* 1.21.2: "You are not allowed to bring a corpse into the city in case the sacred places in the city are polluted. Whoever acts against these restrictions is punished with unusual severity. You are not allowed to bury or cremate a body within the walls of the city." Trans. Hope, *Death in Ancient Rome*, 129. For an example of the Greek counterpart to this idea, see Parker, *Miasma*, 32–73.

31 See Cicero, *De legibus* 2.55: *nec vero tam denicales (quae a nece appellatae sunt) quia residentur mortuis, quam ceterorum caelestium quieti dies feriae nominarentur*. See Toynbee, *Death and Burial*, 292n178. There were, during this period, behaviours that were appropriate and inappropriate. Hugh Lindsay, in his article "Death-Pollution," goes so far as to call some behaviour "taboo," noting that "it seems such matters were closely monitored by the pontiffs" (166), but of course it is more likely that, in most households at least, the responsibility of keeping these days sacred would be up to the family itself.

32 Mary Douglas's work on purity and pollution is helpful in the interpretation of these death rituals. See especially Douglas, *Purity and Danger*. It is clear that these practices are necessary rituals, used to purify the people as well as their space. However, when the discussion turns below to the Christian use of this Roman space, it will be important to bear in mind the ingrained nature of these rituals and the protection they provide the families in question. It would be unwise to assume that, with the change of "spiritual" engagement (through Christianity) the need for purification of space and self – and indeed, the familiar practices that afforded this purification – would disappear or be altered. The danger (to borrow from Douglas) of an unpurified space after the presence of a corpse would be no less palpable to a Roman after conversion to Christianity. The notions of ritual, purity, and space will form an extensive part of the discussion in the coming chapters.

33 Festus-Paulus 68L; see Lindsay, "Death-Pollution," 166.

34 Lindsay, "Death-Pollution," 167. See Lindsay in general for a discussion of the funeral rites, and the problems with their chronology, continued practice, and their literary sources.

35 Toynbee, *Death and Burial*, 49. The funeral couch would be burned with the body only, of course, if the body were cremated. The practices of inhumation and cremation ebbed and flowed from the Republic to the High Empire, according to custom and trend. Inhumation was the norm by the time the Christians started dedicating cemeteries (catacombs) to their dead, and some of the funeral rituals changed accordingly. Purification of the house, however, along with sacrifices and shared meals (usually at the site of the tomb), continued to be a key element of post-funeral rites.

36 Cicero, *De legibus* 2.55 (in Toynbee, *Death and Burial*, 54). It is not clear where this sacrifice actually takes place. It is meant to purify the *Lar* or *Lares*, but whether the sacrifice of a goat or sheep can reasonably be expected to have occurred in the house is up for debate. Whether inside or outside, the fact that the *Lares* demand purification indicates how strongly these gods figured in the life and death cycles of the family.

37 Toynbee, *Death and Burial*, 63. Note also the festivals of the *Parentalia* and the *Lemuria*, which had both private and public aspects to their focus on the celebration of the dead. See especially notes on the *Lemuria*, during which time unhappy spirits, if not appeased, were said to "prowl round the house" (64).

38 The ancestors were present in the home as *imagines*, wax or terracotta portrait busts of deceased family members. These *imagines* will be discussed below.

39 Flower, *Ancestor Masks*, 202.

40 Again, see Petronius's *Satyricon*, "Dinner with Trimalchio," for a typical and popular example of a wealthy freedman who caricatures the type willing to stop at nothing in order to climb the ladder of Roman society.

41 Hillner, "Domus, Family, and Inheritance," 130. Hillner's article discusses the importance of the *domus* as representation of the multi-generationality of the family. It would have been extremely important for a family to retain domestic property in order to maintain their aristocratic status. Moving house did not indicate a move to better and brighter pastures; it meant a loss of the family estate, and with it, a right to claim certain levels of social authority. The ancestor cult would have played, of course, an integral role in this social and domestic maintenance. By the same token, if a wealthy Roman (or social climbing Roman) had acquired an estate by something other than hereditary means, setting up a gallery of ancestral *imagines* in the house – implying that these ancestors too had found their home here – would have sent a message to visitors that the house *belonged* to the family.

42 Eugene Dwyer notes that there was a "usurpation" of the tradition of the ancestor cult by "inferior members of society" ("Pompeian Atrium House," 26).

43 See Giacobello, *Larari Pompeiani*, especially 74–80. Giacobello discusses here what she terms the "larari secondari" – that is, *lararia* dedicated to deities other than the household gods. There are, of course, numerous theories about the importance of these other gods of the Roman pantheon in the city of Pompeii (to say nothing of other cities and towns), but that discussion is too lengthy to be had here.

44 Ibid., 80. Indeed, gods well beyond the *Lares* were worshipped in domestic contexts – not only in the provinces, as one might expect, but also on the Italic peninsula. See, on this subject, Bowes, "At Home," 210–11.

45 *Historia Augusta*, "Alexander Severus," 29.2: *optimos electos et animas sanctiores, in quis Apollonium et … Christum, Abraham et Orpheum et huiuscemodi ceteros habebat.* Unfortunately, no material evidence supporting this claim is extant. However, there is a clear desire to include among his household gods powerful gods from other cultures (subsumed, of course, by the all-powerful Roman Empire).

46 Trans. Klauck, *Religious Context*, 62.

47 A prime example of this fear-mongering associated with "exotic" gods can be seen in Livy's account of the *Senatus Consultum de Bacchanalibus* of 186 BCE, which banned the rites and practices of the Bacchanalia in the city of Rome, on pain of death. See Livy 39. That these official correctives were sometimes deemed necessary is indicative of the popularity of these foreign and mystery gods, although whether they enjoyed more popularity during troubled times, or simply that their worship was more heavily censured in these times is unclear.

48 This and subsequent sections of Cicero's *De Domo Sua* are translated by Klauck, *Religious Context*, 59.

49 Ibid., 58. In this instance, Cicero is arguing for the safe return of his own house, after he has come out of exile.

50 Cicero's lament over his house and the relationship between domestic worship and a sense of belonging will be further discussed below.

51 Boyce, *Corpus of the Lararia of Pompeii*. As with any study of the domestic space of the Roman world, southern Italy dominates the discussion. Pompeii and Herculaneum obviously provide the most evidence for household shrines, but Ostia, Delos, Boscoreale, and Stabia also have excellent examples, and sporadic findings have been recorded in Spain, Hungary, Austria, Roman Britain, Roman Germany, and North Africa. Despite some regional variations, there is a surprising consistency of representation in the household shrines of the Roman Empire. See especially Orr, "Roman Domestic Religion," 1586–90, on this point. The discussion that follows will give some pride of place to the Pompeiian evidence, but it should be noted that the type at Pompeii is very similar to types found in the regions listed above.

52 Orr, "Domestic Religion," 1586. Hundreds of portable altars were also found in Pompeii. See Klauck, *Religious Context*, 60.

53 Foss, "Watchful *Lares*," 196–218.

54 Balch and Osiek, *Families*, 110.

55 Despite its common usage in modern scholarly parlance, the term *lararium* is only used for the first time in the third century. See Bodel, "Cicero's Minerva," 246–75, 271n28, for a discussion of the term, its use in modern scholarship, and its absence in earlier attestations of domestic shrines.

56 Boyce, *Corpus*, 12–17. Note that Bakker, in *Living and Working with the Gods* (14–15), posits that lamps in niches ought to be viewed as the exception, not the rule, in Campanian and Ostian houses. He claims that, while some niches do show signs of lamp-burning, there is only one case (in a Pompeian bath) where a niche can be proven to have been used only for that purpose (that is, not in conjunction with something else, like housing a statuette or similar). The debate, however, is far from conclusive, especially with a lack of concrete evidence. Bowes, "At Home," also discusses the difficulties inherent in "reading" domestic data as ritual data (whether that data be niches, basins, or other objects sometimes associated with domestic cult practice) without accompanying textual data (210).

57 See figure 3.1. This shrine and the building in which it is housed will be discussed in further detail below.

58 See, for example, the wall-niche in the kneading room of the Caseggiato dei Molini. Bakker, *Living and Working*, 66–7.

59 See Bakker's discussion of the Domus del Lارario in *Living and Working*, 85.

60 The *lararium* in the House of the Vettii, Pompeii, is a good example of a wall-painting framed with architectural features.

61 What these serpents represent is the subject of lengthy and inconclusive debate. There is no consensus on the meaning of serpents in *lararia* and other contexts of the household cult, although the most frequently cited options are that the serpents represent the Genius, the *Penates*, or that they perform a general apotropaic function. For a good (if dated) discussion, see Boyce, "Significance of the Serpents." See also Balch and Osiek, *Families*, 85–6.

62 See, for example, the discussion of a *lararium* at the Caupona of Euxinus by Mark Robinson, who has tentatively identified these somewhat faded offerings as a fig, an egg, a pine cone, and a date. Robinson, "Domestic Burnt Offerings," 97 (figure 3).

63 A good example of this type comes from Pompeii, in the Casa del Sacello Iliaco (I.6.4), which boasts a series of vignettes from the Trojan War, picked out in painted plaster relief. Another example of a private space with a dedicated cult room is found at Ostia, at the Caseggiato del Sacello (IV,V,4), discussed at length by Jan Theo Bakker at http://www.ostia-antica.org/regio4/5/5-4.htm, accessed June 2010.

64 See also the sacellum dedicated to Silvanus in the Caseggiato dei Molini. The Caseggiato dei Molini (House of the Millstones) is one of the multi-purpose buildings that are so common in the bustling commercial centre of Ostia. Constructed in the early second century (a dating based on brickwork), it is contemporary to its more famous counterpart, the House of Diana. Like the other complexes, the ground floor was populated predominantly by shops

and work areas; in its earliest incarnation it seems to have housed bakers, and in later years, a guild of carpenters. It is not clear whether the bakers and carpenters who used this space also lived there at some time. However, a small *lararium* and a larger sacellum have been found there, dedicated to various gods and emperors. See Bakker, http://www.ostia-antica.org/regio1/3/3–1.htm, accessed June 2010. See also Heres, "Building History," 37–74.

65 Wooden tripod altars exist mainly in artistic representations on painted *lararia*. See, for example, the *lararium* in the Caupona of L. Vetutius Placidus at Pompeii (I 8,8); and see figures 16–17 in Giacobello, *Larari Pompeiani*, 86.

66 Ulrich, *Roman Woodworking*, 230, figure 11.14. Ulrich discusses the construction of these cabinets and their function as safe or strongbox. He also points out the capability of many of these cabinets to be locked down to the floor with iron rods (231), raising the question again about how freely the term "portable" should be used, especially in the case of these elaborately and finely constructed cabinets. Obviously the housing of valuables makes some kind of permanence or security necessary.

67 Ibid., 228.

68 Ibid., 229. See also Ulrich's discussion of the ways in which the doors opened; the doors could be opened fully in order to display the contents.

69 Ivory diptych, possibly commemorating the consulship of Quintus Aurelius Symmachus, 391 CE. See Gardner and Wiedemann, *The Roman Household*, figure 5 (between pages 116–17).

70 Serpents flanking an altar of a similar type can be seen in the atrium of House VI, xvi, 15, at Pompeii. See Boyce, "Significance," figure 1. See also Casa del Larario di Ercole (also in Fröhlich, *Lararien und Fassadenbilder*, L39, 265, T. 29, 4). The Hospitium del Pulcinella, also, has a niche with serpent painted below and an altar (now missing) in similar configuration. The niches in both of these cases have aedicular details, with painted serpents either positioned below or flanking the altar. See also Fröhlich, *Lararien* (L9: 253, T25.2).

71 Of this type is the very well-known *lararium* at the House of the Vettii, Pompeii, and the House of the Sarno Lararium, among others.

72 Pliny, for example, expresses dissatisfaction with the trend of using costly materials such as bronze or marble, rather than the traditional wax, for the masks of ancestors (*Natural History* 35.2).

73 Flower, *Ancestor Masks*, 202. Flower also notes the blackened grime on some *imagines*, an indication that the cupboards were not always kept closed.

74 For example, the cubiculum in the house of Publius Fannius Synistor, Boscoreale. See figure 5.

75 See Foss, "Watchful Lares," and Giacobello, *Larari pompeiani*.

76 Indeed, Michele George has noted that there is no such thing as a "slave area"; they own nothing, have rights to nothing. They are possessions, not people, and thus exist only where their master wants them. See George, "Domestic Architecture." See also chapter 2, above.

77 Wallace-Hadrill, *Houses and Society*, 110.

78 Ibid., 45. In the House of the Vettii, the location of the *lararium* is on the Western wall of an inner courtyard (there is a central courtyard, and two successive/adjacent courtyards). Even though it is not in the main courtyard, it is still not located in a "private" location in the house (e.g. cubicula, kitchen, or similar).

79 Horace, *Ode* 3.22, *To Diana*: *Montium custos nemorumque, Virgo/ quae laborantes utero puellas/ ter vocata audis, adimisque leto/ Diva triformis: Imminens villae tua pinus esto/ quam per exactos ego laetus annos/ verris obliquum meditantis ictum/ sanguine donem.* Clearly, the owner of a farm estate has dedicated a tree on his property, at which place he offers yearly sacrifices to the goddess Diana. Whether this yearly sacrifice is specifically for the protection of women in labour, or perhaps dedicated in relation to a specific woman in labour is unclear, but given that this particular facet of Diana's protective presence is emphasized, it is not unreasonable to suggest that protection of the children of the *familia* is exactly what the dedication and subsequent sacrificing is meant to achieve.

80 See this volume, figure 3.1.

81 Bodel, "Cicero's Minerva," 249; Rüpke, *Religion of the Romans*, 24–9; Hales, *Roman House*, 18.

82 Hales, *Roman House*, 18.

83 Dwyer, "The Pompeian Atrium House," 33. See Vitruvius 6.5.

84 Petronius, *Satyricon*, 29.8. That the shrine is noticed and commented upon in this satire reveals a connection between true Romanitas and commitment to the household gods.

85 Foss, "Watchful Lares," 197.

86 Klauck, *Religious Context*, 63.

87 Part of the role of place has to do with embodiment; recent work on the body and its movement through space and place lends itself well to discussion here. This conversation will become especially important when the discussion turns to the body of believers and the creation of sacred space in the early house-church communities. See below, chapter 6.

88 Hales, *Roman House*, 19. Hales later states that the Roman owner of a house needed to ensure his proper social standing by advertising that he is "safeguarding his *familia* and *clientes* through his observance of appropriate social and religious ritual" (113).

89 Bergman, "Roman House as Memory Theater," 225–56.

90 Ibid., 225.

91 This idea is already evident from the discussion above, concerning the population of domestic shrines with different gods, emperors, and ancestors.

92 Bodel, "Cicero's Minerva," 249–60.

93 See Klauck, *Religious Context*, on this passage: "the religious value and the consequent right to protection do not come into being through any consecration of the building, but through the forms of religious praxis that are carried out with pious intention by those who dwell in it. A 'holy' house is a 'pious' house that excels in the careful praxis of the domestic cults" (58). In other words, Clodius's attempt to wrest ownership of the house by making it a *locus sacer* (which would restrict it from use as a habitation) is, in Cicero's view, impossible (and redundant). What can be extrapolated from Cicero's argument is that *any* household belonging to a pious Roman is a *locus sacer*, and is indeed inviolate, but not in the way that Clodius suggests; it is, instead, sacred to the Roman who sanctified it through his or her daily rituals. Thus, Cicero argues, there is no "restoration" from exile without restoring his own *locus sacer*; without it, he is subject to a punishment – that of placelessness, homelessness – reserved only for the treacherous and the unforgiven.

94 As above, Aeneas flees Troy in the wake of its destruction, but is sure to bring his household deities with him. See Virgil's *Aeneid* 2. 291–3; Arnobius 3.40.

95 Also of interest in Cicero's entreaty to the priests is the common understanding of the connection between (male) members of the family and the "sacred rites," and the importance of those sacred rites to the continuation of the family line. Cicero is discussing the disinheriting of a son and says, "You are not Fonteius, as you ought to be, nor the heir of your new father; nor, though you have lost your right to the sacred ceremonies of your own family, have you availed yourself of those which belong to you by adoption. And so, having thrown the ceremonies of religion into confusion, – having polluted both families, both the one which you have abandoned and the one which you have entered, – having violated the legitimate practices of the Romans with respect to guardianships and inheritances, you have been made, contrary to all the requirements of religion, the son of that man whom you were old enough to be the father" (*De Domo Sua*, 35). Of interest to the current discussion is the idea that the rites of the family are not to be cast off; the political climber being addressed here is accused of no less than "polluting" the families in question – no small accusation when the sanctity of a family unit is on the line.

96 Stowers, "Theorizing Ancient Household Religion," 11.

97 The discussion will return to issues of space, place, and sanctity in chapters 5 and 6, below.

CHAPTER FOUR

1 See, for example, the installation of chancel screens and the separation of the clergy and the laity in church architecture from the Byzantine period onward, and the increasing ritualization of the liturgy and the congregants. See Kilde, *Sacred Power*, especially 57–9; 73–8.

2 See chapter 3, 55–63, which gives a breakdown of the gods worshipped in Pompeii and the presence of figurines associated with these gods.

3 Even as late as the fifth century, Augustine refers to the accoutrements of the domestic cult as "idols" (*Sermones* 62.12.18).

4 See, for example, Acts 21:25; Gal 5:19–21; Romans 2:22; 1 Cor 5:11, 6:9; 2 Cor 6; Col 3:5; 1 John 5:21.

5 There are many debates about the identification of the strong versus the weak believers. It is not necessarily the case that the weak believers were new converts, and that the strong were those who had converted earlier. There is perhaps a divide between those with polytheistic backgrounds (gentiles) and Jews. See Theissen, *Social Setting*, 121–44; Theissen, "Social Conflicts," 371–91.

6 Even if the meat consumed were purchased later, from a vendor, as opposed to consumed as part of the festal celebration of a deity, a convert from polytheistic practice might be confused by the permissiveness here.

7 Murphy O'Connor, in "Freedom or the Ghetto," argues: "Through fear the Weak would have forced the community into a self-imposed ghetto. Through a destructive use of freedom the Strong would have committed the church to a pattern of behaviour indistinguishable from that of its environment" (573). On this point, see also Horsley, "Consciousness and Freedom," 574–89.

8 In this passage, Paul seems to be referring to sacrificial meals in explicitly "pagan" celebrations, rather than temple meat consumed in a separate, domestic context. In this discussion of sacrificial meals, however, Paul is airing his views both on Roman gods (that they are demons) and the fundamental opposition between rituals performed to those gods and rituals dedicated to Christ.

9 Trans. Sider, *Christian and Pagan*, 30. The *Apologia* is generally accepted as having been written in 197 CE.

10 The accusation levelled against public adherents is mainly that of favouritism and selection; that is, the worshippers choose which deities they wish to honour at a given time, and that they change their allegiance is in itself proof, to Tertullian, that they do not fear their gods (*Apol.* 13.1–2).

11 Trans. White, *Social Origins*, vol. 2, 54. This document is dated to 196/7 CE.

12 The word Tertullian uses here for "church" ("Does a Christian come from idols into the *church*?") is *ecclesia* (*ab idolis in ecclesiam venire*); the words used for house of God are *domus dei* (*in domum dei venire*). The former

seems to indicate the assembly (i.e., of persons); the latter seems to indicate a physical space. On a fifth-century injunction to cease the worship of idols in a domestic context, see Augustine, *Sermones* 62.12.18, discussed further below.

13 Trans. Quinn, "Houses of the Holy," 172.

14 Ibid., 180.

15 Infant baptism may well have been a response to this issue, but at this point its practice is certainly unclear. On the lack of clarity on this issue, see the following: Jeremias, *Infant Baptism*; Everett Ferguson, *Baptism in the Early Church*, especially 362–79.

16 On the function of polemic as relevant to insider communities, see, for example, de Jonge, "The Function of Religious Polemics."

17 Quinn, "Houses of the Holy," 162.

18 Trans. ibid., 180.

19 See Simmons, *Arnobius of Sicca*, especially chapters 6, 7, and 9, for a detailed discussion of Arnobius's conception of the pantheon of Roman deities.

20 Trans. Roberts and Donaldson, *The Ante-Nicene Fathers*, vol. 6, 475. Arnobius discusses the domestic deities at further length in *Adv.Nat.* 3.41–4.

21 Trans. Schaff, *Nicene and Post-Nicene Fathers*, vol. 6, 304.

22 The *Codex Theodosianus*, which collected all of the laws laid down since Constantine, especially with regard to religious practice, mentions (and prohibits) domestic cult practice: "He shall not, by more secret wickedness, venerate his lar with fire, his genius with wine, his *Penates* with fragrant odours; he shall not burn lights to them, place incense before them, or suspend wreaths for them" (*Theodosian Code* 16.2.12; trans. Pharr, *Theodosian Code*, 473). More explicitly even than Augustine's sermon, it is clear here that the domestic cult is to be stopped. As above, however, that this issue is still a matter of concern in the mid-fifth century is an indication of the continued vitality of the domestic cult.

23 As above, the terminology of *domus ecclesiae* here follows White, *Social Origins*, vol. 2, 123.

24 The most complete survey of the Christian building at Dura is Kraeling, *Christian Building*. See also White, *Social Origins*, vol. 1, 123–34.] Peppard's *World's Oldest Church* offers a new and excellent study of the overall structure, its decoration, and an envisioning of the ritual activity that may have taken place there.

25 Kraeling, *Christian Building*, 12.

26 White, *Social Origins*, vol. 2, 123. There is no evidence indicating that the original occupants of the building were Christians; in other words, the Christian community here may have purchased the house outright immediately before performing the extensive renovations.

27 Ibid. See also Kraeling, *The Christian Building*, 5–7. See figure 4.1.

28 See, as a sample of the available scholarship: Jensen, *Understanding Early Christian Art*, throughout, but especially 70, 87–8; Kraeling, *Christian Building*, 45–88; Serra, "The Baptistery at Dura-Europos"; Wharton, *Refiguring the Post Classical City*, 51–63; White, *Social Origins*, vol. 2, 128–9.

29 The figure of a shepherd, bearing a sheep or ram (*kriophoros*), was common in ancient art, but grew especially popular in association with early Christian art. There are many examples of the shepherd figure in the catacombs, for example. There is some debate as to the identification of the figure; it was once assumed that the shepherd represented Jesus, on the basis of John 10:1–21, sometimes bearing eschatological overtones (for example, see Kraeling, *Christian Building*, 213–15). Recent scholarship, however, has suggested that shepherd imagery cannot always be assumed to represent Jesus; indeed, the *kriophoros* symbol continued after the first century CE, and the figure of Orpheus, too, is heavily indicated by the presence of a shepherd figure. Thus, a shepherd is not always "The Good Shepherd," and burials cannot always be identified as Christian on the basis of a shepherd figure or symbol. See Jensen, *Understanding Early Christian Art*, 37–41; Snyder, *Ante Pacem*, 43–5; Wharton, *Refiguring*, 53.

30 Kraeling reads Room 5 as a preparatory chamber for baptizands, based on the connection (via formal doorway) between Rooms 5 and 6. He also suggests, however, that the room could have been used to house the women of the community. In both cases, he notes the apotropaic devices surrounding Room 5, which will be discussed below. See Kraeling, *Christian Building*, 151–5.

31 See chapter 5, below, for an overview of related purification and preparatory rituals.

32 White, *Social Origins*, vol. 2, 128.

33 Kraeling, *Christian Building*, 15.

34 Kilde has suggested that the *bema* represents a growing separation between the clergy and the lay persons in the early Christian communities, and that it also provided visual separation between the two groups in the *domus ecclesiae*. See Kilde, *Sacred Power*, 24–5.

35 Adjacent to this platform was a small plaster socket, the function of which is not known, but which may have housed a stand (as suggested by White) or a cathedra (less likely, according to White). See White, *Social Origins*, vol. 2, 128.

36 Kraeling suggests that the audience would have sat on the floor of the assembly hall while the teacher spoke from the *bema* at the front of the room (*Christian Building*, 143). He also claims that, should the congregants have used reed mats, the assembly hall could have accommodated between sixty-five and seventy-five people (19).

37 Kraeling suggests that the *agape* could have been held in Room 5, though he does not find the suggestion especially compelling, especially given the lack of kitchen facilities (*Christian Building*, 151–2).

38 Ibid., 16.

39 In recent photographs, the section of frieze is no longer *in sitù*; it can be seen, however, in the original photographs from the published field reports (Kraeling, *Christian Building*, plate VI).

40 Ibid., 23.

41 Ibid.

42 Whether a portion of the frieze remained on the east wall is speculative; the only fragment was found on the north wall.

43 The only image available is one taken from a distance, showing the frieze *in sitù* on the wall of the house (Kraeling, *Christian Building*, plate VIa, as above). Other bacchic friezes from around the same area in Dura Europos are provided in detail images by way of comparison (plate VIb,c).

44 White, *Social Origins*, vol. 2, 130; see also Snyder, *Ante Pacem*, 132.

45 Kilde, *Sacred Power*, 28.

46 Ibid., 29. Here she is speaking specifically of the distinctly Christian decoration in the baptistery.

47 Kilde also notes the didactic nature of the baptistery paintings (ibid., 32).

48 Ibid., 24.

49 Hypotheses presented (and rejected) by Kilde include that the unornamented assembly hall could have acted as a cover for the Christian building, should it have been subjected to searches (ibid., 33); she rejects this suggestion on the grounds that there is no evidence of persecution at Dura. One might also note that, should a search have been carried out, the baptistery would hardly have been kept secret, being adjacent to and accessible from the central courtyard.

50 Ibid.

51 Ibid.

52 Discussions of ritual, sanctity, and the gradations of sanctity follow in the coming chapters.

53 Pfordresher, *Jesus and the Emergence of a Catholic Imagination*, 126.

54 Balch, *Roman Domestic Art*; see especially chapters 2 and 3.

55 Ibid., 84–108. He discusses, among other examples, the suffering of Isis or Io as a potential counterpart to the suffering of Christ.

56 Kraeling, *Christian Building*, 144.

57 Ibid., 145.

58 His point of comparison here, of course, is the heavily decorated hall in the neighbouring Durene synagogue.

59 Snyder, *Ante Pacem*, 132.
60 Balch and Osiek, *Families*, 35; italics mine.
61 White, *Social Origins*, vol. 2, 130.
62 Ibid., 130–1.
63 Wharton, *Refiguring*, 61.
64 Kraeling, *Christian Building*, 141.
65 Ibid., 142.
66 This assertion, that rituals are an important part of the process of sacred placemaking, will be discussed in detail in the following chapter.
67 Michael Peppard offers another intriguing example of "foreign" elements in the assembly hall – namely, the presence of graffiti depicting mounted (Persian?) riders. While recognizing the difficulty in dating these graffiti, he points out that their presence in the assembly hall, where the all-important ritual of the Eucharist was celebrated, is puzzling (*World's Oldest Church*, 79–80).
68 The medallion's figure is similar to other female figures found at Dura, usually in a funerary context (Kraeling, *Christian Building*, 32). While the medallion does not necessarily conform to a funerary context, it should be seen as the depiction of an actual person, as opposed to a goddess.
69 Kraeling, *Christian Building*, 31–2; plate XVI, 3.
70 Ibid., 32.
71 Ibid., 31.
72 Ibid. Interestingly, Kraeling rejects out of hand the possibility that the terracottas were given new status by the Christians, saying "it is quite as unlikely as to suppose that the plaster moulding with the bacchic symbols preserved on the north wall of the Assembly Hall was left in place because it was endowed by the Christians with new meaning" (ibid.).
73 Ibid., 32.
74 Ibid., 21.
75 Ibid. The neighbouring synagogue, for example, had a number of apotropaic images embedded in its roof tiles, including eyes and gorgon heads, typically polytheistic but universally apotropaic figures.
76 Ibid., 153. He suggests that the room served as the *exorcisterium* or *pistikon* of the assembly, a function which would certainly be aided by the presence of apotropaic devices.
77 Ibid., 12.
78 See White, *Social Origins*, vol. 2, for many examples of adapted structures after Dura.
79 See Kilde, above, for example, concerning the hierarchization of clergy persons at Dura.

80 Balch's work on domestic art in the house churches underscores the prevalence of wall paintings in upper-class homes of the ancient Mediterranean; see especially *Roman Domestic Art*, 28–9.

81 Meates, *Roman Villa*, vol. 1: *The Site*; Meates, *Roman Villa*, vol. 2: *Wall Paintings and Finds*.

82 See White, *Social Origins*, vol. 2, 245–57.

83 Kim Bowes's book, *Private Worship, Public Values*, is a notable exception here. She discusses Lullingstone at some length, along with other hybrid places of worship. Her focus, however, is on the relationship between private, rural, and estate churches with the orthodox church, focused in the urban centres of the Empire. Her chronological focus is also much later, with the fourth-century data being the earliest.

84 Meates, *Roman Villa*, vol. 1, 24.

85 It has been argued that this owner was in fact Pertinax, governor of Britain and brief, ill-fated emperor after the assassination of Commodus. This argument is based on the tentative identification of two marble busts found in the house, discussed below. See Henig, "Victory-Gem"; de Kind, on the reidentification of the marble busts: "Roman Portraits from the Villa of Lullingstone."

86 Meates, *Roman Villa*, vol. 1, 119. White also suggests the possibility of an absentee owner in the later stages (*Social Origins*, vol. 2, 253).

87 Meates suggested that these figures could have been members of the family that lived in the villa (*Roman Villa*, vol. 2, 14–17).

88 See reconstructions of both the *orans* figures and the *chi-rho* monograms in ibid., vol. 1, 52–4; vol. 2, 34–7; plates 11–15.

89 Here the description follows the reports of ibid., vols. 1 and 2.

90 For a detailed explanation of the loading docks and wooden platforms, as well as the staircase complex, see ibid., vol. 1, 27–31.

91 See plates 4 and 5 in ibid., vol. 2.

92 This and all other building and renovation dates are taken from ibid., vol. 1; Meates bases his chronology on coins and pottery (35–7).

93 Ibid., 35. Interestingly, White suggests that the nymphaeum may have been in use until the final stage of occupation (*Social Origins*, vol. 2, 254). This is contra Meates, who notes that the niche in the nymphaeum was turned into a shelf, likely signifying the end of ritual activity related to the "water spirits" (*Roman Villa*, vol. 1, 33).

94 Meates, *Roman Villa*, vol. 1, 36. Note that Meates also allows for the deposit of one of these bowls in the late second century.

95 The ancestor cult was at least as important as the cult of the *Lares*, especially in the homes of aristocratic Romans. Certainly the ancestor cult had protective functions, just as the *Lares* and *Penates* did; keeping the ancestors satisfied and well-maintained meant that they would protect the home

from malicious spirits, as discussed above, in chapter 3, 59–60. Conversely, of course, refusal to maintain the ancestor cult and to offer the appropriate sacrifices could result in severe consequences for the family, either through harmful actions taken by spurned ancestral spirits, or, perhaps more importantly, through a loss of status.

96 Based on numismatic evidence, Meates actually dates the second deposit to around the same time that the chapel was constructed (ca. 360/85); a coin dated between 345–61 was found in a depression containing one of the pots. He states, "Indeed, when the house-church was erected, two further votive pots were added in the Deep Room for continued pagan ritual purposes. We have here an example of pagan and Christian worship running parallel" (*Roman Villa*, vol. 1, 18).

97 Meates makes an explicit connection between the *manes* of the busts and their continued worship, "right up to the time of final destruction by fire sometime in the early years of the fifth century" (ibid., 39).

98 Also of interest is a small block which was found placed in front of the busts, with a well inside; Meates suggests that it may have been used as a "cresset, with a wick lying in an oil bath … a ritual light might thus have been kept burning before the busts, replenished with oil from time to time" (ibid., 40). Bowes notes the connection between lamplighting and ritual activity in Greek, Roman, and early Christian practice; it is compelling that these lamps, often used as "accompaniment to those particular rituals of family members," were placed before the ancestor busts ("At Home," 216).

99 See Meates, *Roman Villa*, vol. 1, 36: "No entrance from the exterior now remained except possibly by means of the suggested high-level aperture in the centre of its east wall."

100 Ibid.

101 Meates notes that the well was in continuous use until the final stages; access, therefore, must have been possible up to the final occupation of the villa, despite fire having removed any traces of how it would have been achieved. Importantly, he also notes that the well in fact showed signs of repair and ongoing maintenance in the late third century, around the same time that the busts were deposited (ibid., 37).

102 Ibid., 74.

103 Ibid., 85–8.

104 Ibid., 88.

105 Meates prefers to interpret the burial as that of "the workers and menials rather than the owner and his family" (ibid.).

106 Bowes states: "For the dating of the pagan shrine in the cellar, Meates ed. 1979, 38–9, whose adherence to very tight, coin-based chronologies suggested that pagan shrine and Christian chapel overlapped in function.

However, given the relatively broad possible dates for the church and shrine, this remains only a possibility" (*Private Worship, Public Values*, 268n30).

107 Indeed, Meates suggests that the well in the Deep Room may have been the locus for or the source of baptismal water (*Roman Villa*, vol. 1, 39).

108 One could also note that, given the position of Christianity in Roman Britain, we might expect to see a time lag before the developments brought about by Constantine (especially with regard to architecture) really begin to show. Indeed, in Britain, as well as other western provinces (Gaul, Hispania), large-scale building programmes were executed much later than in Rome and the East.

CHAPTER FIVE

1 The story of Eutychus in Acts 20, discussed above, paints a picture of a room packed over capacity.

2 In order to avoid wading into the hotly contested debate about eucharistic origins, or the distinction between *agape* and eucharist as two separate ritual events, I will instead refer to the events of sharing food and drink as "eucharistic meals," following the terminology used by Andrew McGowan (see "Rethinking," 178). I will return briefly to this debate and my choice of terminology concerning the shared meals of the early Christian communities in the section below on eucharistic meals.

3 The rituals of early Christianity certainly changed and developed over the course of the house-church period. This discussion, however, focuses on the placement of these rituals, rather than their origins and development.

4 Chapter 6 will discuss further the essential nature of the gathering in terms of carving out ritual space.

5 Early Christian conceptions of the body of believers as sacred space will be discussed further in chapter 6.

6 See especially Bradshaw, *Search for the Origins of Christian Worship*, and in particular 118–43; Bradshaw, *Eucharistic Origins*; McGowan, "Rethinking." Other discussions of the eucharist and the *agape* meal include Theissen, *Social Setting*, 145–74, 118–43; Smith, *From Symposium to Eucharist*, 173–218; Stringer, *Rethinking the Origins of the Eucharist*; and McGowan, *Ancient Christian Worship*, 31–2.

7 Balch and Osiek, *Families*, 34–7.

8 Ibid., 35.

9 The term "Lord's Supper" is also used, especially by Paul, as will be discussed below.

10 Kloppenborg, "Collegia and *Thiasoi*," 19–22; Stephen Wilson, "Voluntary Associations," 4; Harland, *Dynamics of Identity*, 161–76 (on "transgressive banquets"); Harland, *Associations, Synagogues, and Congregations*, 74–80; Taussig, *In the Beginning was the Meal*, 34.

11 Dunbabin, *Roman Banquet*, 36–71.

12 See also Varro, *Rerum Rusticum* 3.13, on place settings and arrangement at Roman tables.

13 The question of egalitarianism or hierarchy at the banquet table is not the central focus of this chapter, and the discussion of this question will therefore be kept to a minimum.

14 The question of whether or not the Corinthians engaged in a more conventional layout for their eucharistic meals is directly related to the issue of space. If the community adhered strictly to the rules for dining, it would have a direct effect on the number of diners who could participate, which would in turn have an effect on the total size of the group as imagined in the Corinthian house church. The size of the house-church communities, and the connection to the celebration of the meal, will be discussed below.

15 Tertullian's argument is not that they do not participate in banquets, but that they are not guilty of much greater offences. The Christians were occasionally accused of cannibalism, orgies, and other highly improbable acts, although they were not the only group to suffer these characterizations. The same accusations were levelled against mystery cult adherents, especially those affiliated with the bacchic rites. See Harland, *Dynamics of Identity*, 161–76. This type of criticism, of course, was quite common and ought not to be believed. Indeed, Pliny, for example, does not believe them, and says as much in his correspondence with Trajan: "it was their custom to depart and to assemble again to partake of food, but food of an ordinary kind and harmless" (Pliny the Younger, *Ep*. 10.96.7). Calling the food harmless makes it clear that the governor does not believe the accusations of cannibalism which were probably being levelled against the Christians in his community. Pliny's correspondence with Trajan also shows that he is aware of the general order of things in a Christian meeting.

16 Tertullian singles out for criticism the Salii, the banquets in honour of Hercules, the celebration of the Dionysiac mysteries, and the dinners of Serapis.

17 To the reader, the distinction between *agape* and *eros* would have or should have been clear.

18 Tertullian says, "We do not take our places [*discumbitur*] at table until we have first tasted prayer to God" (39.18). Note that the verb *discumbere* means "to lie down, to recline, to recline at table," thereby indicating that, in

Tertullian's mind at least, the meal is shared in a typical banqueting style – that is, with the members of the group reclining at the table. Trans. White, *Social Origins*, vol. 2, 54–5.

19 It could be argued that the image of the banquet as presented by Tertullian is perhaps more akin to a philosophical symposium than a cult banquet, which lends respectability to the event. In symposia, the second half of the banquet is generally composed of recitations, readings, and dialogues, much like Tertullian's description of the *agape*. See Smith, *Symposium to Eucharist*, 47–66, for a discussion of the philosophical banquet as a potential model for the *agape* meal.

20 Trans. White, *Social Origins*, vol. 2, 39. White, among others, has dated the martyrdom of Ignatius to ca. 110 CE. However, a more recent article by Barnes, "Date of Ignatius," dates Ignatius to the reign of Antoninus Pius or, more specifically, to the 140s.

21 Trans. White, *Social Origins*, vol. 2, 37.

22 Ibid., 41.

23 Balch and Osiek, *Families*, 35.

24 See the discussion of the space above the baths in chapter 2, above.

25 There is a distinction made here between host and bishop or other ecclesiastical officer; the latter are mentioned by title throughout the *Apostolic Tradition* of Hippolytus, and therefore, if the bishop were meant, there would be no need to use "host" where "bishop" would do. That the host is not necessarily a church official is made clearer in 28.6, where the assembly and its host are given different rules of behaviour for meetings taking place in the absence of a bishop.

26 The act of ritual demarcation will be discussed in detail below, in chapter 6.

27 David Balch, for example, in his article, "Rich Pompeiian Houses," claims that large Pompeian houses "could have accommodated numbers far greater than 40 persons" (41). He assumes here that a larger house would automatically have increased the number of participants in the rituals, but of course, the *agape* would present a problem here. A triclinium did not necessarily grow exponentially with the size of its domus. Balch is positing larger numbers here in contrast to Murphy O'Connor (*St. Paul's Corinth*, 156). Neilsen has suggested an average of ten to twenty people, with an outside estimate of thirty to forty, if a larger hall or courtyard were available ("Housing the Chosen," 184). On the subject of large numbers, see also Green, *Christianity in Ancient Rome*, 33n118: "The objection that sixty people could not meet in one house is easily countered by the observation that Prisca and Aquila ran a business – tent making – and might have had a warehouse or workshop where a large group could convene." This statement could be convincing

if the assembly did not involve a shared meal, but a warehouse or workshop (the existence of which is dubious in the first place) would not have dining facilities, and even if it did, dining facilities for sixty people is quite demanding. This assumption of Green's is also based on the idea that Prisca and Aquila would have been very successful indeed. Ostia, for example, has a number of *horrea* (large warehouses), but the largest ones seem to have been imperial storehouses. See Bakker, "The Store Buildings (*horrea*)," www.ostia-antica.org/dict/topics/horrea/intro.htm, accessed 10 August 2011.

28 See, for example, McCready, "Ekklesia and Voluntary Associations"; Harland, *Associations*, especially 55–88; Harland, *Dynamics of Identity*, 161–81.

29 Harland, *Dynamics of Identity*, 161–76.

30 Dunbabin, "Triclinium and Stibadium," 125. Dunbabin notes that the couches in the Caseggiato dei Triclinia are laid out in standard fashion, but are much larger than usual, being five or six metres long on each side. Dunbabin asserts that these larger couches would have accommodated as many as six per couch, putting the *triclinia* at eighteen diners each. This caseggiato, of course, also has multiple *triclinia*, as it was likely used as a guild-hall. Again, however, this setup is highly unlikely in a domestic space, and the Christians would not have had access to this specialized architecture, designed and executed purely with the purpose of accommodating large banquets.

31 Harland, *Associations*, 107–12.

32 Dennis Smith, for example, has argued that men and women, masters and slaves, rich and poor, would have been "included as full participants" in the communal meal (*Symposium to Eucharist*, 207). Annette Weissenrieder, "Contested Spaces," has also argued for a kind of communal approach to the shared meal, proposing that the Corinthians, at least, shared a seated, rather than a reclining meal, on the basis that the *ekklesia*, as a legal and social space (and, to some extent, a "pure" space), demanded a rejection of hierarchical meal organization. Since, she argues, the space of the *ekklesia* is structured by practice, and since the practice of the Corinthian group (at least as Paul would wish it to be) "is defined by the acts of serving one another," a seated meal would have been necessary (103). The subject of the constitution of sacred space (and the relationship between space and practice) will be discussed at length below. Here, though, it is worth pointing out that there may have been some communities who practised seated meals for reasons of equality, or perhaps due to available space (as below, with reference to *medianum* apartments).

33 Varro, in fact, states that the ideal number of diners for a party was three at a minimum, and nine at the maximum (for discussion see Smith, *Symposium*

to Eucharist, 25). Plutarch warns against large crowds at parties, saying that "great numbers … interfere with sociability and conversation" (*Quaest.Conv.* 679A-B; trans. Smith, *Symposium to Eucharist*, 25). Some dinner parties may have swelled to well beyond the ideal number. In terms of hierarchy, there was absolutely no issue with the hierarchical arrangement of diners in Roman society; in fact, every seat at the *triclinium* was arranged according to honour and status, and this ordering extended further to the seating of some diners on chairs rather than couches. Certainly Roman banquet hosts had no qualms about the inequality of slave service!

34 It is worth noting also that this "ideal" was perhaps not ideal at all. In the earliest days of the community, eschatological imminence precluded any major reworking of community rules or individual responsibilities. Later, hierarchical organization seemed to rule the day in all situations, including the episcopate (with its eventual culmination in papal and even imperial rule), and thus, discrepancies between members of the community might not have seemed so stark. It could be suggested that the Christians practised a kind of relative equality, wherein each member performed according to his or her station, and was treated fairly and responsibly by the other members. This proposition, too, reflects only an ideal. Again, the situation in 1 Corinthians 11 indicates that community members were indeed taking issue with what they perceived as unequal or unfair treatment.

35 Jewett, "Tenement Churches," 43–58.

36 Indeed, space was likely an issue for the Corinthian community, which was negotiating the tricky boundaries of rich and poor while they shared their *agape* meals.

37 For an excellent overview of the problems inherent in the interpretation of baptismal texts from Paul to the Acts of the Apostles to Tertullian, see Bradshaw, *Search for the Origins of Christian Worship*, 55–7, 59–61. For a discussion of the potential spaces of baptism before purpose-built baptisteries and fonts, see Jensen, "Archaeology of Christian Initiation," 255–6. Jensen notes that the outdoor spaces that likely dominated the earliest baptismal rituals were contemporary with other outdoor initiation rites, such as "Greco-Roman cultic purificatory baths" and some "ancient Jewish ritual baths" (255). As Jensen points out, the spaces of initiatory practices had some influence over the practitioners and initiates who used them, a point to which this discussion will return.

38 The date and provenance of the *Didache* are by no means clear. There is, however, a general consensus on at least a late first-century date (although some still argue for a mid-first century date), and the region of Syria in general.

For a good discussion of the problems with dating the *Didache*, as well as an extensive bibliography on the history of its provenance, see Draper, "The Apostolic Fathers."

39 The *Didache* does instruct believers not to allow those who have not been baptized to partake in the eucharist (*Didache* 9), which is of course an implicit recognition of baptism as a rite of initiation, but it is not described as such in the instructions themselves.

40 Trans. Rordorf, "Baptism According to the Didache," 212.

41 Jonathan Draper argues that purity outweighs the spiritual element of the rite, and that the focus is "on the ritual purity and therefore the purifying nature of the water" ("Apostolic Fathers," 179).

42 *Lavacrum* is the word used here; literally it means a bath. Trans. Roberts and Donaldson, *The Ante-Nicene Fathers*, vol. 3, 669.

43 Trans. White, *Social Origins*, vol. 2, 41.

44 There are a number of possible reasons for this externalization of the baptismal rite. They were most likely practical, in that the space for assembly simply did not have the appropriate resources for baptism. If this place of assembly were in fact an apartment above a bath complex, it would not be hard to believe that a font or an *impluvium* (if such things were even used in Justin's community) would be unavailable there. At the same time, this is perhaps part of the reason why it has been suggested that Justin's community baptized in the baths; it is clearly noted that the baptism is performed elsewhere. While the bath complex may have been a possibility, it is hard to imagine it occurring during busy bathing hours. It could also be that the baptism took place not in a different building, but in a different room. This possibility will be revisited when the layout and function of the rooms in the Christian building at Dura Europos are discussed.

45 Trans. White, *Social Origins*, vol. 2, 49. The dining room is often assumed to be the place of assembly in house churches, as discussed above.

46 Ibid., 50. It should be noted that this text is clearly Gnostic, but the function of the bread seems to be the same as in an orthodox context; that is, the eating of the bread is symbolic to the eating of the body of Christ, and this eating provides the believer with eternal life.

47 That the Christian building at Dura, discussed above, made a baptistery a priority is interesting, given the lack of focus on baptism's placement in these earlier texts.

48 Specifically, Paul refers to the Jerusalem Temple. For a recent excellent discussion on this subject, see Fredriksen, "Judaizing the Nations," especially 246–8. She also argues that this passage does not indicate a supersession of

the physical sanctity of the Jerusalem Temple by the "new spiritual 'temple' of the Christian community" (248). In other words, this passage need not be read as a rejection of sacred space by Paul.

49 Jorunn Økland has argued that the temple metaphor used by Paul is part of an elaborate ritual discourse, specifically referring to the Jerusalem Temple, operating in order to materialize the belief in God in the days of what must have seemed like placelessness. See her discussion in *Women in Their Place*, especially 154–65. She discusses the "replicability" of the Jerusalem Temple and argues that Paul uses metaphor to place this replicated space in the bodies of the believers. For Økland, the "ritual gathering" is the sanctuary, or sacred space (166). Thus, it is not only the body of believers but the specifically gathered and ritually ordered collective body that forms sacred space. The idea of a ritual body and ritually constructed sacred space is a point that will be emphasized below.

50 Paul's choice of *naos*, or temple, to describe the ideological structure of the body of believers is a powerful one, given the associations with sanctity in both the Jewish and the gentile communities. Interestingly, it is this very idea of temple that other commentators wholeheartedly reject, as will be discussed below.

51 See Økland, *Women in Their Place*, 143. Økland carries out a very helpful exploration of the distinction between *oikia* and *ekklesia*, and in the placing of Pauline (specifically, the Corinthian) gatherings in general. See ibid., 131–67.

52 Trans. Glover, LCL, 229–301.

53 The date range here follows White, *Social Origins*, vol. 2, 52. Yasin, *Saints and Church Spaces*, 18, dates this work to ca. 215.

54 Trans. White, *Social Origins*, vol. 2, 52.

55 Rejection of idols is explicitly mentioned here as well; the materials of idol statuary are read as empty and profane (*Stromata* 7.5).

56 See chapter 2, 25–6.

57 Trans. Chadwick, *Origen: Contra Celsum*, 432.

58 The example of Dura, of course, provides evidence that ritual and gathering places were becoming more formalized, and that permanent places were being used for meeting.

59 *Acts of Justin* 3.3; see above, chapter 2, 24.

60 This "new" architecture, of course, was the basilica form, adopted from the structures which housed the magistracies of Rome and her provinces. While the debate over the origins of Christian architecture is far from settled, there is a general consensus that the basilica model carried with it little of the baggage that traditional temple architecture did, and which was deemed unacceptable for Constantine's vision of Christianity. See Finney, "Early

Christian Architecture: the Beginnings"; Krautheimer, *Early Christian and Byzantine*, 41; White, *Social Origins*, vol. 1, 138–9.

61 Trans. White, *Social Origins*, vol. 2, 54.

62 It is not necessary to have purity regulations in order to have sacred space, of course; the exploration of sacred space and its characteristics will be discussed below.

63 Trans. White, *Social Origins*, vol. 2, 61.

64 Ibid., 53.

65 Ibid., 53n9.

66 See chapter 2, 25. Dating follows White, *Social Origins*, vol. 2, 44.

CHAPTER SIX

1 See the introduction, and the discussion of Harold Turner's work.

2 See, for example, the purification of the house used by Simon Magus in the Acts of Peter. On domestic codes, see the very helpful discussion, based on the Corinthian house-church model, in Økland, *Women in Their Place*, 137–43. Økland draws attention to *ekklesia* space, which is ritually constructed, and within which different rules of attire and behaviour apply. She asserts that, "within this space, there is a particular pattern of action and a particular place for everything following a cosmic order – but all this has to be spelled out by Paul since there are no walls or other material texts indicating it" (151). The ritual construction of space will be discussed in detail below.

3 Lewis and Short, *A Latin Dictionary*, s.v. "sacer." For a dramatic rendering of a person who has become detestable (*sacer*), see Plautus, *Bacchides*, 4.6.14.

4 The same could be true of persons as well. Most famously, any person in the Roman Republic who sought dictatorship could be declared *sacer*, or belonging to the gods, which meant that their death was not murder, but rather sacrifice performed for the good of the larger group. See Livy 2.8.2, in Beard, North, and Price, *Religions of Rome: A History*, 59.

5 Lewis and Short, *A Latin Dictionary*, s.v. "profanus."

6 Ibid. Examples of profanus as "wicked" come especially from Christian sources, including the *Octavius* of Minucius Felix (8) and Lactantius 6.23.10.

7 Despite this distinction, however, the fluidity of translation and interpretation in both terms, varying widely over time and source texts, demonstrates the gradations of intensity in the application of both terms. This gradation will be discussed further below.

8 Durkheim, *Elementary Forms*, 38.

9 Ibid., 221.

10 Ibid., 175–6.

11 Ibid., 12–14. He notes that "inherently, there is no right or left, above or below, north or south … All these distinctions evidently come from the different affective values attributed to these regions" (13).

12 Ibid., 13.

13 Ibid., 228–9.

14 Much of the original criticism of Eliade's work came from Jonathan Z. Smith. See "Wobbling Pivot" for an early and incisive critique of Eliade, especially with regard to his claim of an ontological sacred. See also *To Take Place*, 1–10.

15 Eliade, *Sacred and the Profane*.

16 Ibid., 20.

17 Ibid., 26.

18 It is predominantly this view (both ontological and theological in its suppositions) that has garnered the most criticism for his work. It is also this point on which Eliade's theories are most at odds with those of Émile Durkheim, despite their shared categorization of the sacred/profane as dichotomous.

19 Eliade, *Sacred and the Profane*, 26–7. The idea of a connection between underworld, earth, and heaven, is labelled here by Eliade the *axis mundi*.

20 Ibid., 21: "For it is the break effected in space that allows the world to be constituted, for it reveals the fixed point, the central axis for all future orientation."

21 Ibid., 23.

22 Ibid., 27.

23 Ibid., 29.

24 Ibid., 32.

25 Ibid., 43.

26 Ibid., 29–30.

27 Smith, *To Take Place*, 40.

28 Ibid., 41.

29 The essential relationship between ritual and sacred space will be discussed in detail below.

30 Judith Lieu also discusses the difference between ideology and practice. She states, "Perhaps it is better to recognize that in any society there is an interplay between ideal standards and actual behaviour, but that the latter is not necessarily to be seen simply as a falling away from the former" (*Christian Identity*, 159).

31 Smith, *To Take Place*, 41.

32 Ibid., 42.

33 Chidester and Linenthal, "Introduction," 6.

34 The work of Eliade, for example, with its irruptions and hierophanies, may work well within a self-referential system, such as Christianity, but breaks

down in cross-cultural application, where there may not be a close relationship with a revelatory deity.

35 Chidester and Linenthal, "Introduction," 9.

36 Ibid. This view is consistent with that of Jonathan Z. Smith, which will be discussed further below.

37 Ibid., 12.

38 Ibid., 15. See also Michaelsen, "Dirt in the Court Room."

39 Chidester and Linenthal, "Introduction," 15.

40 Smith, *To Take Place*, 103.

41 Chidester and Linenthal, "Introduction," 15.

42 Again, it is the role and process of ritual which is key in implementing difference and ownership.

43 Van Gennep, *The Rites of Passage*, 12. The pivoting of the sacred and its significance will be discussed in further detail below.

44 Chidester and Linenthal, "Introduction," 14.

45 Many temple precincts had graded levels of access, but some dramatic examples can be found in the Greek sanctuary to Asklepios on Kos, and the early Roman temple-theatre complex to Fortuna at Praeneste.

46 Chidester and Linenthal, "Introduction," 13.

47 See Branham, "Bloody Women"; Cohen, "Menstruants and the Sacred," 277; Fonrobert, *Menstrual Purity*, 168.

48 Jonathan Z. Smith argues for a gradation of sanctity in the temple as described by Ezekiel and a parallel hierarchy of political power in the Israelite community; Smith, *To Take Place*, 56–65.

49 See Corbett, "Greek Temples and Greek Worshippers." He notes here the range of access in Greek temples, including the Temple of Apollo at Delphi, among others. It should be noted that, even in those temples where access to the cult statue was open to worshippers, there were nearly always rooms of preparation for ritual and sacrifice, accessible only to members of the priesthood (see, for example, the ground plan of the Parthenon).

50 See Cooper, "Closely Watched Households," 25.

51 Casey, "How to Get from Space to Place," 17.

52 Ibid., 19.

53 Tuan, *Space and Place*, 11–12. Cf. Durkheim, *Elementary Forms*, 13; *supra* 186n19.

54 De Certeau, *Practice of Everyday Life*, 96.

55 Ibid., 98.

56 Casey, "How to Get from Space to Place," 21; italics original.

57 "In fact, the races of Italy are the most perfectly constituted in both respects – in bodily form and in mental activity to correspond to their valour. Exactly as

the planet Jupiter is itself temperate, its course lying midway between Mars, which is very hot, and Saturn, which is very cold, so Italy, lying between the north and the south, is a combination of what is found on each side, and her preeminence is well regulated and indisputable. And so by her wisdom she breaks the courageous onsets of the barbarians, and by her strength of hand thwarts the devices of the southerners. Hence, it was the divine intelligence that set the city of the Roman people in a peerless and temperate country, in order that it might acquire the right to command the whole world" (6.1.11 LCL). A similar argument is made by Aristotle in the *Politics* 1327b.23–33, which justifies the right of the Greek to dominate the non-Greek on the basis of environmental theories.

58 Tuan, *Space and Place*, 17.

59 Ibid., 88. Mythical space (or sacred space) is, for Tuan, an outgrowth of this cosmic anthropocentrism. Tuan's argument is also focused on the difference between space and place, a debate which will not be entered here. In short, however, Tuan views space as something out of which place is created, and that this creation of place is done through the levying of experience and the sedimentation of memory. In other words, place is familiar, tangible, and oriented space. See especially his section on mythical space (85–100).

60 Tuan notes that mythical space is an intellectual construct, a "response of feeling and imagination to fundamental human needs" (ibid., 99).

61 Sanders, "Behavioral Conventions and Archaeology," 44.

62 Casey, "How to Get from Space to Place," 24; italics original.

63 Ibid., 23.

64 De Certeau, *Practice of Everyday Life*, 98.

65 Casey, "How to Get from Space to Place," 24.

66 Ibid.

67 The aristocratic Roman house, as described in chapter 2, had a highly functional layout, connected specifically to the tasks which needed to be performed by an elite member of Roman society. See chapter 2, 37–43.

68 Økland, *Women in Their Place*, 142–3; 166.

69 As will be emphasized below, the preexistent place of the Roman house and its impact on Christian bodies included and was heavily conditioned by the domestic cult.

70 Jonathan Z. Smith's work, *To Take Place*, is a notable exception.

71 See, for example, McGowan, *Ascetic Eucharists*, 1–32; Meeks, *First Urban Christians*, 150–62. On the problems of determining identity through practice, and the possibility of multiple identities, see Harland, *Dynamics of Identity*, 145–60; Lieu, *Christian Identity*, 147–77.

72 Bell, *Ritual Theory, Ritual Practice*. Her more recent volume, *Ritual: Perspectives and Dimensions*, further develops her earlier ideas of practice theory, but also provides an updated and invaluable resource for the dominant theorists of ritual in the past 150 years or so. See especially 3–89.

73 Bell, *Ritual Perspectives*, 2.

74 For Bell's comments on the essentialist schools of thought, as well as the myth and ritual school, see ibid., 3–10. For her discussion of Eliade, including his claim that ritual repetition is a repetition of the primordial or cosmogonic myth (as above, in the discussion of his theory of sacred space), see ibid., 10–12.

75 Ibid., 93–137.

76 Ibid., 138.

77 Ibid., 164.

78 Van Gennep, *Rites of Passage*, 12.

79 Ibid.

80 Durkheim, *Elementary Forms*, 221.

81 Bell, *Ritual Perspectives*, 37.

82 Victor Turner, in *Forest of Symbols*, developed van Gennep's theories further, especially his tripartite ritual structure of separation, testing, and return (with the all-important liminal state being the testing ground). His theories, like van Gennep's, have to do with society and especially, the subversion of hierarchies and categories within it, rather than the relationship between ritual and space, but they also provide valuable insight into the idea of ritual as having an active role. Turner argues that ritual takes the real and dramatizes it and in doing so, actually performs the necessary function. For example, the separation of a young tribesman from his community is what makes him a man, which is the form in which he returns to his community (*Forest of Symbols*, 93–111). As Bell acknowledges, it is Turner's work that propelled a new mode of thinking about ritual as performance, thus giving rise to performance theory in ritual (*Ritual Perspectives*, 42).

83 Van Gennep, *Rites of Passage*, 15–25.

84 Ibid., 13.

85 This reasoning is consistent with Hubert and Mauss, who note in their work, *Sacrifice: Its Nature and Functions*, 96, that the profane becomes sacred and vice versa through the ritual of sacrifice, and that the end of the sacrificial ritual brings with it desacralization.

86 Bell, *Ritual Perspectives*, 74.

87 Ibid.

88 Ibid.

89 Ibid.

90 As will be discussed below, the contradictions inherent in Christian practice in a place normally associated with polytheistic practice are reconciled through the performance of Christian ritual "events."

91 Bell, *Ritual Perspectives*, 73.

92 Ibid.

93 See above, chapter 3, 57.

94 See also Harrill, "Coming of Age and Putting on Christ," 252.

95 Bell, *Ritual Perspectives*, 76. Compare this view to that of de Certeau, above, concerning the interaction between bodies and spaces.

96 Ibid.

97 An example of ritual subversion or reversal is the Roman festival the *Saturnalia*, wherein slaves and masters swap roles. This festival, while affording the slaves some freedom (including, at times, the right to whip their masters), it in fact upholds the structure of Roman society through the recognition that all will be set to rights once the festival has ended. Presumably, only the bravest (and perhaps most foolish) of slaves would have risked their future comfort by engaging in the whipping of their master or mistress, and even if they did, it would clearly be with his or her permission. See Rawson, "Celebrating the Saturnalia," chapter 29.

98 The idea of *habitus* was discussed previously by Mauss, "Techniques of the Body"; and Weber, *The Sociology of Religion*, 158–9. See Bell, *Ritual Perspectives*, 285n77, for a complete bibliography of the history of the term.

99 Bourdieu, *Outline of a Theory of Practice*, 78–9.

100 Bell, *Ritual Perspectives*, 78.

101 By the same token, the practices of the domestic cult were also powerful, because they upheld through their enactment the fabric of Roman society.

102 Bell, *Ritual Perspectives*, 81.

103 The relationship between ritual and the creation of place or sacred space will be discussed in greater detail below, in conversation with Jonathan Z. Smith's work, *To Take Place*.

104 As will become apparent, while Smith specifically engages the relationship between place and ritual, his model works best when applied to purpose-built structures; some interpretive leaps are necessary to apply his ritual theory to house-church space.

105 Smith, *To Take Place*, 45; italics original.

106 Ibid., 83–4.

107 Ibid., 83.

108 Ibid., 84.

109 Ibid., 103.
110 Edward Casey notes a similar function of place, stating that "places also gather experiences and histories, even languages and thoughts … the power belongs to place itself, and it is a power of gathering" ("How to get from Space to Place," 24–5). As bounded space, place is the locus for gathering and holding attention.
111 Smith, *To Take Place*, 103.
112 Ibid., 109.
113 Ibid.
114 Ibid.
115 Ibid., 104.
116 Ibid., 105.
117 Ibid., 91–4.
118 Ibid., 90.
119 Ibid., 92.
120 Ibid., 94.
121 Ibid.
122 Ibid., 95.
123 Casey, "How to Get from Space to Place," 19.
124 Later, of course, the *tituli* would become permanent sacred places, and claim their status via the sedimentation of use as house churches. Archaeologically, however, there is no evidence that any specific *tituli* were in fact in use before the third or fourth century. See Krautheimer, *Early Christian and Byzantine*, 2–12; Lampe, *Paul to Valentinus*, 302–7; Petersen, "House Churches of Rome," 267. See above, chapter 1.
125 The argument for the supersession of so-called belief-based religion over polytheistic ritual has also been suggested as an explanation for the rise of mystery cults in the second century and after. See Stark, "Religious Competition and Roman Piety."
126 Bourdieu, *Outline*, 78–9.
127 Ibid., 79.
128 Ibid.
129 Ibid. This does not mean, however, that the agent has no control over his or her own actions. Bourdieu allows for subjectivity (if not individuality) in an agent, but argues that "personal style, the particular stamp marking all the products of the same habitus … is never more than a *deviation* in relation to the *style* of a period or class so that it relates back to the common style not only by its conformity … but also by the difference" (ibid., 86). This has interesting implications for the study of church leadership; even if a *pater*

were to discontinue his usual ritual practice, or to change it in a way suitable to early Christianity, his position in society would demand some outlet for his disposition of religious arbiter in the home.

130 Bell, *Ritual Theory*, 183.

131 Bourdieu, *Outline*, 79.

132 See also the argument above, chapter 3, 72–6, concerning the material presence of the domestic cult, and the difficulty of removing permanent shrines and wall paintings.

Bibliography

Adams, Edward. "The Ancient Church at Megiddo: The Discovery and an Assessment of its Significance." *The Expository Times* 120, no. 2 (2008): 62–9.

– *The Earliest Christian Meeting Places: Almost Exclusively Houses?* London: Bloomsbury, 2013.

– "Placing the Corinthian Meal." In *Text, Image, and Christians in the Graeco-Roman World: A Festschrift in Honor of David Lee Balch*, edited by Aliou Cissé Niang and Carolyn Osiek, 22–37. Eugene: Pickwick Publications, 2012.

Allison, Penelope M. "Labels for Ladles: Interpreting the Material Culture of Roman Households." In *The Archaeology of Household Activities*, edited by Penelope M. Allison, 57–77. London: Routledge, 1999.

Ascough, Richard S. *Paul's Macedonian Associations*. Tübingen: Mohr Siebeck, 2003.

Bakker, Jan Theo. "Caserma dei Vigili (II,V,1–2)." Ostia Antica. Last modified 7 September 2007. http://www.ostia-antica.org/regio2/5/5–1.htm.

– *Living and Working With the Gods: Studies of Evidence for Private Religion and its Material Environment in the City of Ostia (100–500 AD)*. Amsterdam: Gieben, 1994.

– "Regio I – Insula III – Caseggiato di Diana (I,III,3–4)." Ostia Antica. Last modified 4 April 2004. http://www.ostia-antica.org/regio1/3/3–3.htm.

– "Regio IV – Insula V – Caseggiato del Sacello (IV,V,4)." Ostia Antica. Last modified 12 November 2005. http://www.ostia-antica.org/regio4/5/5-4.htm.

– "The Store Buildings (*horrea*)." Ostia Antica. Last modified 28 May 2005. www.ostia-antica.org/dict/topics/horrea/intro.htm.

– "Topographical Dictionary: Houses and Apartments." Ostia Antica. Last modified 4 October 1999. http://www.ostia-antica.org/dict/topics/houses/houses.htm.

Balch, David. "Rich Pompeiian Houses, Shops for Rent, and the Huge Apartment Building in Herculaneum as Typical Spaces for Pauline House Churches." *Journal for the Study of the New Testament* 27, no. 1 (2004): 27–46.

– *Roman Domestic Art and Early House Churches*. Tübingen: Mohr Siebeck, 2008.

Balch, David L., and Carolyn Osiek. *Families in the New Testament World: Households and House Churches*. Louisville: Westminster John Knox Press, 1997.

Baldwin, Matthew C. *Whose Acts of Peter?* Tübingen: Mohr Siebeck, 2005.

Barnes, T.D. "The Date of Ignatius." *The Expository Times* 120, no. 3 (2008): 119–30.

Beard, Mary. "The Sexual Status of Vestal Virgins." *The Journal of Roman Studies* 70 (1980): 12–27.

Beard, Mary, John North, and Simon Price. *Religions of Rome: A History*. Cambridge: Cambridge University Press, 1998.

Beebe, H. Keith. "Ancient Palestinian Dwellings." *Biblical Archaeologist* 31, no. 2 (1968): 37–58.

Bell, Catherine. *Ritual: Perspectives and Dimensions*. Oxford: Oxford University Press, 1997.

– *Ritual Theory, Ritual Practice*. Oxford: Oxford University Press, 1992.

Bergman, Bettina. "The Roman House as Memory Theater: The House of the Tragic Poet in Pompeii." *The Art Bulletin* 76, no. 2 (1994): 225–56.

Billings, Bradly S. "From House Church to Tenement Church: Domestic Space and the Development of Early Urban Christianity - The Example of Ephesus." *Journal of Theological Studies* 62, no. 2 (2011): 541–79.

Bodel, John. "Cicero's Minerva, Penates, and the Mother of the Lares: An Outline of Roman Domestic Religion." In *Household and Family Religion in Antiquity: Contextual and Comparative Perspectives*, edited by John Bodel and Saul M. Olyan, 246–75. Oxford: Blackwell, 2008.

– "Dealing with the Dead: Undertakers, Executioners, and Potter's Fields in Ancient Rome." In *Death and Disease in the Ancient City*, edited by Eirann Marshall and Valerie Hope, 128–52. Routledge: London, 2000.

Bourdieu, Pierre. *Outline of a Theory of Practice*. Cambridge: Cambridge University Press, 1977.

Bowe, Barbara Ellen. *A Church in Crisis: Ecclesiology and Paraenesis in Clement of Rome*. Minneapolis: Fortress Press, 1988.

Bowes, Kim. "At Home." *A Companion to the Archaeology of Religion in the Ancient World*. Oxford: Wiley Blackwell, 2015.

– "'Christianization' and the Rural Home." *Journal of Early Christian Studies* 15, no. 2 (2007): 143–70.

– *Private Worship, Public Values, and Religious Change in Late Antiquity*. Cambridge: Cambridge University Press, 2008.

Boyce, George K. *Corpus of the Lararia of Pompeii*. Memoirs of the American Academy at Rome 14. Rome: American Academy, 1937.

– "Significance of the Serpents on Pompeian House Shrines." *American Journal of Archaeology* 46, no. 1 (1942): 13–22.

Bradley, Keith. "The Roman Child in Sickness and in Health." In *The Roman Family in the Empire: Rome, Italy, and Beyond*, edited by Michele George, 67–92. Oxford: Oxford University Press, 2005.

Bradshaw, Paul F. *Eucharistic Origins*. Oxford: Oxford University Press, 2004.

– *The Search for the Origins of Christian Worship: Sources and Methods for the Study of Early Liturgy*. Oxford: Oxford University Press, 2002.

Brandenburg, Hugo. *Ancient Churches of Rome from the Fourth to the Seventh Century: The Dawn of Christian Architecture in the West*. Belgium: Brepols Publishers, 2004.

Brändle, Rudolf, and Ekkehard W. Stegemann. "The Formation of the First 'Christian Congregations' in Rome in the Context of the Jewish Congregations." In *Judaism and Christianity in First-Century Rome*, edited by Karl P. Donfried and Peter Richardson, 117–27. Grand Rapids: Eerdmans, 1998.

Branham, Joan R. "Bloody Women, Bloody Spaces." *Harvard Divinity Bulletin* 30, no. 4 (2002): 15–22.

– "Sacred Space Under Erasure in Ancient Synagogues and Early Churches." *The Art Bulletin* 74, no. 3 (1992): 375–94.

Casey, Edward S. "How to Get from Space to Place in a Fairly Short Stretch of Time: Phenomenological Prolegomena." In *Senses of Place*, edited by Steven Feld and Keith H. Basso, 13–52. Santa Fe: School of American Research Press, 1996.

Chadwick, Henry. *Origen: Contra Celsum*. Cambridge: Cambridge University Press, 1953.

Chidester, David. *A Global History of Sacred Space*. San Francisco: Harper, 2000.

Chidester, David, and Edward T. Linenthal. "Introduction." In *American Sacred Space*, edited by David Chidester and Edward T. Linenthal, 1–42. Bloomington: Indiana University Press, 1995.

Clarke, John R. *Houses of Roman Italy, 100 B.C.–A.D. 250: Ritual, Space, and Decoration*. Berkeley: University of California Press, 1991.

Cohen, Shaye. "Menstruants and the Sacred in Judaism and Christianity." In *Women's History and Ancient History*, edited by Sarah B. Pomeroy. Chapel Hill: University of North Carolina Press, 1991.

Cohick, Lynn H. *Women in the World of the Earliest Christians: Illuminating Ancient Ways of Life*. Grand Rapids: Baker Academic, 2009.

Cooper, Kate. "Closely Watched Households: Visibility, Exposure, and Private Power in the Roman *Domus*." *Past and Present* 197, vol. 1 (2007): 3–33.

Corbett, P.E. "Greek Temples and Greek Worshippers: The Literary and Archaeological Evidence." *Bulletin of the Institute of Classical Studies, University of London* 17 (1970): 149–58.

Crook, Zeba. *Reconceptualizing Conversion: Patronage, Loyalty, and Conversion in the Religions of the Ancient Mediterranean. Beihefte zur Zeitschrift für die neutestamentliche Wissenschaft und die Kunde der älteren Kirche* 130. Berlin and New York: Walter de Gruyter, 2004.

Cumont, Franz. *The Oriental Religions in Roman Paganism*. New York: Dover Publications, 1956 [Open Court, 1911].

De Certeau, Michel. *The Practice of Everyday Life*. Berkeley: University of California Press, 1984.

De Jonge, H.J. "The Function of Religious Polemics: The Case of the Revelation of John versus the Imperial Cult." In *Religious Polemics in Context*, edited by T.L. Hettema and A. van der Kooij, 276–90. Leiden: Brill, 2005.

De Kind, Richard. "The Roman Portraits from the Villa of Lullingstone: Pertinax and His Father P. Helvius Successus." In *Otium: Festschrift für Volker Michael Strocka*, edited by T. Ganschow and M. Steinhart, 47–53. Remshalden: Greiner, 2005.

Dix, Gregory. *The Shape of the Liturgy*. Westminster: Dacre Press, 1945.

Dixon, Suzanne. *The Roman Family*. Baltimore, Johns Hopkins Press, 1992.

Douglas, Mary. *Purity and Danger: An Analysis of Concepts of Pollution and Taboo*. London: Routledge, 2002 [1966].

Draper, Jonathan A. "The Apostolic Fathers: The Didache." *The Expository Times* 117, no. 5 (2006): 177–81.

Dunbabin, Katherine. *The Roman Banquet: Images of Conviviality*. Cambridge: Cambridge University Press, 2003.

– "Triclinium and Stibadium." In *Dining in a Classical Context*, edited by W. J. Slater, 121–48. Ann Arbor: University of Michigan Press, 1991.

Durkheim, Émile. *The Elementary Forms of Religious Life*. Translated by Carol Cosman. Oxford: Oxford University Press, 2001.

Dwyer, Eugene. "The Pompeian Atrium House in Theory and in Practice." In *Roman Art in the Private Sphere: New Perspectives on the Architecture and Decor of the Domus, Villa, and Insula*, edited by Elaine K. Gazda with Anne Haeckl, 25–48. Ann Arbor: University of Michigan Press, 1991.

Eliade, Mircea. *The Sacred and the Profane: The Nature of Religion*. San Diego: Houghton Mifflin Harcourt, 1959.

Ellis, Simon. "Power, Architecture, and Décor: How the Late Roman Aristocrat Appeared to His Guests." In *Roman Art in the Private Sphere: New Perspectives on the Architecture and Decor of the Domus, Villa, and Insula*, edited by Elaine K. Gazda with Anne Haeckl, 117–34. Ann Arbor: University of Michigan Press, 1991.

– *Roman Housing*. London: Duckworth, 2000.

Fai, Stephen. "Body/Temple Metaphor: Early Christian Reconciliation with Roman Architecture." PhD diss., University of Ottawa, 2006.

Filson, Floyd V. "The Significance of Early House Churches." *Journal of Biblical Literature* 58 (1939): 109–12.

Finney, Paul Corby. "Early Christian Architecture: The Beginnings (A Review Article)." *Harvard Theological Review* 81, no. 3 (1988): 319–39.

Flower, Harriet I. *Ancestor Masks and Aristocratic Power in Roman Culture*. Oxford: Oxford University Press, 1996.

Fonrobert, Charlotte Elisheva. *Menstrual Purity: Rabbinic and Christian Reconstructions of Biblical Gender*. Stanford: Stanford University Press, 2000.

Foss, Pedar. "Watchful Lares: Roman Household Organization and the Rituals of Cooking and Dining." In *Domestic Space in the Roman World: Pompeii and Beyond*, edited by Ray Laurence and Andrew Wallace-Hadrill, 196–218. *Journal of Roman Archaeology* Supplementary Series 22. Portsmouth: Journal of Roman Archaeology, 1997.

Fredriksen, Paula. "Judaizing the Nations: The Ritual Demands of Paul's Gospel." *New Testament Studies* 56, no. 2 (2010): 232–52.

Frend, W.H.C. "Pagans, Christians, and 'The Barbarian Conspiracy' of A.D. 367 in Roman Britain." *Britannia* 23 (1992): 121–31.

Fröhlich, Thomas. *Lararien und Fassadenbilder in der Vesuvstädten: Untersuchungen zur volkstümlichen pompejanischen Malerei*. Römische Abteilung Ergänzungsheft 32. Mainz: Philip von Zabern, 1991.

Gardner, Jane F., and Thomas Wiedemann. *The Roman Household: A Sourcebook*. London: Routledge, 1991.

George, Michele. "Domestic Architecture and Household Relations: Pompeii and Roman Ephesos." *Journal for the Study of the New Testament* 27, no. 1 (2004): 7–25.

– "Repopulating the Roman House." In *The Roman Family in Italy: Status, Sentiment and Space*, edited by Beryl Rawson and Paul Weaver, 299–319. Oxford: Clarendon Press, 1997.

– "*Servus* and *Domus*: The Slave in the Roman House." In *Domestic Space in the Roman World: Pompeii and Beyond*, edited by Ray Laurence and Andrew Wallace-Hadrill, 15–24. *Journal of Roman Archaeology* Supplementary Series 22. Portsmouth: Journal of Roman Archaeology, 1997.

George, Michele, ed. *The Roman Family in the Empire: Rome, Italy, and Beyond*. Oxford: Oxford University Press, 2005.

Giacobello, Federica. *Larari pompeiani: Iconografia e culto dei Lari in ambito domestico*. Milan: LED Edizioni Universitarie, 2008.

Gradel, Ittai. *Emperor Worship and Roman Religion*. Oxford: Oxford University Press, 2002.

Graham, Emma-Jayne. *The Burial of the Urban Poor in Italy in the Late Roman Republic and Early Empire*. Biblical Archaeological Review International Series 1565. Oxford: Archaeopress, 2007.

Grahame, Mark. "Material Culture and Roman Identity: The Spatial Layout of Pompeian Houses and the Problem of Ethnicity." In *Cultural Identity in the*

Roman Empire, edited by Ray Laurence and Joanne Berry, 156–78. London: Routledge, 1998.

– "Public and Private in the Roman House: The Spatial Order of the *Casa del Fauno*." In *Domestic Space in the Roman World: Pompeii and Beyond*, edited by Ray Laurence and Andrew Wallace-Hadrill, 137–64. *Journal of Roman Archaeology* Supplementary Series 22. Portsmouth: Journal of Roman Archaeology, 1997.

Green, Bernard. *Christianity in Ancient Rome: The First Three Centuries*. New York: T & T Clark, 2010.

Hackworth Petersen, Lauren. *The Freedman in Roman Art and Art History*. Cambridge: Cambridge University Press, 2006.

Hales, Shelley. *The Roman House and Social Identity*. Cambridge: Cambridge University Press, 2003.

Harland, Philip A. *Associations, Synagogues, and Congregations: Claiming a Place in Ancient Mediterranean Society*. Minneapolis: Fortress Press, 2003.

– *Dynamics of Identity in the World of the Early Christians: Associations, Judeans, and Cultural Minorities*. London: T & T Clark, 2009.

Harmon, Daniel P. "The Family Festivals of Rome." *Aufstieg und Niedergang der römischen Welt* 2.16.2 (1978): 1592–603.

Harrill, J. Albert. "Coming of Age and Putting on Christ: The Toga Virilis Ceremony, Its Paraenesis, and Paul's Interpretation of Baptism in Galatians." *Novum Testamentum* 44, no. 3 (2002): 252–77.

Henig, Martin. "The Victory-Gem from Lullingstone Roman Villa." *Journal of the British Archaeological Association* 160 (2007): 1–7.

Heres, T.L. "The Building History of the Caseggiato dei Molini (Reg. I iii 1) at Ostia: A Preliminary Study." *Mededelingen van het Nederlands Instituut te Rome* 48 (1988): 37–74.

Hermansen, Gustav. *Ostia: Aspects of Roman City Life*. Edmonton: University of Alberta Press, 1982.

Hillner, Julia. "Domus, Family, and Inheritance: The Senatorial Family House in Late Antique Rome." *The Journal of Roman Studies* 93 (2003): 129–45.

Horrell, David. "Domestic Space and Christian Meetings at Corinth: Imagining New Contexts and the Buildings East of the Theatre." *New Testament Studies* 50, no. 3 (2004): 349–69.

Horsley, Richard A. "Consciousness and Freedom Among the Corinthians: 1 Corinthians 8–10." *Catholic Biblical Quarterly* 40 (1978): 574–89.

Hubert, Henri, and Marcel Mauss. *Sacrifice: Its Nature and Functions*. Chicago: University of Chicago Press, 1981.

Jeffers, James S. *Conflict at Rome: Social Order and Hierarchy in Early Christianity*. Minneapolis: Fortress Press, 1991.

– *The Greco-Roman World of the New Testament Era: Exploring the Background of Early Christianity*. Madison: InterVarsity Press, 1999.

– "Jewish and Christian Families in First-Century Rome." In *Judaism and Christianity in First-Century Rome*, edited by Karl P. Donfried and Peter Richardson, 128–50. Grand Rapids: Eerdmans, 1998.

Jensen, Robin. *Understanding Early Christian Art*. London: Routledge, 2000.

Jewett, Robert. "Tenement Churches and Communal Meals in the Early Church: The Implications of a Form-Critical Analysis of 2 Thessalonians 3:10." *Biblical Research* 38 (1993): 23–43.

Klauck, Hans-Josef. *The Religious Context of Early Christianity*. Translated by Brian McNeil. Edinburgh: T & T Clark, 2000.

Kloppenborg, John S. "Collegia and Thiasoi: Issues in Function, Taxonomy and Membership." In *Voluntary Associations in the Graeco-Roman World*, edited by John S. Kloppenborg and Stephen G. Wilson, 16–30. London: Routledge, 1996.

– "Membership Practices in Pauline Christ Groups." *Early Christianity* 4, no. 2 (2013): 183–215.

Kraeling, Carl H. *The Excavations at Dura-Europos*. Final Report 8, Part 2: *The Christian Building*. New Haven: Dura Europos Publications, 1967.

Krautheimer, Richard. *Early Christian and Byzantine Architecture*. Baltimore: Penguin Books, 1965.

Lampe, Peter. "Early Christians in Rome: Topographical and Social Historical Aspects of the First Three Centuries." In *Christians as a Religious Minority in a Multicultural City: Modes of Interaction and Identity Formation in Early Imperial Rome – Studies on the Basis of a Seminar at the Second Conference of the European Association for Biblical Studies (EABS) from July 8–12, 2001, in Rome*, edited by Jürgen Zangenberg and Michael Labahn, 20–32. London: T & T Clark International, 2004.

– *From Paul to Valentinus: Christians at Rome in the First Two Centuries*. Translated by Michael Steinhauser. Minneapolis: Fortress Press, 2003.

Lane, William L. "Social Perspectives on Roman Christianity during the Formative Years from Nero to Nerva: Romans, Hebrews, *1 Clement*." In *Judaism and Christianity in First-Century Rome*, edited by Karl P. Donfried and Peter Richardson, 196–244. Grand Rapids: Eerdmans, 1998.

Levine, Lee I. *The Ancient Synagogue*. New Haven: Yale University Press, 2000.

Lieu, Judith M. *Christian Identity in the Jewish and Graeco-Roman World*. Oxford: Oxford University Press, 2004.

Lindsay, Hugh. "Death-Pollution and Funerals in the City of Rome." In *Death and Disease in the Ancient City*, edited by Valerie M. Hope and Eireann Marshall, 152–72. London: Routledge, 2000.

Longenecker, Bruce W. "Exposing the Economic Middle: A Revised Economy Scale for the Study of Early Urban Christianity." *Journal for the Study of the New Testament* 31 no. 3 (2009): 243–78.

L'Orange, Hans Peter. *Art Forms and Civic Life in the Late Roman Empire*. Princeton: Princeton University Press, 1965.

Maier, Harry O. *The Social Setting of the Ministry as Reflected in the Writings of Hermas, Clement, and Ignatius*. Kitchener: Wilfrid Laurier University Press, 1991.

Malherbe, Abraham J. *Social Aspects of Early Christianity*. 2nd ed. Philadelphia: Fortress Press, 1983.

Martin, Dale B. "Review Essay: Justin J. Meggitt, *Paul, Poverty and Survival*." *Journal for the Study of the New Testament* 84 (2001): 51–64.

Mauss, Marcel. "Techniques of the Body." *Economy and Society* 2, no. 1 (1973) [1935]: 70–88.

McCready, Wayne O. "Ecclesia and Voluntary Associations." In *Voluntary Associations in the Graeco-Roman World*, edited by John S. Kloppenborg and Stephen G. Wilson, 59–73. London: Routledge, 1996.

McGowan, Andrew. *Ancient Christian Worship: Early Church Practices in Social, Historical, and Theological Perspective*. Grand Rapids: Baker Academic, 2014.

– *Ascetic Eucharists: Food and Drink in Early Christian Ritual Meals*. Oxford: Clarendon Press, 1999.

– "Rethinking Eucharistic Origins." *Pacifica* 23, no. 2 (2010): 173–91.

Meates, Geoffrey Wells. *The Roman Villa at Lullingstone, Kent*. Vol. 1, *The Site*. Chichester: Kent Archaeological Society, 1979.

– *The Roman Villa at Lullingstone, Kent*. Vol. 2, *Wall Paintings and Finds*. Chichester: Kent Archaeological Society, 1987.

Meeks, Wayne A. *The First Urban Christians: The Social World of the Apostle Paul*. New Haven: Yale University Press, 1983.

Meggitt, Justin J. *Paul, Poverty and Survival*. Edinburgh: T & T Clark, 1998.

Mellor, Ronald. *The Historians of Ancient Rome*. London: Routledge, 2013.

Michaelsen, Robert S. "Dirt in the Courtroom: Indian Land Claims and American Property Rights." In *American Sacred Space*, edited by David Chidester and Edward T. Linenthal, 43–96. Bloomington: Indiana University Press, 1995.

Miller, Patricia Cox. *Women in Early Christianity: Translations from Greek Texts*. Washington, DC: Catholic University of America Press, 2005.

Mouritsen, Henrik. *The Freedman in the Roman World*. Cambridge: Cambridge University Press, 2011.

Murphy O'Connor, Jerome. "Freedom or the Ghetto." *Revue Biblique* 85 (1978): 543–74.

– *St. Paul's Corinth: Texts and Archaeology*. Collegeville: Liturgical Press, 2002.

Neilsen, Inge. *Housing the Chosen: The Architectural Context of Mystery Groups and Religious Associations in the Ancient World* (Contextualizing the Sacred 2). Turnhout: Brepols, 2014.

Neyrey, Jerome. "Spaces and Places, Whence and Whither, Homes and Rooms: 'Territoriality' in the Fourth Gospel." *Biblical Theology Bulletin* 32, no. 2 (2002): 60–74.

– "Teaching You in Public and from House to House (Acts 20:20): Unpacking a Cultural Stereotype." In *The Social World of the New Testament: Insights and Models*, edited by Jerome H. Neyrey and Eric C. Stewart, 183–99. Peabody: Hendrickson Publishers, 2008.

Oakes, Peter. *Reading Romans in Pompeii: Paul's Letter at Ground Level*. Minneapolis: Fortress Press, 2009.

Økland, Jorunn. *Women in Their Place: Paul and the Corinthian Discourse of Gender and Sanctuary Space*. London: T & T Clark, 2004.

Orr, David. "Roman Domestic Religion: The Evidence of the Household Shrines." *Aufstieg und Niedergang der römischen Welt* 2.16.2 (1978): 1557–91.

Osiek, Carolyn, and Margaret Y. MacDonald. *A Woman's Place: House Churches in Earliest Christianity*. With Janet Tulloch. Minneapolis: Fortress Press, 2006.

Peppard, Michael. *The World's Oldest Church: Bible, Art, and Ritual at Dura-Europos, Syria*. New Haven: Yale University Press, 2016.

Petersen, Joan M. "House-Churches in Rome." *Vigiliae Christianae* 23, no. 4 (1969): 264–72.

Pfordresher, John. *Jesus and the Emergence of a Catholic Imagination: An Illustrated Journey*. Mahwah: Paulist Press, 2008.

Pharr, Clyde. *The Theodosian Code and Novels, and the Sirmondian Constitutions*. Princeton: Princeton University Press, 1952.

Pirson, Felix. "Rented Accommodation at Pompeii: The Evidence of the *Insula Arriana Polliana*." In *Domestic Space in the Roman World: Pompeii and Beyond*, edited by Ray Laurence and Andrew Wallace-Hadrill, 165–82. *Journal of Roman Archaeology* Supplementary Series 22. Portsmouth: Journal of Roman Archaeology, 1997.

Quinn, Dennis P. "Houses of the Holy: Roman and Christian Domestic Piety in the Latin West, 100–600." PhD diss., The Claremont Graduate University, 2005.

Rawson, Beryl. "Celebrating the Saturnalia: Religious Ritual and Roman Domestic Life." In *A Companion to Families in the Greek and Roman Worlds*, edited by Beryl Rawson, chapter 29. Oxford: Wiley-Blackwell, 2011.

– ed. *The Family in Ancient Rome: New Perspectives*. Ithaca: Cornell University Press, 1987.

Rawson, Beryl, and Paul Weaver, eds. *The Roman Family in Italy: Status, Sentiment, Space*. Oxford: Oxford University Press, 1999.

Richardson, Peter. *Building Jewish in the Roman East*. Waco: Baylor University Press, 2004.

Roberts, Alexander, and James Donaldson. *The Ante-Nicene Fathers: The Writings of the Fathers Down to A.D. 325*. New York: Charles Scribner's Sons, 1899.

Robinson, Mark. "Domestic Burnt Offerings and Sacrifices at Roman and Pre-Roman Pompeii, Italy." *Vegetation History and Archaeobotany* 11 (2002): 93–9.

Rordorf, Willy. "Was wissen wir über die christlichen Gottesdiensträume der vorkonstantinischen Zeit?" *Zeitschrift für die Neutestamentliche Wissenschaft* 55 (1964): 110–28.

Rüpke, Jörg. *Religion of the Romans*. Cambridge: Polity, 2007.

Saller, Richard P. "*Pater Familias, Mater Familias*, and the Gendered Semantics of the Roman Household." *Classical Philology* 94, no. 2 (1999): 182–97.

Sanders, Donald. "Behavioral Conventions and Archaeology: Methods for the Analysis of Ancient Architecture." In *Domestic Architecture and the Use of Space: An Interdisciplinary Cross-Cultural Study*, edited by Susan Kent, 43–72. Cambridge: Cambridge University Press, 1990.

Schaff, Philip. *Nicene and Post-Nicene Fathers*. Vol. 6. New York: Cosimo, 2007.

Scheidel, Walter, and Steven J. Friesen. "The Size of the Economy and the Distribution of Income in the Roman Empire." *Journal of Roman Studies* 99 (2009): 61–91.

Scott, Sarah. "The Power of Images in the Late Roman House." In *Domestic Space in the Roman World: Pompeii and Beyond*, edited by Ray Laurence and Andrew Wallace-Hadrill, 53–68. *Journal of Roman Archaeology* Supplementary Series 22. Portsmouth: Journal of Roman Archaeology, 1997.

Serra, Dominic. "The Baptistery at Dura-Europos: The Wall Paintings in the Context of Syrian Baptismal Theology." *Ephemerides Liturgicae* 120 (2006): 67–78.

Sider, Robert Dick. *Christian and Pagan in the Roman Empire: The Witness of Tertullian*. Washington, DC: Catholic University of America Press, 2001.

Simmons, Michael Bland. *Arnobius of Sicca: Religious Conflict and Competition in the Age of Diocletian*. Oxford: Clarendon Press, 1995.

Smith, Dennis E. *From Symposium to Eucharist: The Banquet in the Early Christian World*. Minneapolis: Fortress Press, 2003.

Smith, Jonathan Z. *To Take Place: Toward Theory in Ritual*. Chicago: University of Chicago Press, 1987.

– "The Wobbling Pivot." *The Journal of Religion* 52, no. 2 (1972): 134–49.

Snyder, Graydon F. *Ante Pacem: Archaeological Evidence of Church Life Before Constantine*. Macon: Mercer University Press, 2003.

Snyder, Harlow Gregory. "'Above the Baths of Myrtinus': Justin Martyr's 'School' in the City of Rome." *Harvard Theological Review* 100 (2007): 335–62.

Stark, Rodney. "Religious Competition and Roman Piety." *Interdisciplinary Journal of Research on Religion* 2 (2006): http://www.religjournal.com/pdf/ijrr02006.pdf.

Staples, Ariadne. *From Good Goddess to Vestal Virgins: Sex and Category in Roman Religion*. London: Routledge, 1998.

Stewart, Peter. *The Social History of Roman Art*. Cambridge: Cambridge University Press, 2004.

Stowers, Stanley Kent. "Social Status, Public Speaking and Private Teaching: The Circumstances of Paul's Preaching Activity." *Novum Testamentum* 26 (1984): 59–82.

– "Theorizing Ancient Household Religion." In *Household and Family Religion in Antiquity: Contextual and Comparative Perspectives*, edited by John Bodel and Saul M. Olyan, 5–19. Oxford: Blackwell, 2008.

Stringer, Martin D. *Rethinking the Origins of the Eucharist*. London: SCM Press, 2011.

Taussig, Hal. *In the Beginning Was the Meal: Social Experimentation and Early Christian Identity*. Minneapolis: Fortress Press, 2009.

Taylor, Joan E. *Christians and the Holy Places: The Myth of Jewish-Christian Origins*. Oxford: Clarendon Press, 1993.

Theissen, Gerd. "Social Conflicts in the Corinthian Community: Further Remarks on J.J. Meggitt, Paul, Poverty, and Survival." *Journal for the Study of the New Testament* 25 (2003), 371–91.

– *The Social Setting of Pauline Christianity: Essays on Corinth*. Philadelphia: Fortress Press, 1982.

Toynbee, Jocelyn M.C. *Death and Burial in the Roman World*. Baltimore: Johns Hopkins Press, 1971.

Tertullian. *De Spectaculis*. Translated by T.R. Glover. Loeb Classical Library. Cambridge: Harvard University Press, 1931.

Tuan, Yi-Fu. *Space and Place: The Perspective of Experience*. Minneapolis: University of Minnesota Press, 1977.

Turner, Harold. *From Temple to Meeting House: The Phenomenology and Theology of Places of Worship*. The Hague: Mouton, 1979.

Turner, Victor. *The Forest of Symbols: Aspects of Ndembu Ritual*. Ithaca: Cornell University Press, 1967.

Ulrich, Roger Bradley. *Roman Woodworking*. New Haven: Yale University Press, 2007.

Van Gennep, Arnold. *The Rites of Passage*. London: Routledge, 1960.

Vitruvius Pollio. *De Architectura*. Translated by Frank Granger. 2 vols. Loeb Classical Library. Cambridge: Harvard University Press, 2004 [1934].

Wallace-Hadrill, Andrew. "*Domus* and *Insulae* in Rome: Families and Housefuls." In *Early Christian Families in Context: An Interdisciplinary Dialogue*, edited by David L. Balch and Carolyn Osiek, 3–18. Grand Rapids: Eerdmans, 2003.

– *Houses and Society in Pompeii and Herculaneum*. Princeton, NJ: Princeton University Press, 1994.

– "Rethinking the Roman Atrium House." In *Domestic Space in the Roman World: Pompeii and Beyond*, edited by Ray Laurence and Andrew Wallace-Hadrill, 196–218. *Journal of Roman Archaeology* Supplementary Series 22. Portsmouth: Journal of Roman Archaeology, 1997.

Weber, Max. *The Sociology of Religion*. Boston: Beacon Press, 1963.

Wharton, Annabel. *Refiguring the Post Classical City: Dura Europos, Jerash, Jerusalem and Ravenna*. Cambridge: Cambridge University Press, 1995.

White, L. Michael. *The Social Origins of Christian Architecture*. 2 vols. Valley Forge: Trinity Press International, 1990–7.

Weissenrieder, Annette. "Contested Spaces in 1 Corinthians 11:17–33 and 14:30: Sitting or Reclining in Ancient Houses, in Associations and in the Space of *ekklesia*." *Contested Spaces: Houses and Temples in Roman Antiquity and the New Testament*, edited by David L. Balch and Annette Weissenrieder. Tübingen: Mohr Siebeck, 2012.

Wilson, Stephen. "Voluntary Associations: An Overview." In *Voluntary Associations in the Graeco-Roman World*, edited by John S. Kloppenborg and Stephen G. Wilson, 1–15. London: Routledge, 1996.

Yasin, Ann Marie. *Saints and Church Spaces in the Late Antique Mediterranean: Architecture, Cult, and Community*. Cambridge: Cambridge University Press, 2009.

Index